Fundamentalism and Women in World Religions

Blackburn
College

Library
01254 292120

Fundamentalism and Women in World Religions

Edited by Arvind Sharma and
Katherine K. Young

t &t clark
New York – London

T & T Clark International, 80 Maiden Lane, New York, NY 10038

T & T Clark International, The Tower Building, 11 York Road, London SE1 7NX

T & T Clark International is a Continuum imprint.

Library of Congress Cataloging-in-Publication Data

Fundamentalism and women in world religions / edited by Arvind Sharma and Katherine K. Young.
    p. cm.
Includes bibliographical references and index.
ISBN-13: 978-0-567-02533-3 (hardcover : alk. paper)
ISBN-10: 0-567-02533-0 (hardcover : alk. paper)
ISBN-13: 978-0-567-02749-8 (paperback : alk. paper)
1. Religious fundamentalism. 2. Women and religion. I. Sharma, Arvind. II. Young, Katherine K., 1944-
    BL238.F795 2007
    200.82—dc22
                            2007020178

Contents

PREFACE

Arvind Sharma

The great service a book such as this renders, both to the study of fundamentalism and women's studies, is to highlight the fact that while fundamentalism may seem at times to mimic orthodoxy, there is a fundamental difference between the two. Fundamentalism is a religious tradition's response to loss of power, while orthodoxy is a religious tradition's response to loss of piety. However, when such loss of piety is the consequence of the secular disempowerment of religion in the public and the private sphere, then the display of orthodoxy also becomes additionally inscribed with political self-assertion in the face of such loss of power in the form of a massive political pun. This pun has often been missed by observers. The study of fundamentalism and the position of women in world religions is thus more than just an extension of the study of the consequences of phenomenon of fundamentalism to the role of women in the various religious traditions; it has implications that concern the heart of the phenomenon itself.

Once the sights are thus adjusted one realizes that while some loss of power may be induced by globalization, it is nothing compared to the loss of power that was experienced by many religious traditions in the face of imperialism. This fact is obscured from our view by the historical lexical accident that the word "fundamentalism" was chosen to describe which it does. "Fundamentalism" was coined to refer to the reaction of the Christian tradition, as it experienced such loss of power through the forces of secularism and modernity. But *not* through that of imperialism. The term was then extended to cover the cases of other religious traditions, which found themselves in a similar dilemma. One crucial factor is, however, often overlooked in the context of such an extrapolation-that most of the non-Christian religious traditions encountered these forces of secularity and modernity wearing the mask of imperialism.

Perhaps these non-Christian religious traditions would object to this description as too forgiving and claim that they encountered Western imperialism wearing the masks of secularity and modernity. Be that as it may, the study of the interaction between fundamentalism and the position of women in world religions will always be plagued by a "dummy" variable, unless the intervening variable of imperialism is introduced in the equation in some form, directly or indirectly. The various case studies included in this book take on new life when viewed in such a background. This altered perspective, which the book encourages the reader to adopt, grants to these accounts a relevance and a vivacity all its own. The case of Christianity, and to a certain extent Judaism, is rendered remarkable by another phenomenon, which, like imperialism in the case of non-Christian traditions, often gets over-looked-namely, feminism. The nuanced inclusion of this perspective once again has major implications for the discussion of the fundamentalism and the position of women in Christianity.

It is in this spirit of a more sophisticated discussion of fundamentalism and the position of women in world religions-Christian and non-Christian, by incorporating these overlooked perspectives-that this book is offered to the readers.

No one would have predicted, even as late as the 1970s, that a book with such a title as the one this book bears, would see the light of day in the first decade of the twenty-first century. Were one to imagine the appearance of such a book at the time, one would have thought that it would bear a title such as *Secularism and Women in World Religions*. Such a book would then go on to extol the way in which secularism had succeeded in emancipating women form the thralldom to which they had been confined by the world religions. It would have exulted that in this struggle between religious darkness and secular light, light had prevailed and, in doing so, rescued women from their benighted state in the world religions.

We find ourselves however perusing a book with a very different title: *Fundamentalism and Women in World Religions*. What happened?

What happened was that the secular trend in world history, which was initiated by the European Enlightenment in the eighteenth century and which seemed all set to sweep the world, actually gave rise to a countermovement by the 1980s, which was destined to check this trend and may even have reversed it. But this remains to be seen. What seems certain is that the Iranian Revolution of 1979 dramatically signaled trouble in the secular paradise, for it seemed now that secular modernity had spawned a movement to which the label fundamentalism has been applied (though not without some misgivings), which defied many secular expectations.

This fundamentalism is a coat of many colors but it is the color red that catches the eye. That is to say, while fundamentalist movements "can be reactionary in doctrine or social morality or both … it is their militancy which usually prompts the use of the word."[1]

Such militancy has profound implications for the position of women in world religions. The essays in this book explore these implications, and as we read them we discover that when it comes to assessing the implications of this militancy for the position of women in world religions, the color code we may need to employ this time is as often gray as it is black and white.

Notes

1. Willard G. Oxtoby, ed., *World Religions: Western Traditions*, 2nd ed. (Toronto: Oxford University Press, 2002), 314.

INTRODUCTION

Katherine K. Young

The relation of the women's movement to religion is best understood against the backdrop of the changes introduced by modernity and imperialism. Women's critique of hierarchy, after all, can be traced to liberal, egalitarian, and reformist ideals that informed political life in the modern West from the time of the Enlightenment. The women's movement initially spread around the world with Western imperialism. Democracy, socialism, and especially Marxism subsequently inspired movements for national liberation, women's liberation, and lay activism in various countries. Changes brought by the industrial revolution also played a part. The machine, for instance, equalized male and female bodies in the labor force; men's size, strength, and mobility were no longer relevant for many industrial jobs (and even less so with the subsequent advent of the computer age). The development of the condom (and subsequent forms of birth control) contributed to the equalization of male and female bodies, for women no longer had to fear pregnancy and could be a stable member of the work force. Protection against pregnancy gave them the same carefree access to sexual pleasure that men had always enjoyed.[1]

Since the women's movement is a child of modernity (variously characterized as the scientific revolution, industrialization, urbanization, materialism, secularity, and rapid communication and transportation) and fundamentalism is the ostensible rejection of modernity on the part of some major religious movements within the world's religions, then one should not be surprised to find an enormous clash between the two. Their interaction is far more complicated, however, than this simple juxtaposition would suggest. Of one thing we can be sure: modernity has caused enormous stress and provoked three basic reactions: accommodation, withdrawal, or fighting back. The raison d'être of the latter is fundamentalism, although it has connections, as I will show, to the other two.

Fundamentalism is a word created by American Protestants in the early twentieth century to repudiate the secularizing forces of modernity (especially the scientific revolution that undermined the metaphysical basis of religious "truth") by restoring the "fundamentals" of biblical revelation: the literal truth of scriptural doctrines such as the virgin birth of Mary and the vicarious atonement, bodily resurrection, and physical return of Jesus.[2] Because the forces of modernity (especially urbanization with its need for small families, concepts of equality— which led to women's education, personhood under the law and the vote—and entrance into the public sphere of professional work) were also undermining traditional family forms and gender roles, fundamentalists reasserted them as a way to preserve identity.

If modernity posed enormous problems for Christianity, to which it was culturally related, it posed even greater problems for other world religions, which were introduced to scientific, material, and religious claims to superiority through their colonial rulers, thereby creating a conflict of identity and sense of indignity.

Moreover, colonialism was rationalized in terms of freeing native women from their oppressive religions and husbands. The British Raj, for example, rationalized its domination of the Indian subcontinent on the basis of the need to end (mainly elite) Hindu women's lack of education, plight as widows and suttees, and lack of divorce, remarriage, and education. For some Middle Eastern and Asian countries, especially those subject to Marxist revolutions, the damage has been enormous. It has often provoked movements to "fight back" against modernity in general and the West in particular (captured in phrases such as "Eastern religion; Western science").

The word fundamentalism was extended for comparative purposes first in connection with Islam[3] and then other world religions. This was accomplished by the pioneering work of Martin E. Marty and Scott Appleby, editors of *Fundamentalisms Observed*,[4] which included chapters on Christianity, Judaism, Islam, Hinduism, Sikhism, Buddhism, Confucianism, and Japanese religions with special attention given to regional and sectarian differences. In their introduction, the editors defend their use of this word by pointing out that it differs from "traditionalism," "conservatism," "orthodoxy," "orthopraxis," and "extremism." It is a new global phenomenon, they say, with a distinctive "family of resemblances." Therefore, it requires its own terminology and conceptual space. The key features of fundamentalism, according to them, include *fighting back* innovatively and often militantly against threats to central ideas from a "real or presumed past"; *fighting for* their worldview, including the intimate values of family, gender roles, socialization of children, and the like (which marks a transition between passive withdrawal from mainstream society to active control over government and territory); *fighting with* a group of strategies (doctrinal, practical, ritualistic, and symbolic) to define identity and a movement; *fighting against* both outsiders and those insiders considered traitors to the cause (such as moderates); and *fighting under* a *transcendent reality* such as God in theistic traditions. This comparative perspective reveals that scriptural literalism is no longer a distinctive feature of fundamentalism as it has been in Christianity.

Some authors in this book on women focus on how fundamentalisms refer back to some kind of a golden age when life had greater harmony and people experienced more contentment. Others distinguish between formal fundamentalisms (religiously and politically organized) and informal ones (spread by the mass media). Others argue that even the norms defining fundamentalism vary from within; some are invisible, constitutive, and hard to change, and others are visible, regulative, and easy to change. Still others worry about the use of this word altogether, opining as Bruce Lawrence has, that it is "orientalism" or that it just does not fit "their tradition," although they admit to analogues. The interest of all our authors in this book, however, is on the fact that the fundamentalisms and their analogues have all ostensibly upheld the traditional gender role of wife and mother for women. And this response to modernity puts down the gauntlet to women scholars come of age during the heyday of the women's movement, which fought to eliminate such restrictions.

The Authors of This Book

Eva Hellman, an expert on Hinduism, looks at women in the highly politicized setting of today. Advocates of Hindu nationalism, or Hindu fundamentalism (*hindutva*), self-consciously woo women and thus present a challenge to the "autonomous women's movement." Hellman has collected information from field work in the Rashtra Sevika Samiti as well as "policy-documents, hymns, election manifestos and articles published by hindutva organizations" such as the Vishva Hindu Parishad and the Bharatiya Janata Party, which at the time led the central government in India (2003). To be more specific, she has studied the women's groups that belong to these organizations—their power structures and their attempts to promote empowerment or mobilization: character-building activities, schools, training camps, free health services, religious classes (devotional singing, yoga, correct performance of rituals), relief actions, cow protection agitation, and so forth. Hellman discusses six hindutva codes for ideal womanhood: woman as political mother, activist for hindutva, citizen, daughter of Bharat Mata (that is, India), "female cell in the living organism of Hindu society," and the symbol of Hindu society. Out are passive models of womanhood from the past (such as Sita). In are politically active ones from the past (such as female militants or warriors and queens [*virangana*]). Hellman observes that fundamentalist goals are to modernize tradition (by ascribing value and dignity to women) but also to maintain tradition (in clothing, behavior, beliefs) with its underlying view that the sexes are categorically different and their roles complementary (a view that she challenges). Hellman contrasts all this with the orientation of the Indian women's movement toward economic independence, elimination of violence against women, better inheritance laws, and the "foundational similarity between men and women" along with "unconditional equality." Tension between the fundamentalist and secular women's movements will grow, she argues, and Hindu fundamentalists will develop alliances with fundamentalists in other countries or traditions.

Tessa Bartholomeusz, who discusses Buddhism, finds an example of fundamentalism in late nineteenth-century Sri Lanka.[5] For her, fundamentalism refers to keeping women at home, traditionally dressed, and following the traditional rules of decorum. At the same time, however, "feminist" trends encouraged the autonomy of women and their freedom to act in public life. Ironically, this occurred within the fundamentalist turn to religion as a source for women's identity. More specifically, to the "golden age" of Buddhism under the emperor Asoka (third century BCE), who promoted Buddhist nuns as learned teachers and proselytizers. This modern recovery in the public imagination of a golden age inspired the need to restore women's "proper Buddhist education" for both nuns and ordinary women; this would make them both good mothers of children and good mothers of the nation. Bartholomeusz concludes that "religious fundamentalism and feminism are not necessarily antithetical."

Vivian-Lee Nyitray, writing on Confucianism, begins with definitions of fundamentalism. She notes that the word has not been used for Confucianism[6] but comes to the conclusion, albeit "deliberately provocative," that there is a Confucian analogue to fundamentalism in premodern Neo-Confucianism from the Song dynasty through the Ming (twelfth through seventeenth centuries) and its spheres of influence (Korea and Japan). She then examines Neo-Confucian gender constructions, especially their hierarchical nature, which were derived from Han ideas of *yang* (male, strength, growth, light, and life) over *yin* (female, weakness, decay, darkness, and death). These were accompanied by masculine subjectivities and misogyny. Although the social reforms of modern communism led to women's participation in public space, she maintains, they by no means eliminated male domination of political life. Now contemporary Confucians, including academics in the diaspora, want to mobilize Confucian spirituality against the negative effects of modernity: industrialization, urbanization, bureaucratization, and mass communication. She thinks that this modern Confucianism can live with science and democracy. It acknowledges historic problems. It is not militant. And it is not "insensitive to women's interests," although it has yet to account for "new models of family structure, male-female relationality, or a full range of female sexuality." It is hard to know what the future will bring, she suggests. It could be more Confucian humanism or a diffuse fundamentalism might escalate into organized fundamentalism. Whatever the direction, she concludes, "The future is sure to be determined in large measure by contemporary Confucian responses to conflicting demands for both the liberation and control of women."

Sylvia Fishman introduces her study of Jewish fundamentalism with the Haredim (ultra-Orthodox),[7] who look back to the self-enclosed, isolated Jewish communities of premodern Europe as their "golden age" and try to maintain them by rejecting modernity in general and the changing roles of women in particular.

She contextualizes her study of the Haredim, who have considerable power in Israel, by examining their orientation alongside other orthodox communities, Western humanism, and especially feminism. In other words, she examines the spectrum of Jewish communities. Her thesis is that women's problems have a "symbolic valence" in modern Jewish life across the spectrum and that societal transformations crystallize in this context. She then focuses on Jewish strategies for maintaining identity in the face of modernity, their traditional roots, and how they affect women (especially in those communities that maintain sexual segregation). Fishman is particularly interested in Orthodoxy in the right-center of the spectrum because feminism still seeps into it. Finally she shows how rabbinic authorities think about the limits of reform, the goals of feminism, and what all this means for masculine identity.

Reem Meshal provides a microcosm of one key symbol—the hijab—of Islamic fundamentalism in the diaspora. She gave a questionnaire to 129 female university students who identified themselves as Muslim in ten Canadian cities. The study was designed to figure out who is wearing the hijab and why. More specifically, it was designed to see if there is a homogeneous identity among diasporic Muslims wearing the hijab or if there are cross-cutting identities—and how any Muslim identity is likely to fare in the diaspora. She finds that those who wear the hijab do not necessarily see themselves in terms of traditional gender roles. They argue that "ideal/pure/true Islam already acknowledges equality between all humans." Use of the hijab is increasing in the diaspora and its use cannot be accounted for by simple transmission from the country of the immigrant's origin. It has come to symbolize "a new orthodoxy ... against ... colonialism and consolidation of European imperial power." The study found that Canadian-born Muslim women and immigrants of high economic and educational status are less likely to wear the hijab than their immigrant sisters of low status. But she notes that half of the women who currently do not wear the hijab say that they might do so in the future, which suggests that "second generation Canadian Muslim women are, at least in the matter of dress, increasingly accepting of prevailing, twentieth century, Islamic orthodoxy." She concludes that whether or not Muslim women wear the hijab, they use feminist rhetoric in "defending their respective positions."

Heidi Epstein begins her essay on Christian fundamentalist women by throwing down the gauntlet: "'A fine line cleaves bigotry and critical thought,' I once mused to a Pakistani student-friend as we disparaged her parents' old-world marital values. Being 'enlightened' rather than racist, we decided, requires a taste for ambiguity." Feminists have viewed fundamentalist women as part of the patriarchal problem because they endorse the premodern status quo. Feminists explain the fundamentalist position away as a product of false consciousness. Epstein argues that the gulf between feminists and fundamentalists can be narrowed by examining the "paradoxical confluences" between the two (her essay being, as she points out, more a meta-analysis rather than a study of Christian fundamentalism per se); by feminist self-critique; by "producing [unlikely] proximities"; by "reconstructions, and justice-making"; by a "double hermeneutic of suspicion and generosity toward our fundamentalist 'sisters'"; by using the lens of tragedy; and by revalorizing "ambiguity and 'unknowing' as difficult yet necessary preconditions for 'ethical behavior.'" She enters "this hermeneutic circle at one particularly equivocal site: ambiguous vignettes of women flourishing within fundamentalist congregations."

Reading Gender and Fundamentalism from Right to Left

A key theme of fundamentalisms is complementarity between men and women; they are said to be equal but different and this theme often draws on traditional views of gender roles and family. (For instance, in the quasi-fundamentalist Ming-Qing dynasties, according to Nyitray, the ideal wife "complemented her husband.") From the perspective of *hindutva*, says Hellman, men and women (with their respective functions) are of equal worth, necessarily complementary, organic to society (in the sense that family is the building block of society), and the basis for harmony. The underlying premise of all this, she adds, is the assumed difference between men and women. Meshal observes much the same rhetoric among Muslim women in Canada. "Those wearing the hijab often repeat the phrase 'equal but different.'" And Epstein notes that "fundamentalists transhistorically regard men and women as two ontologically distinct groups with different, divinely ordained life purposes."

Our authors cite several authorities to the effect that religious fundamentalisms reaffirm traditional divisions of sex roles and encourage a distinctive semiotics of space, dress, and behavior for women (and men as well). Nyitray refers to anthropologist Lionel Caplan's observation that women "appear to assume a symbolic poignancy in fundamentalism—their dress, demeanor and socio-ritual containment providing eloquent testimony to what is regarded as the correct order of things" (see chapter 3 for Caplan reference). Fishman notes, for instance, that separation of the sexes is nothing new in Judaism; it began in the biblical period in connection with purity and impurity.[8]

She describes how synagogue architecture has expressed sexual segregation. Men and women are separated by a barrier (*mekhitsah*); women worship in sections reserved for them at the back, or on both sides, or on a balcony.

This traditional semiotic of space, dress, and behavior is sometimes given a new gloss by fundamentalist women. Consider the distinctive garb worn by Muslim women. Meshal is quick to point out that the hijab is by no means traditional (the only rule is that the hair and neck be covered) and is not found across the Muslim world. It is *now* becoming a universal symbol of Islam, nonetheless, especially among women in the diaspora. On the one hand, they want to symbolize their rejection of Western fashions (which exaggerate and exploit female sexuality at the expense of female intellect and sexual equality). On the other hand, they want to define their own authentic religiosity as Muslim women, which is based on the Qur'anic notion of sexual equality. This does not mean that they reject all traditional associations. Almost half of those who wear the hijab see themselves as homemakers. In this sense, it represents nothing but a new style for traditional ways. But the fact is that more than half of those who wear the hijab (and virtually all those who do not) see themselves as career women. Central to their identity are education and work outside the home. In this sense, the tug of war between Islamic revivalism and modernism or feminism in Islamic countries has been resolved in at least one diaspora context with a symbolic nod to the importance of women in the former (which I suspect suggests that they still honor the traditions of marriage and family).

The fact that fundamentalist women negotiate the style and meaning of dress suggests that they are combining tradition and modernity. According to Hindu fundamentalists, points out Hellman, Hindu woman who fully develop their potential indicate how hindutva incorporates modernity "without renouncing fundamental Hindu principles and values such as gender specific roles. That women are included in the modern functional systems does not necessarily imply that they have to abandon (ascribed) essential feminine qualities.... Neither does it entail that the traditional gender structure has to be challenged. By 'correct' body language, clothing, sexuality, conduct, morals, values, and social roles, the socially active woman is still the respected carrier of a collective Hindu identity." Women become visible and valuable agents at both the social and transcendent levels. "They are offered jobs, child-care, education, protection, freedom of action, new public roles, responsibility and are accorded tasks in the creation of *hindu rashtra*" (Hindu state). In short, they combine modernity and tradition (domestic responsibilities and *stridharma*, the proper behavior of women including loyalty to family, "chastity, purity, unselfishness, adaptability, service mindedness, and a sacrificial and motherly attitude." But they are also "strong, self-confident, well-educated, patriotic," and responsible in the public realm for transmitting hindutva and contributing to the family income.

Have the fundamentalisms discussed in this volume actually achieved this complementarity (equal but different)? At the moment, Hinduism, in my opinion, is closest to the model of complementarity. There might be two explanations. First, this is a period of low stress, because the Bharata Janata Party has periodically been in power at the central or state level. Second, this party has had to woo women to its cause as part of its political mobilization. Islam in the diaspora, too, comes close to the model of complementarity. Women wear a symbolic head covering, but many also want education, jobs, and careers. Orthodoxy, in the middle of the Jewish spectrum, is heading in this direction. This community has taken several steps to break down sexual segregation and thus distinguished itself from the isolationist haredi community. Epstein notes that Christian fundamentalist women exercise considerable power. They can be ordained (in some churches), they wield enormous financial power in their sex-segregated missionary organizations, and they are strong, media-savvy, college-educated editors, writers, administrators, and social activists. And Nyitray thinks that modern Confucianists, even though they are in search of identity (but are not yet fundamentalists), are sensitive to the interests of women. It would seem, then, that many of the fundamentalisms represented in this book have taken seriously steps toward complementarity, although that may be a fragile balance that might collapse in contexts of stress (see Postscript) and might not be really complementary when the standard of comparison is feminism. This takes us to the next approach.

Reading Gender and Fundamentalism from Left to Right

As scholars, our authors document the values and lives of women in fundamentalist movements. But they do more than this. They evaluate either explicitly or implicitly what is going on. In their essays, in other words, they are speaking as "engaged scholars." Some say so in their introductory paragraphs. By clarifying their own attitudes, they establish boundaries between themselves and their subjects (and thus protect the "bottom line" of their own feminist identities). This is true of Epstein, for instance, who announces that her engagement with the "other woman" should never be misconstrued on important matters: "In teasing out these proximities, however, I in no way condone Christian fundamentalists' demonization of, for example, homosexuality and abortion." Others establish boundaries by dividing their chapters into descriptive and critical sections. According to Hellman, "it has been pivotal to me to strike a balance between an emic and an analytic perspective. In the emic part of the article the intention has been to mirror the insider's point of view. By allowing the 'other' to represent herself, by making a voice heard—a voice with a central standing in the hindutva discourse—I have tried to minimize the orientalist mistake of distorting the picture of the 'other.' In the analytic part, on the other hand, I speak. With the help of feminist theory and a narrativist understanding of religion, I analytically approach questions on gender and power." Still others allow their own evaluations to run throughout their essays. These are indicated by words such as "control," "containment," "regression," and "hierarchy"—certainly not the words of their fundamentalist informants.

Fundamentalisms, point out some of our authors, are selectively modern with reference to education, technology, economy, and polity. Take the example of education in general and religious education in particular. The pursuit of secular education for girls and women seems to be alive and well in most fundamentalist circles, although curricula might vary for boys and girls. Pursuit of higher education is sometimes more problematic if that is perceived to threaten marriage and family life (but even then some fundamentalist women obtain advanced degrees and have careers, which they combine with marriage). Some communities still do not give religious education to girls (Jewish *haredi* schools, for instance, do not teach the Talmud to girls, for instance), though many Orthodox communities now do in day schools, yeshivas, and universities. This has led to some changes in Orthodox religious practice—for example, Bat Mitzvahs for girls to parallel Bar Mitzvahs for boys—and new religious positions for them (although only Reform, Reconstrucitonist, and Conservative Jews have women as rabbis and cantors). The case of Hinduism is even more striking on the religious education front. Hindu fundamentalists are at the vanguard by encouraging women to be trained as ritual specialists in domestic rituals and rites of passage, which demand knowledge of the sacred language (Sanskrit) and sacred texts (the Vedas). Until recently, these had been the prerogative of orthodox Brahmin men. Now that this expertise is in place, women (*stri*) are taking an unprecedented step: becoming gurus (hence the new term *striguru*).

But our authors sometimes argue that fundamentalist women are "anti-modern or regressive" when it comes to the family and the status of women. They note that fundamentalism is primarily about the reestablishment and maintenance of fixed boundaries—that is, separating the religious from the secular, state jurisdiction from family responsibility, and the functions of women from those of men. Bartholomeusz observes, for instance, that a comparative perspective reveals a tendency in fundamentalisms to keep women at home. According to Fishman, "defining and circumscribing women's roles is a way of resealing boundaries between them and the outside world and symbolically rejecting modernity."

Despite the fundamentalist rhetoric of "equal but different," some authors in this volume observe that social organization is, on the contrary, hierarchical; women are under the control of their fathers, husbands, or sons. This is expressed primarily by relegating women to the domestic sphere (therefore reasserting the boundary between private and public) and "female roles." They mention subtle expressions of control as well. "The pedastalization of domesticated womanhood," points out Nyitray, "is seen to be a trait closely related to nostalgia, another distinguishing characteristic of fundamentalism. Nostalgic visions of an idealized past—the representation of which is controlled by men—"'typically lay strong emphasis on the role women played in infusing that bygone time with perfection'" (Nyitray quoting Hawley and Proudfoot: see chapter 3). She observes, moreover, that the *yin* in Neo-Confucianism is understood as a "shadow or an echo," hardly a complementarity in the sense of "equal but different." Where girls were educated, it was mainly to make them more effective mothers. "More recently, in the continuing wake of post-Mao economic reforms," she notes, "the strengthening of the family as not only a viable but a vital economic unit has resulted in the resurrection of the traditional model of ideal wife and mother, transformed slightly into a consumer-oriented one with 'knowledge, skills, and ideas of her own.'" Here, her key word is "slightly."

Hellman, too, observes that sexual hierarchy is the foundation of gender in fundamentalist groups. Men represent the norm, human beings in general; anything connected with men and masculinity is valued. Women represent the "other" and are sometimes considered not fully human; femininity is devalued. She finds this structure in hindutva, because the sexes have different essences, realms of activity, and choices; those of women are always lesser in scope. To be auspicious, therefore, they must be controlled by the male principle (*purusha*). In addition, Hellman notes, an underlying hierarchy that benefits men is an "indigenous, authentic and uncompromisable" fundamental. She is skeptical about just how liberated hindutva women really are. They work outside the home only to add a source of family income, after all, and they volunteer in the public realm only to transmit hindutva (and only if they have extra time). She worries that advocates of hindutva have criticized the United Nations conference on women, which was held at Beijing in 1995. In this context, she mentions Murli Manohar Joshi, then president of the Bharatiya Janata Party, who opines that "free sex, lesbianism, the situation for unwed mothers and artificial insemination were the focus while … the erosion of the family … was neglected." Hellman observes that advocates of hindutva, moreover, silence or demonize dissenters: "The costs for taking part of benefits (such as education) offered by the hegemonic hindutva movement are high indeed but the Indian woman who chooses to be independent faces the risk of having to pay an even higher price." Finally, she observes that "although the hindutva women's room offers freedom zones for women, it is equipped with double locks: a metaphysically legitimated patriarchal gender order and a likewise transcendentally founded organic outlook compels real women to perform like imagined ones."

Similarly Fishman finds the principle of hierarchy evident in Jewish traditions to the right of center, which was inherited largely from traditional forms of Judaism. The rabbis had gradually restricted Jewish women's roles as leaders and from the study of Torah. Fathers (or male substitutes) had taught only their sons, and "intellectualism defines male excellence." In the past, women had been banned from singing in some Jewish gatherings because the Talmud had warned about the dangers of women's voices (although this passage referred originally to spoken voices, which would distract men from study). The superiority of men, observes Fishman, had also been established by excluding women from public rituals.

Epstein takes important steps toward a dialogical approach by scrutinizing the similarities between fundamentalism and feminism. She argues that fundamentalist women occupy "an analytical terrain" somewhere between fundamentalism and feminism, noting that "the patriarchal divide separating fundamentalist and feminist women often obfuscates the common humanitarian causes we share such as addressing problems, especially for children of violence, drug abuse, unemployment, divorce, and inner city poverty." (Fundamentalist women, she points out, drawing on Brenda Brasher's ethnography of them [see chapter 5], have sometimes had more time for volunteer work than today's working women and have a strong record of social activism for these causes.) The approaches of feminism and fundamentalism converge also in the concept of separate spheres; for fundamentalists, sexual segregation has limited the androcentric power of men, providing a refuge from them, a space for self-development, a forum for women's interests, and an arena for mobilizing "collective pressure for reform." Moreover, it has offered emotional religious experiences (giving women an opportunity to find meaning in them), a sense of community, counseling, childcare, continuing education, and weekend retreats. Finally, it has given them opportunities for leadership as preachers, financial administrators, and pastoral counselors. These "rich gynocentric resources of emotional, psychological and material support," notes Epstein, provide the kind of separate space that feminists themselves demand.

In her search for convergences between feminism and fundamentalism, Epstein adds that they share similar faults. One is that they both share a "racist apostasy." To substantiate this point, she cites female African American scholars, who argue that both feminist and fundamentalist perspectives on women have been racist.

And, from her postmodern perspective (see below), she attacks both feminists and fundamentalists for being essentialists. They both essentialize God (presumably by attributing metaphysical reality to a mere name), although the former also essentialize transcendent views of justice or immanent ideals of "originary primal wholeness" or eros.

The descriptions of fundamentalism by Epstein bridge the gap between fundamentalism and feminism by searching for similarities between the two worldviews. Not surprisingly, some feminists call fundamentalist women "quasi-feminists." All this merits the question, Epstein notes, of whether these fundamentalists should really be classified as feminists despite their rejection of that label (though, I would add, fundamentalists themselves would likely reject that label).

But in the final analysis, the standard of comparison still remains feminism. Epstein alludes to the possibility that fundamentalist women still are under patriarchal control: "*However*, when the above examples are read in light of fundamentalism's history, more specifically, its socio-political genesis as a form of patriarchal control, feminism's *historically informed* ethos would recast such positive examples of women's flourishing as a form of betrayal."

In addition, Epstein opines that fundamentalist women's "matrices of resistance" do not contribute in the final analysis to the deep structural changes that are necessary to improve the position of women, because "they maintain that social ills will slowly diminish as one by one, people worldwide submit to God and assume their place in 'His' right order (… [including] heterosexual family life)." These incremental changes will not, she says, bring about the real changes that are necessary. Here Epstein shows her feminist hand by calling fundamentalist women supporters of hierarchy (the Aristotelian household code) and feminist Christians as those who "seek to restore the Jesus movement's discipleship of equals." (But her critics would argue that she compares apples to oranges. Later Christians had to think carefully about family life, whereas early Christians could avoid the topic in view of their belief that the eschaton was at hand, which meant that history and society were about to end.) In still another way, Epstein endorses feminism at the expense of her phenomenology of fundamentalism. Following Rosemary Ruether (see chapter 5), she argues that Christianity is a "living, revisionary tradition," continually offering new interpretations. By default, this means that fundamentalism, by holding to some past "truths," is moribund.

Underlying these feminist readings from Left to Right is the basic assumption that women must be free to choose what to wear, how to act, where to go, and whether to marry. Add to that the assumption that women can do it all (and should). This is a model of radical independence in which men have no necessary or relevant role, except to be women's helpers should they so choose. But our authors reveal a variety of approaches. It is obvious that they do not all belong to the same branch of feminism. Hellman, I suggest, adopts a modernist or liberal approach to feminism, which has focused on equality with men and the reforms necessary to bring it about. Equality, in other words, is her standard of comparison.

Epstein, on the other hand, adopts a postmodernist approach. As a deconstructivist, she wants ambiguity acknowledged along with the "constantly unfolding, deeply interdependent chains of texts and contexts." She criticizes the use of binary oppositions such as insider/outsider, same/other, true/false, liberated woman/not-liberated woman. "Such binary oppositions are the world- or meaning-making apparatuses intrinsic to the broader Western economy of sameness in which fundamentalist and feminist women participate." Now, pluralism and tolerance are central doctrines of contemporary feminism thanks to the fashionable status of postmodernism. When these are combined with that old dictum of feminism, "the solidarity of sisterhood," the result is that other women must be heard and taken seriously. Epstein criticizes what she considers essentialism (ascribing objective reality to a name or concept). The category "woman," for instance, is often essentialized by feminists and fundamentalists, which contributes to an oppositional logic. Following Ellen Armour, she argues that "woman" is a "perpetual site of contestation." As a result, "opacity is to replace clarity, polyvocality univocality, inclusiveness racial exclusion," and so on; thus, we all share an "ungrounded ground."

Some of the other authors, too, have been influenced by postmodernism and deconstruction. Nyitray reveals this, for instance, when she asks of fundamentalists: Is there a "privileging of particular values and how does it occur?" ("Privileging" is a key word in those branches of feminism most influenced by postmodernism and deconstruction, because it signifies *hierarchy of any kind* and is therefore anathema to feminists.) And Nyitray, citing Marilyn Young and Tani Barlow (see chapter 3), observes: "'Woman,' still is not truly a category of analysis."

Bartholomeusz lets us know that she opposes essentializing the category of "woman" (especially as wife and mother), because "woman" has meant different things in different historical periods and so is an unstable category.

Modernist feminists have criticized postmodernist ones by arguing that there can be no project for change to improve the lives of women if everything, including justice, can be deconstructed. Epstein gives the now common, postmodern rebuttal to this:

> Derrida and those who enlist his strategies appreciate the great irony haunting his textual "interventions" within Western metaphysics and psychoanalysis; he accepts the necessity of theorizing (however counter-intuitively) within a metaphysics of presence. Within these constraints, however, he strives to imagine other economies or a least some intimations of a "radical alterity." Indeed, his "solicitations" are precisely meant to illustrate the daunting obstacles that prevent metaphysics from thinking critically about itself.

She quotes Irigaray: "It is still not possible to live without boundaries, not possible to avoid saying no." We all need compassion, says Epstein, even though it too is impure. We have the "moral task" of "making the world go on." Following Kathleen Sands (see chapter 5), Epstein links this to a notion of tragedy: "The moral paradox that beings who want goodness cannot remain uncontaminated by evil, that even faultedness belongs to the enigma of suffering.... The religious and moral risk of tragic consciousness ... is to encounter elemental power/truth in its radical plurality, unmooring the good from any metaphysical anchor, so that it becomes an entirely human, entirely fragile creation." In short, Epstein is postmodernist by the front door, modernist by the back.

Conflicts between fundamentalists and feminists underlie the discussions here, although all our authors are feminists. This conflict is captured in emotional responses to "othering." Underpinning modern and postmodern understandings of hierarchy, suggest many of our authors, is the fundamentalist view of feminist women not only as "others" but also as demons. Because a key feature of fundamentalism in general is the demonization of others (religious communities, modern communities, and so forth), who are considered threats to identity, it comes as no surprise that feminists are demonized as uncontrollable others, symbols of larger problems.

Some of our authors point out that this "othering" of women is nothing new. Bartholomeusz, for instance, recalls how Buddhist monks in late nineteenth-century Sri Lanka did so (drawing on the old ascetic notion of women as dangerous temptresses) and singled out Western women (symbols of whatever was foreign, colonial, secular, and wanton). Listen to Hellman: "Woman as a symbolic capital for hindutva has been used as an ideological weapon against the 'others,' especially the 'west' and Muslims. On the one hand, the ideal Hindu woman has been contrasted to egotistic, greedy and immoral feminists and western women in general." Fishman observes that some Orthodox rabbis consider feminism to be "a pernicious, impious, outside influence. If a suggested change seems to emanate from feminist impulses, it should be rejected even if it is halakhically permitted" (of course, I would add, they might have intuited something important: feminism is sometimes a secular religion and thus a rival of Judaism). They are even more caustic when feminists are found within Orthodoxy itself. One American Jewish newspaper, for instance, referred to Orthodox feminism as "'a movement whose poison, if left unchecked, may seep into the minds of some unaware of its essence,' which challenges the 'root distinctions' between the sexes, and the different roles required of them putatively by divine preference." Whereas those Jews who consider themselves modern and Western support women's equal roles in religious and communal settings, notes Fishman, "The fundamentalists self-consciously reject feminism, which they consider to be licentiousness. Other Jewish groups on the right often are fundamentalist vis à vis women but not in other domains." These Orthodox see women's protests as "as a brazen attempt to undermine rabbinic authority" (which, I would add, sometimes, they are).

Similarly Pentecostal women "found feminism 'too radical, pushy, tied to the gay movement, and a luxury that their working class schedules could not afford" (Epstein quoting Espinosa: see chapter 5).

Sometimes, however, fundamentalist women consider *themselves* "othered" by feminists. Meshal comments that wearing the veil in Canada means wearing a mark; it makes "a Muslim woman more physically conspicuous even as it shrouds her body. In the generally tolerant Canadian social climate, controversies over immigration and multi-culturalism bring intolerances to the fore. Women in hijab are the first identifiable targets as the 'other.'" In addition, she reports that "nearly half the women ... reporting harassment said discrimination rose significantly upon their adoption of the hijab." Why? Because the *hijab* has been seen by many Canadians "as a mark of Islam's oppression of women." As one woman reported, "I fear it [discrimination] is not the superficiality of the veil; it is rather the fear of Islam itself." Surely, these mutual accusations of "othering" suggest that women themselves are part of the polarization. I will give my own reflections on what this all means in the postscript to this volume.

Notes

1. Katherine K. Young, "Introduction," *Today's Woman in World Religions* (Albany: State University of New York Press, 1994).

2. Nancy T. Ammerman, "North American Protestant Fundamentalism," in *Fundamentalisms Observed,* ed. Martin E. Marty and R. Scott Appleby (Chicago: University of Chicago Press, 1991), 2–4.

3. According to John Voll, "The wide diversity of individuals and groups associated with Islamic fundamentalism indicates that it is not a monolithic movement and renders a simple definition difficult. In addition, some contemporary Muslim thinkers and non-Muslim scholars have reservations about using the term because of its original application to a Western Christian movement. Nonetheless, there is widespread recognition of the reality to which the term refers, and many observers and participants find it useful to have a term which can refer to the complex cluster of movements, events, and people who are involved in the reaffirmation of the fundamentals of the Islamic faith and mission in the final decades of the twentieth century. 'Islamic fundamentalism,' then, will here denote the reaffirmation of foundation principles and the effort to reshape society in terms of those reaffirmed fundamentals" (John O.Voll, "Fundamentalism in the Sunni Arab World," in Marty and Appleby, *Fundamentalisms Observed,* 347).

4. Marty and Appleby, *Fundamentalisms Observed.*

5. Donald K. Swearer sees some examples of Buddhist fundamentalism in revivalist movements of the twentieth century in Sri Lanka and Thailand. "Fundamentalisms in Sri Lanka and mainland Southeast Asia have arisen from the collapse and transformation of classical religious and cultural syntheses following upon the colonial period and the introduction of Western values, technology, education, and economic and political systems. Seen from this perspective, fundamentalisms are 'modern' in the sense that they are part of the dynamic of the disintegration of traditional, self-contained societies associated with the processes of modernization. Theravada 'fundamentalism' might be even characterized as postmodern in that it seems to be a direct consequence of, and formed in reaction to, the adjustments that traditional Theravada Buddhism made to the challenge of modernity in the late nineteenth and early twentieth centuries. By critically appropriating elements of modernity alongside transformed traditional elements, fundamentalists have created an innovative and popular synthesis of religion and culture designed to preserve Thai Buddhist identity over against conventional Thai Buddhism and a morally compromised secular society. Indeed, fundamentalistic movements in Theravada Buddhist societies involve a quest for and assertion of identity (national, communal, individual), not merely in a social-psychological sense but at the deepest level of one's (or a culture's) being or personhood. Furthermore, the fundamentalist search for identity assumes the character of a return to roots—to an original situation perceived as a primordial and ideal condition of unity, certainty, and purity—but transformed and adapted in line with a critical posture toward, or rejection of, the contemporary status quo, as well as specific aspects of the historical

tradition.... The ideologies embraced by such movements tend to rest upon simplistic, dualistic, and absolutistic worldviews. Often exclusivistic (although often evangelistic), the movements reject competing groups whether from within the same tradition or from other traditions, as morally evil, spiritually confused, and/or intellectually misguided. Possessed of an almost obsessive sense of their unique role or destiny, these movements may be quasi-messianic or explicitly millenarian in nature" (Donald K. Swearer, "Fundamentalistic Movements in Theravada Buddhism," in Marty and Appleby, *Fundamentalism Observed,* 677–78).

6. Tu wi-ming notes that "fundamentalism," as either theory or practice, seems not to fit the East Asian order of things. "Yet the fundamentalist problematic characteristic of Christian, Jewish, and Islamic societies is obviously relevant to contemporary East Asia.... If we focus on the Confucian revival ... it may become clear that the 'search for roots,' which has been identified as fundamentalistic in nature, proceeds from a critique of modernity that presents a threat to, rather than a confirmation of, values held by the Western academy: tolerance, reasonableness, flexibility, open-mindedness, dialogue, and pluralism. Yet the examination of fundamentalist-like attitudes, if it is to reflect these very values, many not simply proceed as a psychopathological study of radical 'otherness'" (Tu Wei-ming, "Confucian Revival in Industrial East Asia," in Marty and Appleby, *Fundamentalism Observed,* 741–42).

7. According to Samuel Heilman and Menachem Friedman, in the nineteenth century, Jews had found that industrialization, urbanization, and the enlightenment were threatening their values. There were three reactions to all this: assimilation, acculturation, and contra-acculturation. Orthodoxy developed in the last third of the nineteenth century, in central and western Europe, as a movement against this acculturation to modern lifestyles and the reforms it had sparked within some Jewish circles. One tactic "required a resolute attachment to the status quo and a steadfast refusal to accept erosion as an objective, inevitable phenomenon, along with a denial of the process of secularization and acculturation to modernity.... The activists moved beyond traditionalism and toward what may be called active contra-acculturation, or something akin to what today is called 'fundamentalism'" (Samuel C. Heilman and Menachem Friedman, "Religious Fundamentalism and Religious Jews: the Case of the Haredim," in Marty and Appleby, *Fundamentalism Observed,* 214–15). This was the Haredim. The Haredim may be called a radical segment of the "Orthodox." Gradually the Hasidism, at first a spiritualist and charismatic movement, became allies in a contra-acculturationist campaign that sought to reverse the "erosion of Judaism" (210) with "stringent and steadfast attachment to traditions and beliefs" (211). Samuel Heilman and Menachem Friedman note that "we are prepared to describe and analyze a segment of Jewry that has been denoted by many who are concerned with such categories and definitions as fundamentalist. These Jews are often called 'ultra-Orthodox' (i.e., beyond merely Orthodox), but we prefer the term haredim. One might say these Jews believe in the fundamental truths of their religion which they assume are unchanging" (197). Fishman, in her discussion of Jewish reactions to modernity, focuses not so much on the Haredim or "ultraorthodox" but on the middle of the road Orthodox, who

strictly maintain religious law yet also accept some accommodations to modernity (as their willingness to support the education of women demonstrates).

8. The concepts of pure and impure lie at the heart of biblical Judaism's understanding of holiness (the main difference between biblical and rabbinic Judaism, in this respect, is that purity versus impurity was primarily a matter for the priesthood in biblical Judaism but of the entire people in rabbinic Judaism).

CHAPTER 1

Open Space and Double Locks: The Hindutva Appropriation of Female Gender

Eva Hellman

During the last decade, scholars and journalists have given a depressing picture of the situation for Indian women. They have brought to our attention dowry deaths, female foeticide, the higher death rates of girls/women than of boys/men and a sex ratio that is heavily tilted against women—in 1991 there were 927 women for every 1,000 men; in districts with high levels of infanticide less than 700 girls below five years old to 1,000 boys.

In this situation, Hindu nationalist or hindutva[1] organizations are projecting themselves as liberating and empowering forces not only for Hindu women but for all Indian women. Leaders of such organizations maintain that women will have important functions, get better living conditions, and will be met with respect in the Hindu India that is on the agenda of the groups. The Bharatiya Janata Party, BJP, the most important political front of the hindutva movement is projecting itself as a pro-woman political party with a Hindu-inspired program for the uplift of Indian women.[2] By this message, hindutva organizations in the 1990s reached women to such an extent that Indian as well as Western secular feminists have expressed serious concerns and called upon a reconsideration of the strategies of the Indian autonomous women's movement.[3]

One of the aims of the present article is to explore what might be *attractive* to women in the hindutva program on women's issues. A second aim is to identify the boundaries for women's empowerment in the hindutva movement. Which are the costs for women inherent in its alternative for women? In dealing with this problem I will examine the role of religion for establishing non-negotiable norms for female gender.

The article is based on field research in Rashtra Sevika Samiti, RSSa, which is the oldest and one of the largest of the hindutva women's organizations and which operates at the ideological heart of the hindutva network. In addition, previous research on women and hindutva as well as policy-documents, hymns, election manifestos, and articles published by hindutva organizations have been used to contextualise the field material. It has been pivotal to me to strike a balance between an emic and an analytic perspective. In the emic part of the article, the intention has been to mirror the insider's point of view. By allowing the "other" to represent herself, by making a voice heard—a voice with a central standing in the hindutva discourse—I have tried to minimize the orientalist mistake of distorting the picture of the "other." In the analytic part, on the other hand, I speak. With the help of feminist theory and a narrativist understanding of religion I analytically approach questions on gender and power.

The Hindutva Movement and Its Women's Wing

The umbrella concept the hindutva movement refers to groups with a Hindu India on the agenda.[4] The ultimate aim is to transform the secular Indian nation-state into a society informed by allegedly Hindu priciples, values, institutions, and ways of organising social life. At the center of the hindutva network is the Rashtriya Swayamsevak Sangh (RSS), which is a cadre organization with an emphasis on ideology and character-building.[5] In order to transform India into *hindu rashtra*, a Hindu India, the organization provides physical, moral, and intellectual training to its members, and initiates and coordinates think tanks on economy and education as well as grass root organizations such as trade unions and relief organizations. The BJP, which was initiated by the RSS, is the network's most important political front organization. As a government party (1996, 1998–2004), the BJP demonstrated a far-reaching pragmatism that clearly singles it out as the moderate wing of the network. The Vishva Hindu Parishad (VHP), which was founded on the initiative by the RSS as well, is a hindutva organization with still another profile. So far it has encouraged the organization of religious specialists (*sadhus*) for hindutva, and in spectacular, often violent, country-wide campaigns the group has mobilized Hindus for hindutva.

All hindutva organizations have women's groups. They work separately from the main organization that organizes only men (RSS, VHP) or is dominated by male leaders (BJP). Among the most important ones are the Rashtra Sevika Samiti ("The society for female servants of the nation") of the RSS, the Durga Vahini ("The Durga brigade") and the Mahila Samiti ("Women's society") of the VHP, and the Mahila Morcha ("Women's front") of the BJP. In this work the RSSa has been singled out for attention primarily because it is located at the core of the hindutva network.

The Rashtra Sevika Samiti

The Rashtra Sevika Samiti was founded in 1936 by the brahmin widow Lakshmi Kelkar.[6] Deeply impressed by the RSS ideology and the RSS way of organizing

Hindu men for the building of a Hindu India, she believed that a similar organization for women should be initiated. After discussions with K. B. Hedgewar, the founder and the first *sarsanghchalak* (top leader) of RSS, it was decided that a women's organization should be founded and that both organizations should strive for the same aim but be organizationaly separate. In an assessment of Ms. Kelkar´s initiative, the RSSa has emphasized that the women's organization added a new dimension to the work of the RSS: "She also gave a new directions and a larger dimension to Dr. Hedgewar's philosophy. She made him realise the significance of the dormant woman power and how essential it was to evoke and channalise it for the national and social welfare."[7]

Hence eleven years after the foundation of the RSS, Lakshmibai Kelkar, with the approval and the assistance of Hedgewar, established the RSSa as the first affiliate of the RSS. Thereby the two organizations were to work in close cooperation under the banner of hindutva but with different and complementary roles. To the RSS's undertaking of organizing men for the Hindu nationalist cause had now been added the RSSa project of organizing women for the same purpose.

From Marginality to Visibility

From having been a small incognito wing of the RSS with only informal contacts with the RSS, the RSSa has over the years developed into an organization with a recognized position in the Sangh parivar, i.e., the network of the RSS and its affiliates. From its modest inception in the 1930s with only a few activists, the RSSa has today around 300,000 members organized in 3,500 units and is present in almost every Indian state.[8] The organization has even appeared on the international scene with the intention of organizing women with a Hindu background in the diaspora.[9] It is worth noting that the RSSa has been accorded more weight within the hindutva network during the last decade. Now it participates in the *chintan baitak* ("introspection meet") of the RSS where the RSS and its affiliates are gathered to decide on policy questions. In the *baithak* "women's perspective and issues are articulated by the Samiti," the senior RSS leader Mr. Govindacharya has pointed out. In the 1998 *chintan baithak*, Mr. K. S. Sudarshan, the present *sarsanghchalak* of the RSS, stated "that women entering politics will get their values from the Samiti."[10] So in a situation where women's issues have become important in the Indian society the position of the RSSa in the Sangh parivar has been strengthened.

Organization and Leadership

The Samiti is headed by the "main leader" (*pramukh sanchalika*). She is compared to the key-person in a family whose wish is voluntary taken as an order by everyone in the family, who knows everybody's capacity, and who entrusts responsibilities.[11] The *pramukh sanchalika* works in close cooperation with the other members of the central executive committee. At the time of the fieldwork (late 1999) all members of the committee were brahmins. Decisions in the central executive committee of the Samiti are collectively taken by consensus. They are conveyed through the *pramukh sanchalika* and are expected to be morally binding for every *sevika* ("female servant") in the organization.[12]

If the central executive committee is the head of the Samiti, the *shakhas*, the local grassroot groups, constitute its body. In the *shakha* the *sevikas* meet regularly to study and to discuss social issues from the perspective of hindutva, for physical training, for yoga exercises, and for the singing of patriotic and spiritual songs. Every leader is expected to work for the unity of the group and to show concern for the other *sevikas* while the ordinary *sevika* is expected to adhere to the decisions of the leaders.

Two metaphors that are frequently used in the hindutva discourse aptly catch fundamental characteristics of the Samiti's technique of organization, leadership, and decision-making as described above. First, society as an organism is a simile used by hindutva ideologues and also in the Samiti.[13] Every social group (e.g., the family, the *shakha*, the Samiti, the hindutva network, and society at large) is compared to a living organism with a steering function, a brain, which informs the cells, limbs, and organs how to perform their respective functions in order to enhance the well-being of the organism in its totality. The *pramukh sanchalika* and the executive body exercise the steering function in the Samiti. They decide what is good for the organization. Like cells, limbs, and organs, the individual *sevikas* and *shakhas* are expected to accept their place in the organization and to carry out as well as they can the tasks being entrusted to them by the governing body. At the grassroots level, the executive committee of the *shakha* performs the steering function and the *sevikas* heed to the advice given to them. While the organism simile puts an emphasis on the unity of the group, the necessity of a central leadership, the functionality and the complementarity of the parts, the second simile of the family (*parivar*) lays down additional aspects of leadership.[14] In the family as well as in the Samiti there is, according to the RSSa, an emphasis on informal, close personal contact between individuals. Mutual respect, consideration, team spirit, and devotion to the mother bind the family members together. In the family and in the Samiti there is one key person who is loved and respected, who knows the strengths and weaknesses of every family member, and who cares for them. By her/his natural authority, they entrust responsibilities to each family member according to their capacities. The considerate leader and the sense of community transmitted by the family metaphor cleverly balance the harsher demands of the organism simile.

The Samiti way of organization, leadership, and decision-making is an example of what Durkheim has termed "organic solidarity." There is a relative equality between the members of the executive committee, and a hierarchical solidarity between the members and groups at different levels of the Samiti. This implies that the power over ideology, organization, and appointment of leaders are solidly in the hands of the central executive body, leaving the ordinary *sevikas* with the choice of working within the established boundaries or quitting the organization. Since the power to pass resolutions and to appoint functionaries is in the hand of a small body of senior leaders who are firmly established in the organization, major changes of policy are rendered unlikely and dissident voices are effectively silenced. The caring and responsible attitude that is expected by the leader does of course not change the basic imbalance in power.

Activities

Character-building activities in the local group (*shakha*) are at the center of the RSSa work. By her training, the *sevika* is expected to inspire the members of her family and to serve as an instrument of social transformation. In order to contribute to the spread of hindutva outside of the family, the RSSa runs several social and cultural projects.[15] Schools for small children and for girls, training camps for teachers, and free health care for exposed women and their children are examples of such activities. Classes for women on the singing of *bhajans*, devotional hymns, on yoga, and on the correct performance of *puja* ("worship") are examples of popular cultural programs run by the Samiti. Further, the organization participates in relief actions—during my fieldwork *sevikas* were sent to the flood-striken state Orissa—and in mass campaigns launched by the broader hindutva movement. Campaigns for the protection of cows (*goraksha*), for local production (*swadeshi*), for a Hindu Kashmir, and for the building of a Rama temple in Ayodhya can be mentioned as examples. The RSSa also cooperates with other women's organizations within the hindutva network. Thus several RSSa leaders spoke at the Matri Sangam ("meeting of mothers") rally celebrating the "spirit of motherhood." The rally that was held in early 2000 gathered approximately 50,000 women from more than 1,000 villages in Karnataka.[16]

In summary than, the main objective of the RSSa is to empower and to mobilize women for hindutva. The group encourages women's agency and self-respect. It is a top-down brahmin-dominated organization with an influential position on women's issues in the hindutva network. Through its various activities at grassroot levels, it has the potentiality of gaining a foothold among ordinary Indian women.

The Rashtra Sevika Samiti and Female Gender Scripting: Six Codes for Ideal Womanhood

In October–November 1999 I carried out a fieldwork at Devi Ahalya Mandir, the RSSa national headquarters in Nagpur, Maharashtra. The center owes it name to Ahalyabai Holkar (1725–95) the legendary queen who ruled the princely state of Indore after the deaths of her husband and her son. She is one of the role models of the Samiti and represents efficient and accountable administration (*kartitva*). On top of the large, multistoried building of Ahalya Mandir flutters the *bhagva dvaj*, the orange-colored flag that symbolizes *dharma*[17] and serves a guide for the RSSa (and for the RSS as well). To the visitor the emblem and the name clearly positions Devi Ahalya Mandir in the hindutva discourse and as an association for women stressing the importance of administration, organization, and female role models.

At the time of my field research Ahalya Mandir was buzzing with activity. Besides the daily assignments a training camp (*shibir*) for young *sevikas* was taking place at the center. For this objective most of the twenty-eight *pracharikas*,[18] full-timers, and most members of the executive committee of the RSSa appeared at the site. A visit by Mr. K. S. Sudarshan, the then joint general secretary of the RSS, added an extra impetus to the camp.[19] Simultaneously *sevikas* in charge of the foundations managing the various Samiti projects met at Ahalya Mandir to discuss the running of schools, program of health care, etc. Hence during the fieldwork I had the chance to observe the annual *shibir* for *pracharikas* and *pracharikas* to be, to meet with leaders at the central level and with *sevikas* responsible for *seva* projects while also participating in the regular activities carried out at Ahalya Mandir.

Since the aim of the case study was to highlight the official RSSa voice on ideal womanhood and women's issues, I decided to interview central leaders of the group. In a kader organization such as the RSSa it would besides be problematic to identify radically divergent opinions and attitudes.[20]

Six Hindutva Codes for Ideal Womanhood

On the basis of interviews with official RSSa representatives, RSSa policy-documents, hymns, pamphlets, conference souvenirs, study material, articles but also official BJP material, six hindutva codes for ideal womanhood have been iden-tified. In order to come across that which might prove appealing to women the codes are formulated from an emic perspective.[21]

To the Rashtra Sevika Samiti, *woman as political mother* is a centrality. The strong, self-confident, well-educated, and patriotic mother is over and over held to be pivotal in the family as well as in society. Ms. Pramilatai Medhe, who was then the general secretary of the RSSa (she was named Pramakh Sanchalika of the RSSa in 2006), saw her as the pillar of society:

> The female powers or qualities should be used firstly in the family to control, to mould the family and make it fit for social life. In our tradition family has been given the most prestigeousness and importance and in that woman is the centre-point. When we want to draw a circle with a compass we have to be very firm on the centre-point, otherwise the circle will not be formed. If woman is firm, if she has got a clear conception of life then the family and

society at large becomes fruitful. The family circle, the social circle, the universal circle, so she can control one after another circle. She can make them fruitful. When women loose their womanly qualities there will be chaos in society.[22]

With female qualities such as love, devotion, modesty, unselfishness, and the readiness to serve she cares for the family, and by raising her children in the spirit of hindutva she makes an essential contribution to the building of *hindu rashtra*.

Other informants used the metaphor *Vishvam Bhara* ("The one who carries the world")[23] to communicate the same idea. Ms. Sindhu Risbud, who is the vice president of the RSSa's educational wing, explained:

Also after marriage the girl goes to another family. If the girl is properly trained she can train the whole household. When she is in the home where she was born she can be a guide to her father and brother. And when she goes to her husband's house she can also … of course not teach but influence her husband and her sons. She is the whole support for the family and influences the whole system. She is Vishvam Bhara, i.e., she is moulding the world by moulding her family.[24]

The fact that hindutva leaders—female and male[25]—over and over again emphasise the importance of women as political mothers is not surprising in a movement that aims at minimizing the role of the State. In the envisaged Hindu India, the family is expected to care for children, the elderly, and the handicapped, thereby reducing the need for a state-sponsored public sector. In this scenario it is taken for granted that women carry the family: it is her duty as a woman (*stridharma*) to care for the needs of its members and to transmit basic hindutva values and the hindutva brand of patriotism to them. To fulfill her duties it is a must that she is educated and ideologically firm. In her spare time she is invited to carry out social work or to work publicly for hindutva. If the economy of the family demands it, she could work, but should never forget that her primary duty is to care for the family.

The second code, *woman as activist for hindutva*, implies that women are encouraged to use their talents for promoting hindutva outside the family. By working in a Samiti group, they are invited to participate in the social projects launched by the Samiti or to militantly defend hindutva values in times of emergency. All the *sevikas* I met during the fieldwork were activists for hindutva. Most of them were peaceful ideologues and ambitious social workers, not demagogues, hecklers, looters, or carriers of karosene. They were engaged in *seva* ("service") projects directed at exposed women and their children. As examples of such activities can be mentioned the running of free medical centers, chreeches, nursery schools in slum areas, schools for girls, tailoring classes, small home industries for women, computer classes, family counselling centers, reading rooms, hostels for tribal girls, for daughters to leprosy patients, and for low-caste girls. Some of them were working with the education of female *purohits* (orthodox "priests"), an office that traditionally has been the privilege of male brahmins.[26] The Samiti is responsible for the education of such female ritual authorities, and their training is led by experienced senior female *purohits*. The enterprise is regarded as a revival of a Vedic acceptance of female ritual experts. On the invitation from families, individual women or the Samiti the female *purohits* perform *pujas* ("worship"), *yajnas* (Vedic sacrifices for public welfare), and *samskaras* (rites of passage), even *antyeshti*, the last rites. Their *dakshina* (fee) is donated to the Samiti. The female *purohits* are proud of their vocation and are definitely aware of being pioneers. This picture of hindutva women activists as working for the empowerment of individual women, as expounding women's public roles, as building an alternative social network among women and as hindutva propagandists in the neighborhood is to be contrasted with Tanika Sarkar's and Sikata Banerjee's studies of militant hindutva women.[27] However, the RSSa importance attached to militant female role models, to violence, and to weapon training makes clear the potentiality of women's violence in furthering the hindutva project.

The Samiti holds out three women from the past as main role models for contemporary women.[28] Jijamata (seventeenth century) embodies the ideal of the political mother. In the RSSa discourse she represents *matritva*, "enlightened motherhood" or "the mother as an architect and builder of a nation."[29] She is praised for having brought up her son Shivaji[30] to become a crusader against Mughal rule and to work for a *hindu rashtra*. The other two models represent two aspects of woman as activist for hindutva. Ahalyabai Holkar (eighteenth century), after whom the Samiti's national headquarters Devi Ahalyabai Mandir is named, is to be emulated in times of peace. She represents the ideal of *kartitva*, the capacity to work hard. She is glorified for her effective administration of the sovereign Hindu kingdom of Indore, for having cared for her people as a mother and for having renovated temples destroyed by the Mughals. In times of crises Rani Lakshmibai of Jhansi (nineteenth century) is the model to be inspired by. She represents *netritva* ("leadership") and is praised for her militant struggle against the British colonial power during the mutiny 1856–57. The RSSa female role models as described above are socially active women performing public roles and having a public influence. The hindutva cultural icons and female role models stand in stark contrast to prevalent traditional role models for Hindu women such as Sita, Savitri, and Sati who all personify the *pativrata* ideal, i.e., the woman who is devoted and subservient to her husband and regards him as God. In a speech Ms. Usha Chati, the third top leader of the RSSa (from 1994 through 2006), encouraged women to become socially active: "When a woman develops the qualities of enlightened motherhood, the capacity to work and leadership she will become the source of strength in the nation."[31] In her declaration there were no reference to the submissive and docile wives of Sanskritic Hinduism. Instead she stressed the qualities represented by the three RSSa role models.

The historian Tanika Sarkar, the sociologist Paoloa Bacchetta, and the political scientist Sikata Banerjee have addressed the question why women have chosen to be actively involved with hindutva organizations. One reason mentioned by all three scholars is that female hindutva activists actually experience benefits from their involvement with the hindutva movement. In their research they have encountered other kinds of activists than the ideologues I met with in Devi Ahalya Mandir. I will briefly summarize those aspects of their studies that increase our understanding of the hindutva movement's appeal to women.

In her pioneering and influential article "The Woman as Communal Subject,"[32] Tanika Sarkar focuses on the active, militant women who were mobilized by Hindu organizations during the last years of the Ayodhya campaign. Sarkar declares that the middle-class women of the hindutva network during this phase of hindutva escalation were encouraged to (re)claim public spaces—they acted as political subjects, as leaders, and they were trained to view themselves as citizens. Some of them acted in front positions, while others took part in the Ayodhya-campaign as grassroot activists. Sarkar has highlighted the benefits experienced by female hindutva activists. Her interviews with young members of the RSSa reveal that the women regard the daily physical training in *shakha* as a preparation for a civil war against Muslims and as a protection against Muslim rapists. However, behind these ideologically correct answers Sarkar identifies other motifs. She makes the contention that these urban, upwardly mobile, affluent middle-class women experience the self-confidence and the physical training they get in the group as means of handling problems they face in daily life—spousal abuse, dowry murders, discrimination, and sexual harassment.

Sarkar's reflections, which are of a general nature, are corroborated and illustrated by Paola Bacchetta's case study of Kamlabehn, a relatively young engineer and an activist of the RSSa.[33] Kamlabehn is described as an enterprising and independent woman, who, by her commitment to the hindutva and the RSSa, has an aim of life outside the family. She is actively involved in the training of other young women in the martial arts. To propagate hindutva she travels alone in India, gives public speeches, and discusses *hindu rashtra* with primarily male activists. She dresses untraditionally in jeans, in men's shirts and sneakers, and drives a motorbike. She chooses where to live, if to marry, and when she eventually marries she does not allow her new status to restrict her independence. By her whole-hearted and successful involvement with the organization, Kamalabehn acquires freedom of choice and gets an outlet for her enthusiasm and talents. In spite of the fact that she transgresses the boundaries of a traditional role for a Hindu woman, she is assigned great status in her family, in the RSSa, and in the RSS as such. Women such as Kamlabehn are tolerated within the movement, but they are to be assessed as the exception that proves the rule.

Sikata Banerjee has spelled out that Hindu women from poorer sections also may experience benefits from projects launched by hindutva organizations.[34] In a micro-study on the Shiv Sena's (SS) activities among women in Mumbai she has pointed out that the organization runs income-generating projects for Hindu women and offers day care and medical help. Thereby, she contends, the organization has provided poor, powerless, and exposed women in slum areas with opportunities for a better life. However, at the same time as female members of the Shiv Sena have gained greater control over their personal lives and have been given access to the public arena by the alternative infrastructure provided by the SS, they have also been mobilized by the organization for violent actions. After the destruction of the Babri Masjid in 1992, a large number of women took an active part in the riots that followed. Women blocked the arrest of Shiv Sena leaders, prevented fire engines from going to Muslims areas on fire, looted stores, and are even reported to have attacked Muslim women.

A third code, which I call *woman as citizen,* is also evident in the material. The RSSa activities make it easier for individual women to take part in public life. In the RSSa schools for girls, the education in general subjects prepare them for college and university. And the training in practical affairs provides them with the possibility of earning money by their practical competence.[35] Likewise the RSSa classes for women on tailoring and computers train them for jobs outside the home. The creeches, the small-scale industries for women and the health care clinics run by the RSSa facilitates such a choice. More important, in the local grassroot group, the *sevika* systematically develops personality traits that help her to deal with challenges she might face in everyday life. In the group she learns to work hard, to take responsibility, to lead a group, to speak publicly, and to defend herself physically. The confidence and discipline gained are valuable assets when applying and competing for employment.

The RSSa however does not work politically for women's rights. Like most hindutva organizations, it projects itself as a socio-cultural organization working for the implementation of Hindu values in society. Character-building, not political rights, is the means per se to reach this objective. In fact, the demand for individual rights is condemned as a non-Hindu Western ideal detrimental for social harmony, a foundational quality of the utopian *hindu rashtra.*[36]

The Bharatiya Janata Party, which is the political wing of the hindutva network, on the other hand works politically to empower women and to protect the rights of women by law. It should come as no surprise that a hindutva organization working within the political system addresses women's issues. To gain numerical strength it is important to win women's votes. In its 1996 election manifesto, the party launched an ambitious twenty-nine point agenda titled *Nari shakti: Towards Empowerment of Women.*[37] The program suggested that all major political decisions should be gender analysed; that 33 percent of seats in elected bodies should be reserved for women; that equal opportunities for women and men in employment and promotion should be aimed at; that equal wages for equal work should be enforced; that the same legal and economic rules for women and men should be actively promoted; that different programs to give women work outside the family should be initiated; that educational and medical resources should be directed specifically at women and girls; that measures to tackle the problem with woman beating should be taken; that efforts to eradicate female foeticide and female infanticide should be intensified and that a common civil code that eradicates the discrimination against women in the present private laws should be introduced.[38] By these proposals the BJP announced its intention to improve the conditions for women and to make them into "real participants in a resurgent India of the 21st century."[39] In the 1998 election manifesto the demands were repeated and some more were added. A development bank to cater for the financing need of women entrepreneurs and self-employed women was suggested, as was the promise for free education for women up to graduation, including professional studies like medicine and engineering.[40]

The three codes for ideal womanhood dealt with so far (woman as political mother, activist for hindutva and citizen) are all located in a practical, social context. They deal with qualities, roles, tasks, and arenas held to be appropriate for women. The fourth and the fifth codes (woman as the daughter of Bharat Mata and woman as female cell in the living organism of Hindu society), on the other hand, add a metaphysical dimension to the lives of women. With the help of two nonhistorical symbols for an assumed female essence, ideal womanhood is inscribed into a religious context.

Woman as the daughter of Bharat Mata is a fourth code of ideal womanhood to be expounded. Bharat Mata, "Mother India," is a central symbol in the hindutva discourse.[41] As a modern form of Devi, The Great Goddess, she represents fertility and prosperity and is regarded as an embodiment of *prakriti* ("matter") and *shakti* ("energy," "power"). To the *hindutvavadis*, proponents of hindutva, she is above all regarded as a personification of the holy land and as the mother inspiring her daughters and sons to implement *dharma*, the eternal cosmic law, i.e., Hindu principles and values, in life. In her activist form Bharat Mata is an inciting war goddess.[42] She blows her conch and urges her children to fight against nondharmic elements. Her sons and daughters march in rank and file toward the enemy and the goddess's war lion attacks. In the hindutva discourse the enemy or the "other" can be Muslims or Christians refusing to individualize and privatize religion; secularists drawing a sharp line of demarcation between the political and religious systems; liberals denouncing the subordination of the rights of the individual to the interests of the collective; Marxists and socialists regarding class as an important element in the analysis of conflicts; feminists critical of gender-based inequalities; capitalists being accused of encouraging greed and reducing people into mere machines and people identifying as *dalits*, "down trodden," rather than as Hindus.

They are all charged with undermining Hindu unity and threatening the dharmization or Hinduization of India.

The expression "Bharat Mata's daughter" is of central importance in the *Prarthana* ("prayer"), the hymn of Rashtra Sevika Samiti, which is recited daily and collectively by the members of the group.[43] After having hoisted and saluted the *bhagva dvaj*, the saffron-colored flag, which is regarded as the guru of the organization and as a symbol of *dharma*, the *sevikas* recite the *Prarthana* in unison. One of them acts as precentor—the *sevikas* take turn at leading the recital since everyone is trained in leadership. She chants the text and the others repeat her words. During the recital everybody stands at strict attention in front of the *bhagva dvaj* with the right arm placed horizontally in front of the chest.

In the hymn the *sevikas* eulogize the goddess Bharat Mata and identify themselves as her daughters (*sutah*). They also dedicate themselves to become Bharat Mata's instruments in the dharmic struggle against alleged enemies. The recital closes with the *sevikas'* resolve to become fiery makers of *hindu rashtra*. In this scenario woman is accorded a cosmically meaningful task. As a child of the inciting Bharat Mata, she, like her male siblings, is to work for the implementation of the dharmic order in the world and to fight anything that poses a threat to this order. As the *daughter* of Bharat Mata and as a *female* soldier in her army she in addition has a specifically *female* function to perform in the mission of establishing *dharma* in Bharat.

The RSSa conception of women's gender bound tasks in the dharmic project is further clarified by the fifth code to be reiterated—*woman as female cell in the living organism of Hindu society*. This code is based on the hindutva idea that every Hindu, be it woman or man, is a constituent of a metaphysical entity referred to as Hindu society (*hindu samaj*). It is perceived as a living, divine organism consisting of limbs, organs, and cells representing different social units, institutions, and individuals. Ideally, according to the organistic hindutva worldview all these units should be imprinted with hindutva, i.e., dharmic values, and thus work in a manner that enhance the unity and the harmony of the social body.[44] In order to actualize the potential divinity of the organism, it is held to be necessary that each one of its parts performs its specific function optimally. Men are encouraged to develop and use their masculine qualities in furthering the hindutva project while women are supposed to refine and direct their feminine essence for the building of *hindu rashtra*.

Ms. Pramila Medhe, the general secretary of the RSSa, illustrated this line of argumentation.[45] After having stressed the importance of activating women for the Hinduization of India and having delineated the Samiti as an organization working for this end, she gave vent to a conception of femininity that is prevalent in the Sanskritic tradition. She stated femininity to be radically different from masculinity and took for granted a female inborn essence, which is not culture bound but which is present in every woman. She further stressed the complementarity of femininity/masculinity and of women/men. The sexes are certainly radically different in essence as well as in qualities, but they are at the same time complementary to each other and are accordingly given gender-based functions and responsibilities. In laying out the conception of gender, Pramila Medhe made explicit use of Hindu concepts. The assumed female essence was identified with the cosmological principles *prakriti* and *shakti*, i.e., matter without form that is the physical prerequisite of universe, and the creative but unconscious power necessary for bringing forth and maintaining the universe. The male principle was equated with *purusha*, the conscious subject that gives direction to the creative power and accords form to matter. In arguing for the ontological and the functional complementarity between the sexes, she referred to the established Hindu symbol *Ardhanarishvara*, god as half male (with Shiva representing the male qualities of divinity) and half female (with Parvati representing the female attributes of divinity). When speaking about the necessity of controlling or directing the female essence in order to make it beneficial, she made use of Hindu symbols as well. It is symptomatic that she referred to *Durgasaptashati* ("The seven hundred verses on Durga") when arguing that a woman's *shakti* or strength should be used for attacking that which is detrimental to social harmony and for patronizing that which is conducive to it. Likewise the female *trimurti*, i.e., the combined form of the goddesses Sarasvati, Lakshmi, and Kali, was depicted as representing the proper utilization of the female essence. A woman thus endowed with controlled femininity brings about social harmony and wealth. She has an understanding of the aims of life and of the duties to be performed. She knows the proper use of material resources, fights against evil tendencies, and inspires others to lead righteous lives. The epithet *Ma*, "Mother," is used for designating any woman who uses her feminine nature in this auspicious manner. If women do not live accordingly, chaos will be the result. Hence Ms. Pramila Medhe formulated a conception of woman that is said to be in rapport with the Hindu tradition; that is characterized by the radical difference between femininity and masculinity and between women and men, by an essentialistic outlook, by the complementarity between the sexes; that refers to the metaphysical as well as the mundane/social level; and that ascribes high value to controlled femininity.

The goddess Astha Bhuja ("The one with eight arms") is a RSSa symbol of auspicious femininity as delinated above. Astha Bhuja is a new Hindu goddess that was created by Ms. Lakshmi Kelkar, the founder of RSSa. In RSSa pamphlets she is described as the combination of Lakshmi (representing wealth), Sarasvati (representing knowledge/intellect), and Kali (representing strength). She is also referred to as *matrishakti*,[46] which in the RSSa connotes the essential female power, which is being contained for positive ends. But Astha Bhuja is also regarded as a symbol of the ideal Hindu woman.[47] In this capacity the goddess represents an inherent divine and positive female nature that should be cultivated by every woman. For the objective of protecting *dharma* and *samskriti* and for establishing *hindu rashtra*, a woman should develop and direct her female nature as represented by Astha Bhuja[48]:

> The eight arms of Astha Bhuja signify her capacity for hard work and in her hands are symbols representing the fully developed qualities of the ideal Hindu woman: the sacred fire (*agnikunda*)—the ability to sacrifice; the string of beads (*japmala*)—to constantly focus on the goal of life; the double edged knife (*khadga*)—to protect herself and dharma and to fight adharma; the protective hand (*varadhasta*)—to punish evil doers and to bless good people; the saffron flag (*bhagvadvaj*)—to live according to hindutva and to work for the establishment of *hindu rashtra*; *Bhagavadgita*—to combine *gyan* (insight), *karma* (work), and *bhakti* (devotion); the bell (*ghanta*)—to be alert and the lotus (*kamala*)—to live a detached and pure life.[49]

As *matrishakti* the goddess represents auspicious *shakti*, the feminine essence, which is controlled and used for the benefit of Hindu society. Since she in addition represents the ideal feminine form she denotes that every woman is expected to develop and to make perfect her inherent female nature and to use her womanly qualities for hindutva. In the discourse of hindutva organicism Astha Bhuja represents the fully developed female cell that functions perfectly for the benefit of the living organism of Hindu society.

Lastly, I draw attention to a sixth code—*woman as symbol for Hindu society*. From the insider's point of view the Hindu woman who has developed her full potential as woman (*narishakti/matrishakti*) as delineated above illustrates hindutva's ability to initiate change, reforms, and modernization without renouncing fundamental Hindu principles and values such as gender specific roles. That women are included in the modern functional systems does not necessarily imply that they have to abandon (ascribed) essential feminine qualities such as chastity, purity, unselfishness, adaptability, service mindedness, and a sacrificial and motherly attitude. Neither does it entail that the traditional gender structure has to be challenged. By "correct" body language, clothing, sexuality, conduct, morals, values, and social roles the socially active woman is still the respected carrier of a collective Hindu identity.

Woman as a symbolic capital for hindutva has been used as an ideological weapon against the "others," especially the "West" and Muslims. On the one hand the ideal Hindu woman has been contrasted to egotistic, greedy, and immoral feminists and Western women in general.[50]

Already Ms. Lakshmi Kelkar, the founder of the RSSa, strongly denounced Western ideas about women's liberation that stressed equal rights and economic freedom. Such values were according to her related to individual progress and self-centeredness and made women lose their inborn female qualities such as a commitment to sacrifice and service. She warned that this eventually might lead to the disintegration of the family, which she regarded the primary social unit for imparting correct *samskaras* (read: values, traditions, customs). The Samiti was started to counter such tendencies.[51] My informants condemned "Western feminism" on similar grounds. The polarization against Muslims has as well been common in the hindutva movement. Scholars such as the Indian historians Urvashi Butalia and Purshottam Agarwal have argued that woman as symbol has been used by the hindutva movement for the sake of mobilizing against and for demonizing the Muslim minority.[52] Under the pretext of defending chaste Hindu women from Muslim rapists, Hindu men have been urged to mobilize for the defense of the Hindu community. And in the debate in the wake of the Shah Bano case in the mid-80s (on the right of divorced Muslim women to alimony) hindutva organizations branded the Muslim position in women's issues as oppressive and contrasted it with the allegedly woman-friendly Hindu attitude.[53]

A Pro-woman Alternative?

In the preceding sections I have explored six hindutva codes for ideal womanhood, i.e., social roles, mythological conceptions, and ideological constructs relevant for female gendering. Woman as political mother, as activist for hindutva, as citizen in a Hindu India, as daughter of Bharat Mata, as female cell in the body of Hindu society, and as symbol for the Hindu community have been investigated. Woman as political mother has been identified as a code with direct consequences for women's everyday lives. The prime duty of a woman is to be the "circle point" of the family, to care for it, to keep it together, to suppress her personal aspirations, and to transmit hindutva values to its members. She is thus supposed to carry on the organistic worldview of hindutva with its insistence on harmony that is held to be in concord with *dharma*, or the eternal transcendent principle; she is to rely on interpreters of *dharma* for guidance in mundane matters, to accept the injunction that individuals and social groups are to strive for the well-being of society at large as defined by leading *hindutvavadis*, to carry on a collective identity, to live according to an ethics of duty, and to mark against individuals and groups challenging fundamental hindutva norms.

The hindutva codes for ideal womanhood certainly offer women some degree of "empowerment" and better living conditions, facts that partly explain the success of the movement among women during the last years. First, the codes make women visible. They all take women's lives, experiences, and issues seriously. Second, the codes ascribe value to women. They are recognized as pillars of the family and of society at large. Third, women's agency is encouraged and supported in the codes. She may break the traditional roles for women as daughter, wife, and mother economically dependent on her father, her husband, or her sons. Lastly, women's lives are assigned meaning at the social level and at a transcendent level.

In the Indian society the hindutva alternative for women might appear to be a radical and progressive one. In comparison to the contemporary situation for girls and women, it offers prospects of improved living conditions. Women within the movement get visibility, appreciation, and are presented with positive self-images. They are offered jobs, child care, education, protection, freedom of action, new public roles, responsibility, and are accorded tasks in the creation of *hindu rashtra*. This implies that women have a certain degree of freedom to choose how to live their lives as political mother, activist, and citizen, and that individual women are provided with resources for improving their lives. The fact that men are supposed to be reliable heads of the household and the prime breadwinners in addition gives many women the prospect of better living conditions.[54]

However, we have come across some of the costs implicit in the hindutva option for women. To gain acceptance they have to adapt to a collective female identity according to which women are expected to carry the honor of the group, mainly by transmitting and conforming to the culturally conservative hindutva values identified in this article. Women are expected to restrain their personal aspirations and to make the needs of the family a priority. If a woman works outside her own household, she is encouraged to work on a voluntary basis or only in order to add to the income of the family. What happens to the woman who refuses to be a cultural icon of the hindutva movement? What happens to the woman who questions the hegemonic hindutva ideology and advocates a secular and multicultural India? What happens to the woman who questions the idea of an essential difference between women and men and stresses the similarities, i.e., the common humanness of women and men and opts for women and men to have equal chances of giving shape to their lives? The hindutva construction of female gender undoubtedly empowers women to a certain extent, but is the movement really prowoman in its deeper layers? We now turn to explore this question.

Hindutva Boundaries for Female Gender

After thus having depicted and preliminary assessed six codes for ideal womanhood in the hindutva discourse, it is now time to locate the boundaries and the conditions for the empowerment of women inherent in the codes.

The Hindutva Brand of a Patriarchal Gender System

The Swedish historian Yvonne Hirdman has introduced the concept of gender system for the analysis of power relations between women and men. With gender system Hirdman understands a system that "arranges" the sexes into their respective genders and that seems to show a regularity based on two types of rules. One is the rule of distinctive separation, which can be seen in the division of virtually all areas and levels of life into male and female categories. The second rule is that of the male norm, i.e., the way that "higher value" is almost automatically accorded to things masculine.[55]

The relationship between the sexes in a patriarchal society is, according to Hirdman, characterized by a gender system based on two principles.[56] The principle of "distinctive separation" implies that the dichotomy masculinity-femininity defines the relation between women and men. By this logic women and men are ascribed separate qualities, directed into separate social arenas, and are assigned separate tasks. The hierarchization between the sexes is the other principle for gendering. Man is the norm representing human being in general: that which is connected with men and masculinity is valued, while woman is defined as the "other" and sometimes even as a not fully human being, and femininity is devalued.[57]

What about the hindutva construction of gender in the light of the two principles identified by Hirdman as features of a patriarchal gender system? The principle of "distinct separation" is obvious in the codes that have been dealt with in the article. Men and women are accorded radically different inborn essences as well as psychological and physical features. In society they are directed into separate arenas where they are expected to perform gender specific tasks. Thus "distinct separation" between the sexes is a strong and visible rule in the hindutva gender system. In questions of power, the principle of "keeping apart" is operative as well. The home and the women's organization being the main arenas imply that women systematically are faced with fewer options than men, that their freedom of action is restricted, and that they are absent from the locations where the overall agenda for the hindutva movement is settled. The fact that women are accorded the responsibility to carry on a set of prescribed culturally conservative values to the family and are regarded as symbolic capital for hindutva further entail that women have to keep well within the the fixed boundaries of hindutva. Consequently they run the risk of being punished if transgressing them. Men, on the other hand, work in public space, and in the main organizations that set the agenda for the hindutva movement at large, or in one of its numerous affiliates. A man's failing to live a morally impeccable life can be blamed on the slackness of his wife. The code woman as female cell in the social body conveys the idea that the female essence (*shakti*, *prakriti*), which every woman is endowed with, has to be controlled by the male principle (*purusha*) in order to be auspicious. In matters of authority the idea makes women second to men. Men set the agenda, and women are instrumental in carrying out and maintaining plans designed by men. To put it bluntly, men direct women who in their turn might be delegated the authority to direct other women.

However, the gender asymmetry to women's disadvantage exemplified above is not to be equated with the principle that Hirdman calls "man-as-norm." To Hirdman this rule states that men and masculinity are highly valued while women and femininity are systematically devalued. This is not the case in the hindutva gender system. According to the hindutva worldview, masculinity is radically different from femininity, and the difference is metaphysically founded. But masculinity and femininity as well as man and woman are regarded as necessary complements to each other. Each category reflects a special quality of the divine. The interplay between them is regarded as necessary for the harmonious functioning of society. This implies that masculinity and femininity as well as men and women are held to be of equal worth. Although the sexes are accorded gender-bound tasks in everyday life, male tasks and female tasks are ascribed the same value.

Starting from Hirdman's concept of gender system, I have characterized the hindutva gender system as a patriarchal one with three distinct characteristics: a far-reaching separation between the sexes, a gender assymetry to the benefit of men in questions of authority, and a complementarianism assigning equal value to the innate qualities of women and men, and to the gender-bound tasks performed by them. This is a gender system that can be qualified as a patriarchal gender system with *equity*, not equality, as one of its distinguishing mark. The idea of equity assigns the same value to every individual but holds that they, due to different innate qualities, are fit to perform different social tasks. Actually the idea of equity is foundational in the hindutva organic worldview. In this article the equity between the sexes is in focus. However, other constructions of primal identities such as race and caste can also be structured according to the equity scheme.

Constitutive and Regulative Norms for Female Gender

To carry on the investigation of girders and ground-stones of hindutva's patriarchal gender system I turn to the Scandinavian sociologist Eva Lundgren's theory on the process of constituating or making gender. To answer her overarching questions "How does the constituating of *gender* take place and how to analyze the constituating of *gender* as a lifelong process?" Lundgren distinguishes between constitutive and regulative norms for gender.[58] With such norms she understands cultural norms for gender, which women (and men) follow or break, thereby constituting or destabilizing gender. I apply her distinctions to further examine the rules or norms for gender that we have identified in the hindutva patriarchal gender system. Lundgren defines constitutive norms as being presupposed, relatively stable, and often invisible. The cost for breaking them is generally high. Regulative norms on the other hand are more flexibile and also more easily recognizable. Let us see what Lundgren's distinctions add to the understanding of the hindutva patriarchal gender system!

The codes woman as activist for hindutva and woman as citizen demonstrate that the principle of "distinct separation" is not an absolute one in hindutva's women's room. Women may choose not to become mothers and instead work for hindutva in various capacities, sometimes together with male activists. Women are neither deprived of civil rights. Like men they are accorded the right to education, to political positions, and to employment outside the home. The female *purohit* is an example of a woman adopting a traditional male role that we have encountered in the material. Thus in the case of tasks and social arenas the principle of "keeping apart" should be regarded as a regulative norm. It works as a relatively strongly structuring principle for women's lives. But women may transgress the norm without being harassed or expelled from the community. In the fields of power and authority, however, the principle of "distinct separation" operates as a constitutive norm. The code woman as female cell in the social body gives a conception of how women are and how they shall act. The essentially feminine is said to consist of a potential destructivity and an inherent inability to set boundaries while the essentially male is said to represent opposite qualities. This implies a dichotomy between the sexes where men are privileged with stating the "real" problems, to formulate "acceptable" solutions to the problems, and to define the boundaries of social space. Women can act relatively freely within these boundaries, but they are not in the position to set the agenda in a radical manner nor to redefine the boundaries.

I have argued that the principle of "distinct separation" is a regulative, i.e., flexible, norm in matters of social tasks and social space. It can be transgressed and it gives scope for a reformative potential of hindutva in women's issues. In questions of power and authority is it, however, a constitutive, i.e., firm, norm for women's empowerment. In the process of writing I have come across still another norm for gendering in hindutva's gender system, which is of a constitutive character, namely the ideological contextualizing of gender. Gender (male as well as female) is inscribed into the overarching hindutva organic ideology in which the view of society as a living divine organism and its corollaries complementarianism, the stress on equity, harmony, and conflict reduction are some of the main characteristics. As the daughter of Bharat Mata, controlled *shakti*, or female cell in the body of Hindu society, a woman is expected to contribute to the hindutva project in various ways: as mother she is supposed to raise her children into hindutva patriots and to instill hindutva values into her family, as symbolic capital for hindutva she carries the honor of the community, as activist she is allowed freedom of action only within the framework of the hindutva movement, and as a citizen she is supposed to accept the fundamentals of hindutva.

As distinctive scripts for gender in the hindutva discourse we have noticed the principle of distinct separation, the gender assymetry to the benefit of men, the ideal of equity in matters of the valuation of female and male qualities and tasks, and the ideological contexualization of gender. Two of these scripts have been found to be of a constitutive nature: the gender assymetry to the benefit of men in questions of authority and the hindutva ideology. To hindutva women's groups it is crucial to keep within these non-negotiable boundaries when organizing women and when issuing directions for the everyday life of women. Actually the legitimacy in the hindutva movement of the women's groups as representatives for women and as guides for women depends on this adaptation. And the individual woman in her part runs the risk of being branded as a destructive force if her behavior and actions are not in concord with the constitutive norms of the hindutva gender system.

The Hindutva "Grand Narrative" and Female Gender

The fieldwork in the RSSa revealed the religious praxis of the *sevikas* to be multifarious. For her spiritual development the *sevika* is free to choose her own *sadhana*, or means of realization. There is no prescribed Samiti way for spiritual development, but it is a matter solely for the individual woman. The *sevikas* I had the privilege to meet with were all pious women whose personal spirituality was in tune with orthodox advaita vedanta or its more recent adaptation neo-vedanta. They all meditated in privacy on the *nirguna* ("formless") aspect of *brahman*, the divine hidden ground of reality, and on *atman*, the inner divine self. At the same time the women were careful about performing the household rites in a ritually correct manner. For the well-being of their families they daily carried out the prescribed *pujas* to the *kuladevatas*, the family deities, in accordance with Sanskritic ritual manuals. It was also important for the women to carry out or to let the appropriate Hindu rites of passage be carried out to mark the various life stages of the individual. By practicing, preserving, and transmitting the orthodox Sanskritic tradition, the *sevikas* saw themselves as safeguarding an unbroken Hindu tradition. The adherence to Sanskritic orthopraxi hence functioned as a cultural marker for them. Although it might be important for the individual *sevika* to increase her spirituality and to carry on the Sanskritic ritualism in the family, the prime concern of the RSSa is to encourage the *sevikas* to take part in the building of a Hindu India. When observing the regular activities in the local group, I soon discovered that rituals, symbols, and concepts from the Sanskritic tradition were central. The meetings in *shakha* always began with a collective rite. With words and bodily gestures the *sevikas* paid homage to the saffron-colored flag representing *dharma* and to the goddess Bharat Mata. In the ritual they identified as her spiritual daughters dedicated to establishing a society based on *dharma* and fighting against anything counteracting the "eternal, cosmic law." The interviews disclosed that the *sevikas* saw their everyday life in the light of this worldview. Practical activities like the raising of children, caring for the family, social work among deprived Hindus, and the mobilization of women for hindutva were carried out as *seva* ("service") to Bharat Mata.[59] The *sevikas* thus located their everyday activities within a metaphysical frame.

The examples of the *sevikas'* ritual activities—meditation, the performance of Sanskritic rituals, and devotion to *dharma*/Bharat Mata illustrate three different types of religious narratives: the first has a spiritual center, the second a cultural one, and the last one is a narrative with a sociopolitical focus.[60] For clarifying the role of religion in the hindutva discourse on gender, the third kind of religious narrative is crucial.

At the heart of the hindutva discourse is a religious narrative with a sociopolitical focus.[61] By prescribing an allegedly transcendent principle (*dharma*) as normative for human life, it provides a blueprint for the structuring of every aspect of social life, i.e., the functional social systems as well as that which falls between them. The building blocks of the narrative are a selection of Hindu elements such as concepts, symbols, motifs, texts, and rituals, which are being reused and adjusted for new purposes. The Hindu collective is depicted as involved in a cosmic drama being carried out within the sacred territory of Bharat (the Indian subcontinent or the land "between the Himalayas and the sea"). The long-term goal is to mould Bharat in accordance with *dharma*, thereby implementing eternal values and insights. In the struggle the individual is assigned utmost importance. To carry out her duty properly she needs guidance from role models and people with the competence to interpret *dharma* in various situations.

As can be inferred from the RSSa devotion to Bharat Mata as described in this article, women's lives are inscribed into the hindutva narrative. Thereby binding beliefs, values, and behavior for women are provided, and women are assigned socially and cosmically important roles. The RSSa narrative on women

(1) assigns meaning to the life of the individual woman. Answers are given to questions such as "who am I?" "how should I act?" "why?" "what is the purpose of my life?" As the daughter of Bharat Mata, a Hindu woman partakes in the overall project of building *hindu rashtra* in accordance with eternal principles and values. Her prime contribution to the undertaking is to care for the family in a proper dharmic manner.

(2) mobilizes women for social and political ends. Hindu women are ascribed the sacred mission of implementing *dharma* in Bharat.

(3) polarizes between "we" and the "other." Hindu women are expected to take a standpoint against allegedly adharmic or destructive forces, be it feminists, Muslims, or the "West."

(4) copes with reforms in women's issues. Since *dharma* is identified with a general principle that gives overall directions for the organization of society—and not with the static injunctions of the classical *dharmashastra*-literature—it is flexible and hence applicable in new situations.

(5) facilitates the recruiting of women for hindutva. The hindutva message about the dignity and the responsibility of women in contemporary India is

formulated in a religious language familiar to most women with a Hindu background.

(6)   positions the Samiti as *striguru*, i.e., as the guide for women on appropriate female behavior and values to be adopted by women.

(7)   gives legitimacy to female gender scripting. The metaphysically informed narrative is crucial for ascribing legitimacy to constitutive norms for female gender that we have recognized. Two such norms are held to be in tune with *dharma*. The first one is the essentialistic outlook taking for granted inborn male and female qualities, a fundamental difference between men/masculinity and women/femininity, and the complementarity between the qualities and functions of the sexes. A woman who develops her feminine qualities in the proper manner thereby lives according to *dharma*. Women (and men) are supposed to keep well within the organic worldview of hindutva, which is held to be in concord with *dharma*. Hence they are to take for granted a rule from above, to rely on interpreters of *dharma* for guidance in mundane matters, to strive for the well-being of society at large as defined by those in power, to carry on a collective identity, to live according to an ethics of duty, and to mark against individuals and groups challenging or refuting norms inherent in the hindutva organicism. Since both norms are metaphysically legitimated, they are non-negotiable. If transgressing these normative scripts, women are held to pose threats against a dharmic social order. Such women are branded as adharmic or demonic. However, within these constitutive norms women are faced with opportunities for reform and empowerment.

The Hindutva Alternative for Women in a Global Setting

Previous research on women and hindutva has by and large emphasized the Indian context, and hindutva has been analyzed as communalism. The commitment of the hindutva movement to women's issues has been seen as an attempt by the upper castes of the middle class to increase their economic and political influence, and has been identified as a prime mover in the polarization between Hindus and Muslims.[62] In this section I analyze the hindutva alternative for women neither in the Indian context nor in terms of ethnicity as Hindu communalism. Thereby I of course do not reduce the importance of this aspect of hindutva. But here I am interested in discussing the official women's room of hindutva from a global perspective and as located in a religious context.

Globalization implies that the world becomes a smaller place, and that a multiplicity of outlooks, cultures, identities, and competing grand narratives appear on the same arena. The sociologist Peter Beyer has stated that media, communication, and trade changes the world into "global metropolis in which things that do not belong together nevertheless live side by side."[63] In the case of conceptions of female gender, the pluralism is striking as well. In the globalizing process a feminism with universalist claims has been challenged by a variety of feminisms. Different kinds of feminism,[64] contextual feminisms,[65] and religiously informed alternatives for women coexist and claim to give voice to women's experiences of marginalization, subordination, and oppression. In a global perspective hindutva's women's room is one among the manifold alternatives that include women in the vision of the good society.

In the late modern world the Western ideological systems (capitalism, communism, liberalism, secular nationalism, feminism) are no longer taken for granted. They have been tried out and have failed to bring about the good society. In the void after the eroding –isms, religious narratives with a sociopolitical focus grow all the more important. By launching religion for social guidance, they represent a reaction against the functional differentiation that characterizes the modern secular way of organizing society. Some of them are of a limited extent, or to use a terminology introduced by Bruce Lincoln, they are minimalist.[66] They inform only a limited number of social systems (e.g., systems for education and health) or issues that fall outside the systems (e.g., the relation between children-parents, women-men, human being–God, rights-duties, freedom-authority, equality-hierarchy, individual-group, solidarity, identity, and so forth). Other narratives are more comprehensive or maximalist. Those with the widest reach constitute what I call "grand narratives." They are maximalist in Lincoln's sense since they cover all the social systems and that which falls between them. I hold that the hindutva religious narrative is launched as a new "grand narrative" prescribing a religiously maximalist blueprint for social life that includes a transcendentally legitimated conception for the organization of gender.

Against this background it is not surprising that hindutva leaders, male and female, have presented hindutva's women's room as an alternative to Western feminism. In the article "Women's Liberation: The Indian Way" Mr. Murli Manohar Joshi, the then president of the BJP, vented his criticism against the UN conference on women and development that was held in Beijing in 1995.[67] In 2003 Joshi headed the important ministry of Human Resource Development, which handles women's issues. In the article Joshi drew a sharp line between an Indian way of women's liberation and a feminism "rooted in the consumerist culture of the western world." He maintained that the agenda of the Beijing conference was set by women from the G7-countries and that it consequently came deal with "the wrong kind of issues." Free sex, lesbianism, the situation for unwed mothers, and artificial insemination were in focus, while "real" problems such as the physical and economic exploitation of Indian women, the erosion of the family, and women's roles in the peace movement were neglected. Similar conceptions of Western feminism have been found in the RSSa material.

Under the pretext of representing an authentic Indian alternative for women, the hindutva movement claims a place and legitimacy in the heterogenous global society. It makes a pretence of presenting a radical, Indian, Hindu-inspired program that treats seriously women's problems in the local context, makes women visible, offers reforms, education, space, and makes women into participants of the social project. In global society the hindutva movement hence demands respect for its very alternative for women. In the Indian context on the contrary there is no question of a generous pluralism. By inscribing gender issues into the hindutva "grand narrative," the hindutva movement claims the privilege of formulating problems and solutions in matters concerning Indian women. Thereby every dissenting voice is effectively silenced or demonized. The costs for taking part of benefits (such as reforms, education) that women are offered by the hegemonic hindutva movement are high indeed, but the Indian woman who chooses to be independent faces the risk of having to pay an even higher price.

Summary and Conclusive Reflections

In this article has been considered the official women's room of the hindutva movement. Primary material for the study has been drawn from the Rashtra Sevika Samiti, RSSa, which is the oldest and one of the largest hindutva groups for women.

The six hindutva codes for ideal womanhood that have been identified (woman as political mother, as activist for hindutva, as citizen in a Hindu India, as daughter of Bharat Mata, as female cell in the body of Hindu society, and as symbol for the Hindu community) certainly offer women some degree of "empowerment" and better living conditions. Women get visibility, appreciation, and are presented with positive self-images. They are offered sisterhood, jobs, child care, education, protection, freedom of action, responsibility, and are accorded agency in the creation of *hindu rashtra*. These facts partly explain the success of the movement among women during the last years.

We have, however, realized that the dignity and the empowerment offered to women is associated with costs. Women get benefits and respect on the condition that they accept the overall hindutva ideology and the hindutva gender order that keeps men and women apart and systematically bars women from positions of power outside the family and the women's group.

One purpose of the article has been to investigate the role of religion in the hindutva appropriation of female gender. For that end the hindutva "grand narrative" has been identified and discussed from a gender perspective. It is a religious narrative with a sociopolitical focus providing a transcendentally legitimated blueprint for social transformation. Gender is a vital theme in this holistic religious narrative. The RSSa metaphysically informed narrative on women has been found to ascribe legitimacy to the foundational scripts for female gender. It projects the hindutva patriarchal gender system, with its insistence on the difference but complementarianism between the sexes, as an eternal and divine gender order. It also projects the hindutva organicism with its insistence on social harmony as such. Although the hindutva women's room offers women freedom zones, it is equipped with double locks: a metaphysically legitimated patriarchal gender order and a likewise transcendentally founded organic outlook.

In this work the notion of equity has been used to distinguish the hindutva patriarchal gender system. It should be regarded as one instance of an overall ideology that is constructed in opposition to the Western enlightenment or liberal ideal of equality. The idea of equity accords the same value to every individual or group but holds that they, due to different innate qualities, are fit to perform different social tasks. Such a system makes women into participants in the functional social systems (such as health, education), gives them a place in the social project, and views men and women as of equal worth. In a deeper sense, however, it broadens the gap between the sexes. By stressing the difference and the complementarity between the sexes, it proposes a far-reaching keeping apart of men and women and invites a hierarchization in matters of authority. A patriarchal gender system in which the idea of equity is central can be contrasted to feminisms stressing the value of unqualified equality between individuals. The latter kind of feminism emphasizes the similarities between men and women ("we are all human beings"). It opts for equal rights and equal opportunities for individuals, regards gender as a cultural construction, i.e., refutes the idea of gender as a primordial category, and attempts to undo any gender-based asymmetry of power.

The article is finished off with the hypothesis that the kind of alternative for women projected by the hindutva movement is emerging as an important option in the globalization process. Modernity in the sense of the functionally differentiated social systems poses no problem to such movements. However, seen as problematic are the ideas and values connected with modernity, i.e., the primacy of reason, the privatization of religion, the insistence on the rights of the individual, including the right of women to choose how to live and whom to marry. Regarding gender, patriarchal movements of protest against the "soft" constituents of modernity launch religiously informed alternatives in which transcendentally anchored ideas of an inborn femininity/masculinity and the equity between the sexes are noticeable. The complementarity between the sexes, an essentialistic understanding of masculinity and femininity, and an underlying hierarchization to the benefit of men are launched as indigenous, authentic, and uncompromisable fundamentals. Women are ascribed value and dignity, reforms for women are initiated, and women are appreciated primarily as political mothers, but the underlying power structures between the sexes are left intact. Such movements stand in stark contrast to secular feminisms rooted in the modernity discourse. The latter insist that women's ability to support themselves economically is a presupposition for their empowerment, and they employ a perspective from below (issues such as sexualized violence, women's rights to inheritance are on the agenda). On a more general level they stress the foundational similarity between men and women, strive for an unconditional equality between the sexes, and work for the eradication of any gender-based inequality. I am convinced that the idea of equity between the sexes will come to play a prominent part in polemics against secular women's movements, and for building alliances between different partiarchal movements protesting the values of modernity. What becomes of women's real lives under these movements is quite another question.

Notes

1. In the article, the concept of "hindutva" ("Hinduness") is used as an umbrella term for groups and ideologies with the overall aim of hinduizing India. V. D. Savarkar (1883–1966), one of the early ideologues of the movement, coined the concept. In the pamphlet *Hindutva* (1923) he defined "Hinduness" in terms of one country (*bhumi*), one people (*jati*), one culture (*samskriti*), and one nation (*rashtra*). V. D. Savarkar, *Hindutva* (Pune: S. R. Date, 1949), 95. Within the hindutva movement, hindutva is equated with "cultural nationalism," which is distinguished from "merely" geographical or political nationalism (*The Hindu*, April 11, 2001). Hindu nationalism thus represents one type of German romantically inspired nationalism that is to be contrasted to a territorially conceived nationalism with the social contract as the criterion for citizenship.

2. *BJP's election manifesto 1998: Nari shakti. Empowerment of women* <http://bjp.org/manifes/chap10.htm>.

3. Basu et al., *Khaki Shorts and Saffron Flags* (New Delhi: Orient Longman, 1993), 42, 44; B. Cossman and R. Kapur, "Women and Hindutva," *Women against Fundamentalism* 5, no. 1 (1994): 1; P. Jeffrey, "Agency, Activism and Agendas," in *Appropriating Gender: Women's Activism and Politicized Religion in South Asia*, ed. A. Basu and P. Jeffery (New York: Routledge, 1998); P. Mukta, "Gender, Community, Nation: The Myth of Innocence," in *States of Conflict: Gender, Violence and Resistence*, ed. S. Jacobs, R. Jacobson, and J. Marchbank (New York: Zed Books, 2000), 176.

4. For a study of the hindutva movement from the perspective of political science, see C. Jaffrelot, *The Hindu Nationalist Movement in India* (New Delhi: Viking, 1996).

5. For a study of the RSS, see W. Andersen and S. D. Damle, *The Brotherhood in Saffron: The Rashtriya Swayamsevak Sangh and Hindu Revivalism* (New Delhi: Vistaar Publications, 1987).

6. *Rashtra Sevika Samiti: An Organisation of Hindu Women* (Nagpur: Sevika Prakashan, 1998), 2.

7. *Life Sketch of Vandaniya Mausiji* (Nagpur: Sevika Prakashan, 1996), 25.

8. V. Radhika, "Emerging from the Shadows: Sangh Sewikas," *The Week Magazine*, January 24, 1999; *Rashtrasevika Samiti* a <http://hssworld.org/seva/sevadisha/sevadisha1/sevika_samiti.html>.

9. *Rashtrasevika Samiti* b <http://rss.org/samiti/press__1.html>..

10. Radhika, "Emerging from the Shadows."

11. *Rashtra Sevika Samiti: An organisation of Hindu women*, 73.

12. *Ibid.,* 74.

13. M. S. Golwalkar, *Bunch of Thoughts* (Bangalore: Jagarana Prakashana, 1980), 133; V. V. Nene, *Pandit Deendayal Upadhyaya: Ideology and Perception* (part II) (New Delhi: Suruchi Prakashan, 1991), 12, 49f., 52; *Rashtra Sevika Samiti: An organisation of Hindu women,* 16, 37.

14. The family metaphor is used by the RSS to delineate the relationship between RSS and the *swayamsevaks*, the (male) members of the RSS, and between the RSS and its affiliates. H. V. Seshadri, ed., *R.S.S.: A Vision in Action* (Bangalore: Jagarana Prakashan, 1988), 315.

15. *Rashtra Sevika Samiti: An organisation of Hindu women,* 9; *Samiti Shiksha Varg,* speech by *sanchalika pramukh* Usha Chati, 1997, 10.

16. D. Kamath, World Peace Is Bharat's Goal, *Organiser,* January 14–20, 2000.

17. *Rashtra Sevika Samiti: An organisation of Hindu women,* 69.

18. Though it was decided during the inception of the Samiti that there would not be any full-timers, in the mid-1970s some *sevikas* expressed their desire to work full-time for the organization. And finally in 1980 the issue was settled and *pracharikas* ("propagators") were allowed. A *pracharika* works full-time for the Samiti, is unmarried, celibate, and has undergone a *diksha* (initiation ceremony) in which she has given the vow to sacrifice her "body, mind and wealth" (*tan, man, dan*) for the sake of the organization. Some remain *pracharikas* for life while others marry and continue their work as lay *sevikas*.

19. A couple of months later K. S. Sudarshan was appointed as the fifth *sarsanghchalak* of the RSS.

20. When conducting interviews, I experienced that the informants were eager to and encouraged to provide "correct" answers. One of the *sevikas* regarded it as unnecessary for me to conduct multiple interviews since "we all say the same thing." Control mechanisms for ensuring conformity or consensus were amply demonstrated during the work. A central senior leader was always present during interviews with *sevikas* who were not members of the executive committee. In a collective interview with the young *pracharikas*, the leader of the group turned off the tape recorder when a question had been formulated and urged the question to be discussed by the members of the group. The discussion (*charcha*) implied that the leader commented on suggestions made by the younger *pracharikas*. When the recorder was turned on, the *pracharikas* provided ideologically correct answers (and had been given a lesson in the official policy of the RSSa).

21. A fuller account of the RSSa construction of female gender is found in E. Hellman, *Hindu Women as Religious Agents* (forthcoming).

22. Interview with Ms. Pramila Medhe, November 2, 1999, Devi Ahalya Mandir, Nagpur.

23. The concept of *Vishvam Bhara* was given visible form by Ms. Pramila Moonje during her tenure as one of the joint secretaries of the RSSa. The picture depicting "woman as the one who carries the world" was first published as front cover of the souvenir of the fourteenth (1996) RSSa all-India conference. *Vishvam Bhara,* souvenir of the fourteenth RSSa all-India conference, 1996.

24. Interview with Ms. Sindhu Risbud, October 30, 1999, Ahalya Mandir, Nagpur.

25. For the opinions of male hindutva ideologues on women as political mothers, see Golwalkar, *Bunch of Thoughts*, 485–93; A. Singhal, "Mothers' Role in the Establishment of Dharma," *Hindu Vishva* 23, no. 1 (1987): 9.

26. In Mumbai there are around 1,000 female *purohits*, in Nasik 300–400, and in Nagpur 300. At the time of the fieldwork, ten to twelve women were being trained in Devi Ahalya Mandir to qualify as *purohits*. Their teacher Ms. Sarita Prakash Rajurkar, who is the secretary of the trust running Devi Ahalya Mandir, started her own training in 1982 and has been a *purohit* teacher since 1989. Personal communication from Ms. Sarita Prakash Rajurkar.

27. S. Banerjee, "Hindu Nationalism and the Construction of Woman: The Shiv Sena Organises Women in Bombay," in *Women and the Hindu Right*, ed. T. Sarkar and U. Butalia (New Delhi: Kali for Women, 1995); T. Sarkar, "The Woman as Communal Subject," *Economical and Political Weekly*, August 31, 1991. During the last years of the Ayodhya campaign, women were actively involved in the hindutva agitation against Muslims.

28. *Rashtra Sevika Samiti: An organisation of Hindu women*, 4f., *Samiti Shiksha Varg*, 33.

29. *Samiti Shiksha Varg*, 32.

30. Shivaji, ca. 1630–80, founded the Maratha empire in 1674. Already as a young man he fought against Muslim supremacy. Within the hindutva movement, he is hailed as one of the main Hindu patriots.

31. Speech by *sanchalika pramukh* Usha Chati. Translation by the author.

32. Sarkar, "Woman as Communal Subject."

33. P. Bacchetta, "All Our Goddesses Are Armed," in *Against All Odds: Essays on Women, Religion and Development from India and Pakistan*, ed. K. Bhasin, R. Menon, N. S. Khan (New Delhi: Kali for Women, 1996).

34. Banerjee, "Hindu Nationalism."

35. In India a parallel educational system is presently being built by hindutva organizations. In the more than 13,000 schools ranging from elite schools to slum and village schools from primary schools to senior high schools and colleges run by hindutva organizations a Hindu value–based education is at the heart of the curriculum. *Alternate model of national education* (New Delhi: Vidya Bharati Akhil Bharatiya Shiksha Sansthan, 1990), 20. The RSSa participates in the hindutva educational project mainly through the foundation Bharatiya Shrividya Niketan ("Indian center for learning," BVN) dedicated to developing models schools for girls. During the fieldwork I visited Shishu Gyan Mandir ("Children's temple of knowledge") in Nagpur, one of the schools run by the BVN. I also interviewed Ms. Sindhu Risbud who is the vice-president of the foundation and one of the motors behind the RSSa educational program.

36. See e.g., Golwalkar, *Bunch of Thoughts*, 50f. My informants expressed the same opinion.

37. *BJP's election manifesto 1996: Our agenda for women*.

38.. Indian Muslims are entitled to their own civil law, which is based on *sharia*. It primarily covers matters concerning the family and the private sphere such as marriage, divorce and inheritance. Agnes 1995 and Kumar 1995 have argued that disagreement over women's rights and the idea of a common civil code were instrumental in polarising between Hindus and Muslims during the 1980s.

39. *BJP's election manifesto 1996: Our agenda for women.*

40. *BJP's election manifesto 1998: Nari shakti. Empowerment of women.*

41. See *bharata ekatmatastotra* 1994:2; C. P. Bhishikar, *Pandit Deendayal Upadhyaya. Ideology and Perception* (part V) (New Delhi: Suruchi Prakashan, 1991), 110, 114; Golwalkar, *Bunch of Thoughts*, 116–18, 121f., 161f. The American historian of religions Lisa McKean has noticed this characteristic of Hindu nationalism, which she accordingly refers to as "militant matriotism." L. McKean, "Bharat India and Her Militant Matriots," in *Devi: Goddesses of India*, ed. J. S. Hawley and D. M. Wulff (Berkeley, Los Angeles: University of California Press, 1996).

42. In pictures and texts Bharat Mata is depicted in her ideal, her activist, and her exposed forms. The different forms reflect the dharmic condition in Bharat as interpreted by hindutva sympathizers.

43. For the *Prarthana*, see *Rashtra Sevika Samiti: An organisation of Hindu women*, 47f. The *Prarthana* was composed by the *sevika* Kusum Sathe from Maharashtra in the late 1940s. By studying classical Sanskrit texts she had earned the prestigeous title *shastri*, "scholar of the scriptures." Personal communication from Ms. Pramila Moonje, a former jt. secretary of the RSSa. The prayer is written in Sanskrit and is made up of five four-line stanzas. It comprises two functional entities: an eulogy of Bharat Mata and a painting of the ideals set before the *sevika*. Throughout the hymn the goddess Bharat Mata is praised with attributes that are common in the hindutva discourse. She is eulogized as *matribhumi* ("motherland"), *punyabhumi* ("holy land"), *hindubhumi* ("land of Hindus"), *vishvashakti* ("the power that is held to be the creative spirit behind *hindu rashtra*"), and as the giver of *samskriti*, "culture," to her daughters.

44. Golwalkar, *Bunch of Thoughts*, 132ff. The organic outlook characterizes the "Philosophy of integral humanism" (PIH), which is the BJP's official philosophy. PIH was created by Deendayal Upadhyaya who was one of the leaders of the RSS as well as the political party Jan Sangh, a predecessor to the BJP. For representative pictures of PIH, see Bhishikar, Pandit Deendaval Upadhyaya, and V. V. Nene, *Pandit Deendayal Upadhyaya: Ideology and Perception* (part II) (New Delhi: Suruchi Prakashan, 1991). The books are based on lectures by Upadhyaya.

45. Interview with Ms. Pramila Medhe, November 2, 1999, Devi Ahalya Mandir, Nagpur.

46. *Rashtra Sevika Samiti: An organisation of Hindu women*, 34.

47. Ibid., 4, 34.

48. The first stanza of the *Astha Bhuja stotra* reads: "Every lady should become your copy in character and beauty. Women should save dharma and samskriti and by that make Bharat great." *Samiti Shiksha Varg*, 42. Translation from Sanskrit by Ms. Sindhu Risbud.

49. Interview with Ms. Sindhu Risbud, October 30, 1999, Ahalya Mandir, Nagpur. The *Astha Bhuja stotra* is recited daily in the BVN schools and in *shakha*.

50. M. M. Joshi, "Women's Liberation: The Indian Way," *Manthan*, December 24, 1995.

51. *Rashtra Sevika Samiti: An organisation of Hindu women*, 1f., 31.

52. P. Agarwal, "Surat, Savarkar and Draupadi: Legitimising Rape as a Political Weapon," in Sarkar and Butalia, *Women and the Hindu Right*; E. Butalia, "Muslims and Hindus, Men and Women: Communal Stereotypes and the Partition of India," in Sarkar and Butalia, *Women and the Hindu Right*.

53. Cossman and Kapur, "Women and Hindutva," 101f.

54. This is a similarity between hindutva and other culturally conservative or "fundamentalist" movements. With examples drawn from evangelical Christianity in Colombia and Neo-Orthodox Judaism in the United States. E. Brusco, "The Peace that Passes All Understanding: Violence, the Family, and Fundamentalist Knowledge in Colombia," in *Mixed Blessings: Gender and Religious Fundamentalism Crossculturally*, ed. J. Brink and J. Mencher (New York: Routledge, 1997), and L. Davidman, *Tradition in a Rootless World: Women Turn to Orthodox Judaism* (Berkeley: University of California Press, 1991) exemplify how "fundamentalist" men are engaged in the education of their children and take a responsibility for their families.

55. Y. Hirdman, "Om genussystemet," *Kvinnovetenskaplig tidskrift*, 1988, 63.

56. To steer clear of the methodological trap in Hirdman's model, that is an outcome of the mixing of generic and specific instances of gender system, I notice that the gender system, which she uncovers, is merely *one* of a number of possible *patriarchal* gender systems. Gender systems may differ on important points; the gender asymmetry to the benefit of men, which Hirdman locates, is not a necessity in every possible gender system. And, as will be argued in this work, there is a plurality also of patriarchal gender systems. Hence the specific rules for gendering ("distinct separation," "male-as-norm") that Hirdman, with the help of her material, identifies as basic in the gender system are specific for one kind of patriarchal gender system only. This precise reading of Hirdman, in which I distinguish between the concept of gender system and specific instances of gender systems, does not contradict Hirdman's overall reasoning on gender, but it removes a major flaw in her use of the concept of gender system.

57. Hirdman, "Om genussystemet," 51f.

58. E. Lundgren, *Det må da være grenser for kjønn* (Oslo: Universitetsforlaget, 1993), 210ff.

59. Interview with *pracharikas*, November 4, 1999, Devi Ahalya Mandir, Nagpur.

60. In this article a narrativist understanding of religion is being employed. Drawing on the work of Gavin Flood, religion has been understood as a narrative presenting binding beliefs, values, and behavior in which the dichotomy transcendental-immanent is central. In the generic sense religion is hence understood as one type of narrative. Furthermore, every single religion is held to be a culturally located narrative of this kind. G. Flood, *Beyond Phenomenology. Rethinking the Study of Religion* (New York: Cassell, 1999), 47ff. Here I go beyond Flood by distinguishing between types of religious narratives on the basis of their focus.

61. See E. Hellman, "Dynamic Hinduism: Towards a New Hindu Nation," in *Questioning the Secular State: The Worldwide Resurgence of Religion in Politics*, ed. D. Westerlund (London: Hurst, 1996).

62. Sarkar and Butalia, *Women and the Hindu Right*.

63. P. Beyer, *Religion and Globalization* (London: Sage Publications, 1997), 2.

64. E.g., "similarity feminism" and "difference feminism." The former stresses the similarities between the sexes and strives for a nonconditional equality between the men and women in regards of rights and opportunities. The latter presupposes a radical difference between the men and women, but argues for the positive valuation of female qualities and tasks.

65. By contextual feminism is meant feminisms formulated from specific standpoints such as race, caste, religion, class, sexuality, culture, anticolonialism. Postcolonial feminism, womanism, Islamic feminism, lesbian feminism, left feminism, liberal feminisms are examples of contextual feminisms.

66. See B. Lincoln, *Holy Terrors. Thinking about Religion after September 11* (Chicago: University of Chicago Press, 2003), 59.

67. Joshi, "Women's Liberation: The Indian Way."

CHAPTER 2

Women as Fundamental and Fundamentalist Women: The Case of Buddhist Sri Lanka

Tessa Bartholomeusz

Introduction

Denise Riley has suggested that "'women' is an unstable category, [and] that this instability has a historical foundation."[1] This is as true of the category of women in America as it is in Sri Lanka (formerly Ceylon), as true among Catholics as it is among Buddhists. For instance, in nineteenth-century America, Catholics debated what it meant to be a woman in the context of the reevaluation of the family in a new economic era. Indeed, during the early nineteenth century, Catholic Americans focused on the nature of women as they grappled with how to educate the female who, for them, in many ways represented the condition of their religion.[2] At that time, Catholic women's colleges were founded with the rationale that women possessed a distinct nature and thus needed a "specifically feminine education"[3] geared toward matrimony and motherhood. In late nineteenth-century Sri Lanka, Sinhala Buddhists similarly debated the category of women, yet they did so as they evaluated their own position vis-à-vis British colonial rule. In other words, for both nineteenth-century American Catholics and Sri Lankan Buddhists, the category of women was contested in particular historical circumstances. More importantly, as we shall see, in the Sri Lankan case, as was the case in American Catholicism, the category of women came to represent the condition of religion.

In this essay, I shall highlight the contours of the debate over the definition of women in late nineteenth-century Buddhist Sri Lanka to argue that anxiety about "women" intersected with religious fundamentalism. As Jack Hawley and an ensemble of scholars have pointed out, in and of itself, such an intersection is not surprising. Indeed, Hawley has demonstrated that in India, for instance, the 1987 debate surrounding the suttee of Roop Kanwar, called into focus anxiety over the category of women, who, according to Hindu fundamentalists, are "natural vessels of religion."[4] In short, Hindu fundamentalist ideology alleges that to control women is to control the religion.

However, the situation in Sri Lanka, as we shall see, has been somewhat different, particularly because while Buddhist fundamentalism in nineteenth-century Sri Lanka sought to control the female—to privatize them—in some cases such control resulted in women's empowerment in public culture. Though scholars have argued that a "family resemblance" of religious fundamentalism worldwide is the "resistance to the idea that women are autonomous beings,"[5] and that in cross-cultural manifestations of religious fundamentalism there are attempts to confine women to the home,[6] in the case of late nineteenth-century Buddhist Sri Lanka, a different situation cohered—namely, the intersection of religious fundamentalism with a burgeoning feminist discourse, that encouraged women to be both autonomous beings and free from the constraints of the home life. Thus, in this essay, I shall underscore the intersection to argue that religious fundamentalism and feminism are not necessarily antithetical, at least not in the case of Buddhism in Sri Lanka. Indeed, what I also hope to demonstrate is that, as Riley has argued regarding the category of women in general, in late nineteenth-century Sri Lanka "feminism [was] the site of the systematic fighting-out of [the category's] instability."[7]

Notwithstanding the Sri Lankan case of an intersection between religious fundamentalism and feminism, however, when we survey the sources available to us, we find that the anxiety over the condition of the female among Sinhala Buddhists toward the end of the nineteenth century hinged on the rhetoric of shame and promise, rhetoric not unique to the case of Sri Lanka. For instance, Lata Mani has argued that the Hindu woman in nineteenth-century British India represented both "shame and promise": sometimes in that period her low status was a barometer for the degradation of Hinduism; at other times, her reform assured that those very traditions could be protected. In short, in nineteenth-century Hindu India, women were officially evoked as repositories of tradition.[8] The Hindu preoccupation with the status of the female is not unique to nineteenth-century India; the responsibility of Hindu women to safeguard religious tradition is reflected in the ancient text, the *Bhagavad Gita*, with its focus upon social and religious duty. The text warns that ultimately women are responsible for social order: "When unrighteous disorder prevails, the women sin and are impure; and when women are not pure ... there is disorder of castes, social confusion."[9] It is possible, as some scholars have argued and as is widely accepted, that the text has captured a period in which religious traditions were challenged, in which the status quo was threatened. It is equally possible that, as was the case in nineteenth-century India—also a period of intense social change—the *Gita's* anxiety over the condition of culture and religion called into focus the category of women.

In much the same way, at various periods of great social change in Buddhist Sri Lanka, the female has represented either the corruption of "tradition" or the hope that it can be safeguarded. I have described elsewhere the ways in which Buddhist women in the late nineteenth century came to represent tradition for all those concerned.[10] Here, I explore why late nineteenth-century Sinhala Buddhists constructed the female as the "other," or as antithetical to Buddhism and Buddhist tradition, that is, as a symbol of shame. But to stop there would be to tell only half the story. Indeed, as we shall see, at the very same time that the category of women came to represent the other, it also symbolized the "self," that is, the "promise" (to use Mani's term) that Buddhism, and eventually Sri Lanka, could be restored to the glory of the precolonial context. In order to complete the story, I shall examine late nineteenth-century Buddhist fundamentalism in Sri Lanka to illuminate fundamentalist attitudes about the Buddhist female as the self.

Following Martin E. Marty and R. Scott Appleby, by fundamentalism I mean among other things "a movement in conscious, organized opposition to the disruption of … traditions and orthodoxies."[11] As we shall see, late nineteenth-century Buddhist fundamentalists in Sri Lanka[12] alleged that, above others, woman—as the self of the nation—had the power to correct dangerous tendencies in Buddhist society. At that time, otherness was cast in terms of the foreign, while the debased condition of woman served as a symbol of foreign corruption; during the late nineteenth century the female represented for Buddhist fundamentalists all that is "other," or alien to Buddhism, including westernization and secularization. Her "condition"—the "alien" way she acted—was a powerful source of shame. Which prompted Anagarika Dharmapala, one of the architects of Sinhala-Buddhist fundamentalism, to suggest in his *Gihi Vinaya* ("The Daily Code for Laity") thirty rules—more rules than he urged for any of his other categories—for how females should conduct themselves, including how to dress: in the *Gihi Vinaya*, amongst the 200 rules that Dharmapala recommended, the manner of eating food, with twenty-five suggestions, is second to the category of women in terms of the number of rules; how children should treat their parents, with fourteen, is third.[13] In other words, for Dharmapala in 1898 and presumably others since then—the nineteenth edition of the *Gihi Vinaya* appeared in 1958[14]—women needed more control than any other category in Sinhala society.[15]

Notwithstanding Dharmapala's preoccupation with the category of women, and his attempts to control them, the outcome was different than in other religious fundamentalisms: in the case of Buddhist Sri Lanka, one concomitant of stricter control of the female was the ideology that she should be a public exemplar of religion. Indeed, harkening back to a time when the Buddhist female allegedly contributed to the life of the island, Buddhists argued that women in ancient times were an integral component of society. For instance, according to Dharmapala in 1898, in the religion that Emperor Asoka sent from India to neighboring countries—namely, Buddhism, "Women took part in everything that was good and noble equally with man. She became a public teacher for the first time, and with man she spread the blessings of Buddha's religion."[16]

In another 1898 example of the rhetoric regarding women and the condition of Sri Lanka, we learn the "true" condition of women in days past, and their contribution to society at home and abroad:

> In the glorious days of the Sinhalese there were in Ceylon women of great learning and piety. The "Mahavamsa" mentions instances of the devotion of Sinhalese women to the cause of religion. The Tibetan history records the introduction of the order of Buddhist nuns into Tibet by the Sinhalese bhikkhunis [nuns]. Seven hundred years ago Sinhalese women were sent as nurses, like the Sisters of the Red Cross Society of the present day, to nurse the wounded in the battlefield in the war which took place in Lower Burma at the time of Parakrama the Great of Ceylon.[17]

Whether the historical allusions are correct or not, in this late nineteenth-century example of gender attitudes, women's status—in part based on a reading of an authoritative text—symbolized the condition of Buddhism in the island. Though the *Mahavamsa* is not a sacred text, in the sense that it is neither revealed nor canonical, in the late nineteenth century it authorized Buddhist fundamentalism.[18] From readings of it, Buddhists were (and are) able to claim that ancient Buddhism, which empowered women, provided the foundation for a prosperous and strong Sri Lanka. Recreation of the glorious days, which meant attending to the debased condition of the female, now the other, was on the agenda of fundamentalists in the 1890s.

Like the late nineteenth-century social construction of women, one dimension of doctrinal Buddhism also views the female as other. This is not surprising. Buddhism advocates a path of celibacy, especially for males. The female, perceived in the Pali texts as a temptress who can veer men from that path, is an impediment to the goal of the path, or *nibbāna*. Because she reproduces, she embodies rebirth—*samsāra*—and thus all that Buddhism seeks to transcend, all that is other.[19] Put differently, according to doctrinal Buddhism, woman's biology—her life-giving capacity—is her destiny in that her biology determines that she perpetuates *samsāra*. And because woman embodies rebirth (Buddhism's nemesis), she thus perpetuates tradition, and consequently embodies tradition and represents society and culture. In the canon, the category of women represents both other and self at *the same time*. Which perhaps helps to explain the complicated gender imagery of canonical Buddhism.

Education and the Guardians of Buddhism

Complicated gender imagery is not confined to textual Buddhism. It is refracted through a view of late nineteenth-century Sri Lanka, in which one of the main foci of Buddhist fundamentalists then and there was the elevation of women, the self of Buddhist society, despite efforts to control them. While Buddhists evaluated the condition of their religion under the British, they alleged that the female's lack of access to a proper Buddhist education indicated the demoralized condition of Buddhism. As Buddhists negotiated a Buddhist identity, they construed ancient Buddhism as an egalitarian religion that did not "inflict any indignity upon women."[20] In recreating an ideal, mythical past, a cross-cultural concern of fundamentalists,[21] these Buddhists, as we have seen in the allusion to the *Mahavamsa*, urged women to take a more active role in the resuscitation of Buddhism. They also argued that Buddhism could be restored to its former glory if Buddhists granted females a Buddhist education. Though females had had access to an education, it was in Christian missionary schools, schools that Buddhists argued undermined Buddhist "tradition."[22]

Despite the 1870s' focus upon education for boys, in the 1880s and 1890s Sri Lankan Buddhists shifted their attention to girls, for "the prosperity of a state or country are largely dependent upon the intellectual and moral elevation of its women."[23] The elevation of Buddhist women meant the assurance of maintaining tradition and thus the hope of reestablishing Sri Lanka as a Buddhist country. The need to "elevate their sisters"[24] became a great source of shame for Buddhists at that time. To correct inequities so as ultimately to preserve tradition, Buddhists began the task of elevating women by educating girls, spawning in 1889 the first four Buddhists schools for girls on the island.[25] But female education included a curriculum that would prepare girls for gender-determined work: they were taught "cooking, housekeeping, plain sewing, cutting, fitting, lace making, embroidery, etching, and thread-work." In addition, however, they studied "English Literature, Mathematics, History, Geography, Grammar, and Chemistry," to name only a few of the subjects.[26] Unlike the case of nineteenth-century Catholic America, and as the inclusion of a curriculum of mathematics and chemistry suggests, in late nineteenth-century Sri Lanka Buddhists supplied girls with an education designed for the girls' own personal, intellectual development. Yet, the curriculum was fashioned to benefit the country as well. Learning "female" subjects would begin the process of educating female children to be good mothers of the future generation.

Within the next year, the Women's Educational Society (WES)—established in 1889 to "educate Sinhalese ladies"—had "brought under its direction the education of *nearly one thousand girls*."[27] Among the schools the WES had established, the one of which they were the most proud, and which became an international and multi-ethnic project, was the Sanghamitta English School for Girls, which opened in 1890. The WES invited Colonel Olcott, the American cofounder of the Buddhist Theosophical Society (BTS), to preside over the school's opening. He accepted the invitation with enthusiasm and looked forward to the event.[28]

According to the description of the school's opening, "A square *pandal* was run up the entrance with the motto 'From daughter to wife, from wife to mother.'"[29]

In short, the banner proclaimed that well-educated Buddhist girls would make good wives. Above all, they would make good mothers. This late nineteenth-century valorization of motherhood, however, was not intended to confine women to the home. Though, as we have seen, Buddhists argued that girls should learn to be good mothers—to instill Buddhist values in children—they also had the task of mothering the nation,[30] of safeguarding tradition. As we shall see, this awesome responsibility entailed active exhortation of the Buddhist *dhamma*.

"Elevating the status of the Sinhalese woman"[31] continued to be one of the main tasks of Buddhists throughout the 1890s. As I have argued elsewhere,[32] Buddhists alleged that education would empower women to participate in the Buddhist revival: Buddhists encouraged women to preach and teach the *dhamma*, thereby invigorating lapsed Buddhists. Basing their ideas on religious texts, another typical characteristic of fundamentalism,[33] they alleged that just as women in the days of the Buddha preached and taught the *dhamma*, so should women in the 1890s. In other words, these Buddhists urged women to be active purveyors of tradition, in addition to instilling Buddhist values in the home. They achieved these two goals in the latter days of the Sanghamitta School.

It is necessary to recount in full the details of the Sanghamitta School's establishment, for the particulars of the history of the school suggest that, while Buddhist fundamentalists took the lead, others joined the bandwagon of Buddhist female education as a way to air their grievances under the British. Which goes to show that the category of women in late nineteenth-century Sri Lanka was a source of anxiety for fundamentalist and nonfundamentalists alike. As the sources indicate, over one thousand Sri Lankans, among them (predominately Buddhist) Sinhala, as well as (non-Buddhist) Burghers and Tamils, all of elite families, and a few international visitors, attended the school's opening.[34] Like the Sinhalas and others, non–Sri Lankan Buddhists (particularly Theosophists) at that time argued that Sri Lanka was home to the oldest and purest form of Buddhism.[35] And like Sri Lankan Buddhists, they longed to reestablish Buddhism along the lines of the *Mahavamsa*. In short, they shared Sinhala Buddhists' fundamentalist concerns, which converged in debate over the category of women, the impetus for the creation of the school. Established with a view to "ameliorate [the] social and moral condition and to inculcate the high principles of [the] noble religion on [the] rising [female] generation,"[36] the Sanghamitta School had a very auspicious beginning. Its opening coincided with the launching of what the WES referred to as the "Women's movement" in Sri Lanka.[37] Buddhists and others hailed the Sanghamitta project and "women's education" as the "corner-stone of civilization," as the "material for building up a nation."[38]

Applications poured in from interested parents while the WES searched for a principal. The school formally opened in October 1890 with twenty children in attendance.[39] The first principal of the school was Miss A.J. Ferdinands, "an accomplished Burgher Lady,"[40] which demonstrates the degree to which Buddhist fundamentalist concerns had permeated non-Buddhist, non-Sinhala society. Indeed, as Ferdinands' participation in the school suggests, and as the guest list for the school's opening alleges, many traditionally non-Buddhist ethnic communities consolidated to "build up the nation" by empowering Buddhist women through education.

Due to the untimely illness of her mother, Ferdinands had to resign her post as principal six months after the school's opening. The WES replaced her with a European, who was eventually replaced by an Australian Theosophist, Kate Pickett. Two weeks after Pickett arrived, she was found dead in the bottom of a well on the school's premises in Maradana,[41] a district of Colombo, presumably from stumbling while walking in her sleep. Pickett's replacement was Mary Museus Higgins, an American Buddhist Theosophist, who agreed to help in the cause to "advance the position of women [in Sri Lanka] both socially and morally."[42] She abruptly left her position (as clerk in the dead letter office in Washington), and enthusiastically agreed to help elevate Buddhist women in Colombo.[43] Foreign involvement of Pickett's and Higgins's ilk in the school points to the anxiety—even of non-Buddhist, non-Sri Lankans—over the category of women.

Despite Higgins's enthusiasm about the Sanghamitta School, she resigned her post shortly after she was hired.[44] Though it is difficult to discern the reasons for her resignation, it is clear, however, that the WES tried to prevent the collapse of the school upon Higgins's departure, and began the search for Higgins's replacement. Higgins, in the meantime, opened a rival school in the prestigious Colombo neighborhood, Cinnamon Gardens; that school, Museus College for Girls, has continued to attract students to the present. The Sanghamitta School, unlike Museus College for Girls, was not able to overcome the problems it faced in its early years. Though the WES with great difficulty kept the school functioning for a while after Higgins's departure, they closed its doors, if only temporarily, in 1895.

As the history of the Sanghamitta School thus far suggests, Sri Lankan Buddhists and non-Buddhists zealously endeavored to put their ideas about Buddhist women into practice. As the history of the school implies, the goal of empowering women was by no means a mere philosophical or intellectual enterprise. Rather, it was a crucial matter that warranted considerable attention, despite all the impediments.

Buddhist Female as Self and Other

Buddhist fundamentalism, with its anxiety of the condition of the female, had affected late nineteenth-century Sri Lankans to such a great extent that many were not willing to abandon the Sanghamitta project. For them, as we have seen, the Sanghamitta School represented the hope that girls could become good Buddhists, and eventually good wives and mothers, both of their own progeny and of Sri Lanka. It is significant that these Buddhists chose to name the school after the

Buddhist nun, Sanghamitta. She is alleged to have brought the nuns' lineage to Sri Lanka from India, which firmly helped to establish Buddhism on the island. A question here as to why the WES named their school—which they had established to produce good Buddhist wives and mothers—after Sanghamitta, who had renounced both matrimony and motherhood, can hardly be escaped. In this context, I discuss the 1898 reopening of the Sanghamitta School and the way that many of the WES's early ideas about the Buddhist female—based on their readings of Buddhist texts—merged in a later construction of the "good Buddhist woman."

In the late nineteenth century, when Sri Lankans constructed the female as the guardian of Buddhist tradition,[45] heroines of Buddhism and Buddhist texts such as Sanghamitta became role models for women. Buddhists argued that women should be more like the women immortalized in the texts, as we have seen. Their textually based, late nineteenth-century revitalization of Buddhism in Sri Lanka resembles fundamentalist concerns in other religious traditions, as I have noted. Yet, it is worth remembering how it challenges contemporary ideas about religious fundamentalism—namely, that religious fundamentalism urges the control and thus privatization of the female. Though the identity of the female figured critically in the discourse of late nineteenth-century Buddhist fundamentalism, much as it has in other fundamentalisms,[46] women in Sri Lanka in fact were given new freedoms. Rather than concluding that women are to be dependent on men, nineteenth-century Buddhists argued that men and society in general were dependent on women, the repositories of Buddhist tradition. Indeed, Buddhists in Sri Lanka in the 1890s maintained that women should be good mothers and good wives. The sources of the period also suggest, however, that Buddhists supported women who became itinerant preachers—unquestionably autonomous women— to the same degree that they supported men.[47] The sources also record that the Buddhists of the period believed that theirs was the first such instance of supporting female world-renouncers in over seven centuries. In other words, they prided themselves on their empowerment of women, echoing their pride in the Sanghamitta School for Girls.

It was not until the school's resuscitation in 1898, however, that the themes of world-renunciation and its seeming antithesis, world-affirmation, converged in the symbol of the Buddhist female. In 1898, the Sanghamitta School, named after the Buddhist nun who, according to the *Mahavamsa*, introduced to Sri Lanka the monastic lineage for women, came to represent the female's empowerment both in, and away from, the home life.

Though the school lay dormant from 1895 until 1898, it remained a topic of conversation among many.[48] In 1898, the Buddhist Theosophical Society (BTS) took control of the school, and relocated it to Cinnamon Gardens, in the area of Colombo that Higgins earlier had established her institution. The BTS, much like WES and their supporters,[49] maintained that the elevation of women meant the reformation of Buddhism, and ultimately the reformation of the country. Basing their ideas on religious texts, and as I have argued elsewhere,[50] Buddhist Theosophists argued that this reformation would entail reestablishing the defunct order of nuns. They claimed that in much the same way that early Buddhism was based on four communities, namely monks, nuns, laymen, and laywomen, each of the four was necessary for the prosperity of Buddhism in any age.[51] Thus motivated to resurrect the defunct order of nuns, and to continue with the task of educating females, the BTS combined both goals in its renovation and revival of the Sanghamitta School.

In 1898, the school reopened with much fanfare. The brainchild of two leading Buddhist Theosophists, Dharmapala and an American, Miranda de Souza Canavarro,[52] the school attracted the attention of the Colombo elite, much as it had in the early 1890s. At the school, the BTS achieved, at least in attenuated form, both of their goals: they placed Buddhist "nuns" in charge of girls who, they hoped, would eventually embody the religious identity of Buddhists in Sri Lanka. Sybil LaBrooy, a Burgher, acted as Canavarro's confidant and colleague; like Canavarro, she became a Buddhist nun. Their "convent" attracted many students. In June 1898, just after its opening, the convent housed "135 pupils, including nineteen borders, with the excellent daily average of 130."[53] The convent functioned for nearly three years and attracted the attention of aspiring Buddhist nuns from Australia, England, and North America, all of whom worked for the elevation of Buddhism in Sri Lanka. At the convent, the nuns wore ochre robes, while the girls "dressed uniformly in white with a red spotted cloth thrown across the shoulders, making the general effect more Eastern in appearance."[54] In other words, the females' outward appearance symbolized the reestablishment of tradition, the elevation of Eastern ways, the mending of the nation. In short, in Theravada Buddhist Sri Lanka, in the years yielding interest in female education, the female had represented corruption, or all that is "other." Yet at the Sanghamitta School the female—as world-renouncer/nun and world-affirmer/future mother—embodied the "self," or the traditions of the religion, the people, and the country.

Conclusions

A definition of the woman's role was central to the discourse of the late nineteenth-century Sri Lankan Buddhist fundamentalism, much as it has been in fundamentalist discourse worldwide.[55] At that time, however, women had the option to be autonomous, a choice that has often evaded women in both non-Buddhist and Buddhist societies. Rather than being perceived solely as other, women—both as world-renouncers and world-affirmers—were perceived as the embodiment of Buddhism. As world-renouncers they affirmed, and became the repositories of, the Buddhist ascetic ideal, despite being female. Highlighting positive images of women in the canonical texts, Buddhists hailed women as exemplars of religion, rather than as impediments to the path of liberation, another common image of the female in the texts.[56] Yet, for Sri Lankan Buddhist revivalists in the late nineteenth century, women represented Buddhist tradition, rather than solely its corruption; self and other converged in the construction of the female, who, if only briefly[57] and rather paradoxically, was empowered by fundamentalism. Indeed, Buddhist fundamentalists saw the liberation of woman as linked to the destiny of the nation, a matter for the whole society. Yet, they also took personal interest in the individual female, as discussion of her education suggests. She was the valiant keep of tradition, the hope that Sri Lanka might again establish itself as a Buddhist country. And as much as her nation, she was to benefit from her newly granted education.

It remains to be seen whether the Buddhist fundamentalism that I have charted in Sri Lanka, with its focus on female education, was a theme in other Theravadin countries. Dharmapala, who, as we have noted, played an important role in elevating the status of women through education in late nineteenth-century Sri Lanka, pioneered similar projects in Burma to do the same. Yet, while Burma and Sri Lanka share a colonial legacy, in the present they struggle with different sets of problems. The extent to which Buddhist fundamentalist concerns about the category of women continued to capture Burmese attention—in the wake of Dharmapala's trips there—remains an open question. Further research is needed in Burma, as well as in the other Theravada Buddhist countries, to see whether or not Sri Lankan Buddhist history—especially its fundamentalist stripe—is unique in its emphasis on the empowerment of both woman and the nation through female education.

Notes

1. Denise Riley, "Am I That Name? Feminism and the Category of 'Women' in History," in *Feminisms*, ed. Sandra Kemp and Judith Squires (Oxford: Oxford University Press, 1997), 244.

2. For more on this, see Antoinette Iadarola, "The American Catholic Bishops and Woman," in *Women, Religion and Social Change*, ed. Yvonne Yazbeck Haddad and Ellison Banks Findly (New York: State University of New York Press, 1985), 475–76.

3. Ibid., 458.

4. "Hinduism: Sati and Its Defenders," in *Fundamentalism and Gender*, ed. John Stratton Hawley (Oxford: Oxford University Press, 1994), 102.

5. This is implied in ibid., 99.

6. See John S. Hawley and Wayne Proudfoot, "Introduction" in ibid., especially pp. 27–30.

7. Riley, "Am I That Name?" 244.

8. Referenced in Sara Suleri, *The Rhetoric of English India* (Chicago: Chicago University Press, 1992), 75.

9. *The Bhagavad Gita*, trans. Juan Mascaro (London: Penguin Books, 1962), 47.

10. Tessa Bartholomeusz, "Sri Lankan Women and the Buddhist Revival," *Iris: A Journal About Women* 26 (Fall/Winter 1991): 43–47.

11. Martin E. Marty and R. Scott Appleby, eds., *Fundamentalisms Observed* (Chicago: University of Chicago Press, 1991), 14.

12. For more on Buddhist fundamentalism in Sri Lanka, see Tessa J. Bartholomeusz and Chandra R. de Silva, ed., *Buddhist Fundamentalism and Minority Identities in Sri Lanka* (Albany, NY: State University of New York Press, 1998).

13. For more on the *Gihi Viyaya*, see Richard Gombrich and Gananath Obeyesekere, *Buddhism Transformed* (Princeton, NJ: Princeton University Press, 1988), 214.

14. Ibid.

15. Dharmapala's ideas about the female are indeed complicated. For instance, though Dharmapala agued that women should be allowed to don the ochre robe of the Buddhist mendicant—which by definition entails a certain degree of autonomy—he also urged in 1917 that women should follow the duty of the female "laid down in the 8th Nipata of the Anguttara Nikaya." Which, according to Dharmapala, entails the following: "She has her duties at home. She has to learn to be a help to her husband, she is expected to be clever in some kind of art or craft," etc. See *Anagarika Dharmapal: Return to Righteousness*, ed. Ananda Guruge (Colombo: Ministry of Cultural Affairs and Information, 1991), 344–46.

16. Quote from Dharmapala's writings of 1897–98. Cited in ibid., 206.

17. "The Inauguration of the Sanghamitta Convent in Colombo," *Journal of the MahaBodhi Society* 7, no. 2 (June 1898): 15.

18. For the *Mahavamsa* as a the equivalent of a sacred text, see Tessa J. Bartholomeusz and Chandra R. de Silva, "Buddhist Fundamentalism and Identity in Sri Lanka," in *Buddhist Fundamentalism*, 4–5.

19. For more on the idea of the female as the embodiment of *samsāra*, see Lorna Rhodes Amarasingham, "The Misery of the Embodied: Representations of Women in Sinhalese Myth," in *Women in Ritual and Symbolic Roles*, ed. Judith Hock-Smith and Anita Spring (New York: Plenum Press, 1978).

20. "Women's Place in Buddhism," *The Buddhist* (1903): 277–78.

21. Marty and Appleby, *Fundamentalisms Observed*, 814–42.

22. "It was the duty of all parents to send their children to Buddhist schools, and not to Christian Mission schools where the young minds are poisoned against their beautiful ancestral Buddhism" ("Activities," *The Buddhist*, 4, no. 8 [February 19, 1892]: 64). For more on this, see Tessa Bartholomeusz, *Women under the Bo Tree: Buddhist Nuns in Sri Lanka* (1994; repr., Cambridge: Cambridge University Press, 1996), especially chapters 3 and 4.

23. "A Retrospect and an Appeal," *The Buddhist* (1889): 246.

24. "History of the W.E.S.," *The Buddhist* (February 2, 1894): 26. W.E.S.=Women's Education Society.

25. Ibid., 25.

26. "The Sanghamitta Convent School and Orphanage," *Journal of the MahaBodhi Society* 7, no. 4 (August 1898): 30.

27. "Sanghamitta Convent School and Orphanage," 30; italics are in the original.

28. Ibid., 26.

29. Ibid.

30. For more, see my *Women under the Bo Tree*, chapter 3 and chapter 6.

31. "History of the W.E.S.," 27.

32. See my *Women under the Bo Tree*, especially chapter 2.

33. See Marty and Appleby, *Fundamentalism Observed*, 814–42. See also Bartholomeusz and de Silva, "Buddhist Fundamentalism and Identity in Sri Lanka," 4–6, for a discussion of the relationship between Buddhist fundamentalism and religious texts.

34. The description of the opening is replete with Burgher names such as Buultjens and Ferdinands; Tamil names, such as Ramanathan; and Sinhala names, such as Weerakoon, Wijesinhe, and de Silva. In addition, an American, Mrs. Susan A. English attended, as did an Englishman, Dr. Daly. A Tamil, the Honorable P. Coomaraswamy, became a permanent trustee of the school.

35. For more on this, see Tessa Bartholomeusz, "Real Life and Romance: The Life of Miranda de Souza Canavarro." *The Journal of Feminist Studies in Religion* 10, no. 2 (Fall 1994), 24–47.

36. "Activities," 63.

37. Ibid., 64.

38. Ibid.

39. "Changes of Principals," *The Buddhist* 6, no. 4 (February 2, 1894): 26.

40. Ibid.

41. Ibid. For more on the death of Pickett, see *Women under the Bo Tree*, chapter 3.

42. "Activities," p 63.

43. "Mrs. Higgins Appointed Principal By W.E.S.," *The Buddhist* 6, no. 4 (February 2, 1894): 28.

44. "The Sanghamitta School," *The Buddhist* 6, no. 4 (February 2, 1894).

45. Along these lines, Kumari Jayawardena argues that in the late nineteenth century, the female was also considered the guardian of the Sinhala people. For more, see Kumari Jayawardena, "Some Aspects of Religious and Cultural Identity and the Construction of Sinhala Buddhist Womanhood," in *Religion and Political Conflict in South Asia*, ed. Douglas Allen (Delhi: Oxford University Press, 1993), 161–80.

46. See Hawley, *Fundamentalism and Gender*, 27, for more on the construction of a female identity in fundamentalist discourse.

47. See my *Women under the Bo Tree*, chapter 3.

48. Anagarika Dharmapala's diaries from the mid to late 1890s suggest this. I would like to thank the MahaBodhi Society, Colombo, for allowing me to read Dharmapala's handwritten diaries.

49. Actually, the W.E.S. was a satellite of the Buddhist Theosophical Society.

50. See *Women under the Bo Tree*, chapter 3.

51. For more on this, see ibid., chapter 4.

52. For more on Canavarro, see Tessa Bartholomeusz, "Real Life and Romance"; and Thomas Tweed, *The American Encounter with Buddhism 1844–1912: Victorian Culture and the Limits of Dissent* (Indiana, PA: Indiana University Press, 1992).

53. "The Sanghamitta Convent School and Orphanage," 30.

54. Ibid.

55. For more on this topic, see Betty A. DeBerg, *Ungodly Women: Gender and the First Wave of American Fundamentalism* (Minneapolis: Fortress Press, 1990).

56. A typical specimen is "Monks, a woman, even when going along, will stop to ensnare the heart of a man; whether standing, sitting, or lying down, laughing, talking or singing, weeping, stricken or dying, a woman will stop to ensnare the heart of a man." For the entire text, see *Anguttara Nikaya,* vol. 4, ed. E. Hardy (London: Luzac and Company, 1968), 67–68.

57. For changes in this construction, see my *Women under the Bo Tree,* chapters 7 and 8.

CHAPTER 3

Fundamentalism and the Position of Women in Confucianism*

Vivian-Lee Nyitray

"Confucianism" and "fundamentalism" are terms not often paired, and to date there have been no studies that simultaneously engage "Confucian fundamentalism" with women's studies or gender studies concerns. The invitation to explore these intersections was therefore both welcome and daunting, and the process of exploration has proven provocative at every step. The present study reflects that process, beginning with a working definition of fundamentalism and a brief discussion of the role of gender in fundamentalist discourse. In considering the problem of employing "fundamentalism" as a category of inquiry with respect to Confucianism, the present study investigates alternative applications of the term to the Confucian tradition past, present, and future. I first suggest that Song-Ming Neo-Confucianism (twelfth through seventeenth centuries) bears a greater resemblance to modern fundamentalisms than do twentieth-century Confucian ideologies—leaving the Confucian cultures of modern industrial East Asia more accurately understood as "post-fundamentalist" legacies of Neo-Confucianism. I then examine whether the persistence of Confucian ideologies might not betray either a quasi-institutional fundamentalism represented by "New Confucianism," or else a diffuse fundamentalism comprising deep conceptual structures that subtly control sex and gender systems in Confucian cultures.

Definitions and the Gendered Discourse of Fundamentalism

The term "fundamentalism" originated in early twentieth-century American Protestant Christianity as a self-designation by certain sects whose leaders hoped to fend off the secular forces of a modernizing world through the restoration of "fundamental" beliefs and practices derived from an inerrant Bible.[1] Contemporary scholarship has broadened the term's parameters considerably. "Fundamentalism" is now a theoretical concept employed in the comparative analysis of religious groups ranging from Christians, Jews, and Muslims to Hindus and Theravadin Buddhists—all of whom define themselves as defenders of orthodoxy, the vanguards of a "return" to an idealized tradition.[2] A survey of the growing literature on religious fundamentalism yields a cluster of characteristics, including the following: (1) the perception of a tradition under threat from secularism and modernism, although not necessarily all aspects of modernity; (2) charismatic leaders who articulate the threat; (3) advocacy of active and often political responses to threat; (4) a strong and urgent sense of solidarity among members of the group; and (5) nostalgia for a glorified past coupled with the achievable prospect of an equally glorious future, an historical vision in which the present is a remediable degeneration of fundamental belief and practice.[3]

Fundamentalist faith is neither necessarily primitivist nor a religion of the marginalized. A more apt appreciation of fundamentalism, according to Karen McCarthy Brown, is that it develops among people "caught off balance," often arising in places where social, cultural, and economic power is up for grabs. "Far from essentially marginal to the societies in which they exist, fundamentalists are often directly involved in the political and economic issues of their time and place."[4] The boundary between religious fundamentalism and politics is therefore indistinct at best, and may be obliterated by a group's militant sense of mission. In contrast to traditionalists and conservatives, who distance themselves to varying degree from modern cultural trends in order to more fully embrace tradition and preserve its positive aspects, fundamentalists focus their attention just as much, if not more, on the condemnation and combating of negative aspects of modern secular culture.[5] Moreover, they are not disheartened. In the words of Martin Marty, fundamentalists "no longer perceive themselves as reeling under the corrosive effects of secular life. On the contrary, they perceive themselves as fighting back, and doing so rather successfully."[6]

What fuels the fundamentalist fighting spirit are interlocking anxieties regarding faith, family, and the state—loci of concern that individually encompass private and public aspects. Certain issues, such as marriage and family law, cut across the private and public dimensions in every area, strongly reinforcing the linkage of religious and political ideologies. It must be emphasized, however, that fundamentalism is not unequivocally antimodern; in fact, it can be, and is, both modern and antimodern. In her comparative study of Islamic and Christian fundamentalisms, Shahin Gerami asserts that in concerns regarding the public domain, such as the economy or polity, fundamentalism often shows itself to be quite modern and surprisingly open to technological innovation. On the other hand, "when it looks toward the private domain—the family and women's status—fundamentalism is anti-modern or regressive."[7] At the heart of fundamentalist concerns is the re-establishment and maintenance of fixed boundaries: the demarcation of the religious from the secular, the delineation of state jurisdiction from family responsibility, and the clear differentiation of sex roles. Anthropologist

Lionel Caplan has observed that women "appear to assume a symbolic poignancy in fundamentalism—their dress, demeanor and socio-ritual containment providing eloquent testimony to what is regarded as the correct order of things."[8]

Several theories have been advanced to account for the prominence of gender in the discourse of fundamentalism. Discussions by John Stratton Hawley, Wayne Proudfoot, and Karen McCarthy Brown, for example, suggest that fundamentalist groups are led by men "whose identity is constructed in important ways by their confrontation with an external other" and who will naturally attempt to assert control over women, "the more accessible other in [their] midst."[9] Here, "otherness" is not a perception of difference but a recognition of threat, fanning the flames of militant response. Women tend to carry the projections of "all that is undesirable or threatening in human existence: sexuality, emotion, pollution, sin, and mortality"—necessitating their control and containment.[10] On the flip side of the demonization of uncontrolled women is the subtle control manifest in the fundamentalist construction of supposedly positive images of woman. The pedestalization of domesticated womanhood is seen to be a trait closely related to nostalgia, another distinguishing characteristic of fundamentalism. Nostalgic visions of an idealized past—the representation of which is controlled by men—"typically lay strong emphasis on the role women played in infusing that bygone time with perfection."[11] Further explicating this position, Brown adopts a psychoanalytical approach:

> Fundamentalist religion, more than most, capitalizes on the strength of the connection between religion and childhood. In its devotion to restoring a golden age—a time better structured and more innocent than the present—it pulls toward the center of religious experience the more broadly felt adult need to solidify ties with a nurturing childhood. The figure massively responsible for nurturance in childhood—mother—is often given a prominent symbolic position in religious groups for whom this act of reconnection is a very substantial concern.[12]

For fundamentalists, then, the affective pull of nostalgia and the intense concern for boundary definition divide men from women, and masculine from feminine—structural sex and gender divisions that Confucians would find familiar.

In the Confucian tradition, a man's identity is constructed within the family and then displayed in the outside world of employment and public responsibility; in contrast, the roles a woman assumes—daughter (-in-law), wife, and mother—are all located within the domestic sphere, a situation that renders her devoid of independent subjectivity and of any public identity other than one derived from her relation to father, husband, or son. In the normative roles of "virtuous wife and good mother" (*xiangqi liangmu*), she is the representation of that which comforts, complements, and thereby completes the dominant males in her life; she is also the quintessential "other" over whom control must be exercised.

Gender and Relationality in the Confucian Tradition

The present paper focuses on Confucianism primarily as it developed in China, although reference will be made to conditions in Japan and Korea.[13] In every context it is vitally important to bear in mind that "Confucian" attitudes and dispositions toward women and gender—as well as actual practices and customs—are not now, and never were universal. Historically, certain practices, such as foot binding, never spread beyond China; other customs developed in China but were differently interpreted, encouraged, or enforced when adopted elsewhere within the sphere of Confucian influence. In Japan, for example, matrifocality was only gradually displaced by imported Confucian patriarchal structures, and in Korea, Confucian bureaucrats regulated widow chastity with legislation that was more severe than was ever the case in China. Even within China, there never was a monolithic Confucian culture: issues of class always mitigated appropriation of ideal practice, the distinctive demands of urban vs. rural life mandated differential belief and practice, and certain historical periods were more or less "Confucian" in overall orientation.

At this point, it would be reasonable to ask just what "Confucianism" is. In the West, the seventeenth-century Latinization of "Confucius" from a supposed *Kongfuzi* ("Master Kong") led to the reification of "Confucianism"—an entity that did not previously exist.[14] In China (and in Chinese), what the West calls "Confucianism" refers to a body of teachings, ascribed to Master Kong Qiu (c. 551–479 BCE), which was transmitted to a small group of students and later espoused and revised by competing lineages of enshrined scholar-officials. Canonical Confucian texts and teachings changed markedly over time; nevertheless, what any given generation of *ru* ("genteel") scholars understood as "Confucianism" was for them a cohesive explanation of the way the world had been (whether in a real or mythic past), the way the world of their own time ought to be, and the way the world ought to proceed in the future.[15] A hallmark of the Confucian canon is its oddly atemporal character: its texts provide a cosmological vision and ethical program wherein past, present, and future are subtly conflated—a point to which we shall return below.

For the purposes of the present paper, "Confucianism" will refer to a complex cultural system that developed in China in the fifth century BCE and was codified initially during the first century CE. After a period of quiescence, the *ru* tradition expanded geographically as well as metaphysically from the tenth century on down to the present day. According to Tu Wei-ming, the most prominent contemporary proponent of "the Confucian project," *ru* teachings are still at the core of social mores and values in Confucian East Asia:

The majority of East Asian intellectuals embrace the ideas that the person is a center of human relationships, that family is an indispensable institution for human development, that society ought to be a fiduciary community [i.e., based on trust], that politics should be characterized by exemplary leadership, and that cultural life should be shaped in part by the symbolic resources of the past.[16]

Confucius emphasized his own traditionalism. He was, he said, simply one who "followed the Ancients" (*Analects* 7.1). To follow their teachings meant that an individual would undertake a dual process of formal education and ritual self-cultivation in order to become a true *junzi*, or "gentleman," who would manifest sincere and complete humaneness or cohumanity (*ren*). Later Confucian orthodoxy stressed cultivation of a balanced harmony of five reciprocal relationships (ruler-subject, parent-child, husband-wife, older brother-younger brother, and friends or peers), symbolized by *yin-yang* complementarity.

In the Confucian schema, the fruits of one's self-cultivation radiate outward in ever-widening circles of influence until all of human society "mirrors Heaven." The family—locus of three of the five cardinal relationships—is much more than a mere political or economic unit; it is where one first learns ritual interaction, and it is the first recipient of one's cultivated virtue. The Confucian family, therefore, is a profoundly religious unit—a venue for self-transformation and the springboard to public application of virtuous action.

Regarding women, it is by now well-known that Confucius himself had little to say about them other than to observe that, like "small men" (*xiaoren*), they were difficult to deal with, presumably because they lacked education and ritual refinement (*Analects* 17.25). There is little in the early texts of the *ru* school to deny women access to the education that would make them virtuous and ritually refined, but the canon is rife with references to popular customs that make plain a female's subordination and lack of value relative to males.[17]

It was with the grafting of popular cosmological speculation, particularly *yin-yang* theories of binary opposition, onto the core of Confucian ideas during the Han dynasty (second century BCE–second century CE) that gender hierarchy took root within the tradition. The complementary yet hierarchical relationships of Confucianism took on a new tone. *Yang* originally connoted strength, growth, light, and life, but was now extended to encompass "superior" and "male." Likewise, *yin* originally designated weakness, decay, darkness, and death; now, it extended to "inferior" and "female." The pre-Han distinction between emotion and rationality was already complicated by a belief in their physical location within the same organ—the *xin* or "heart-mind"; now, in the great Han synthesis, *yin*-associated emotion was seen to cause confusion and error, and *yang*-rationality was deemed morally superior. In this way, pre-Confucian customs of patrilineality and patrilocality fused with the Confucian imperative to educate, cultivate, and control the self—to the detriment of traits and persons associated with *yin* temperament.[18] Up until the Han, however, women were perceived as able to cultivate virtue and knowledge. Liu Xiang's (77–6 BCE) *Lienü zhuan* (Biographies of Exemplary Women) offers evidence: among the virtuous lives cataloged are those of women who were "wise" and "able in reasoning." These women remonstrate with their husbands, their rulers, and one of them—the woman washing at Agu—demurely but decisively stands up to the intrusive attentions of Confucius and his disciples.[19] Beginning with the Han, and intensifying during periods when China was divided or under foreign rule, the tendency to essentialize women and associate them with *yin* firmed up to more consistently result in the diminution of female virtues or in their valorization primarily within the context of family or state needs.

With notably few exceptions in the premodern period, Confucian ideologies have focused on patriarchal needs and have been born of masculine subjectivities, even when the standard-bearers have been female. Every student of women's history in China knows well the female Han scholar Ban Zhao (c. 48–c.120 CE), author of the first explicitly didactic text for women, the *Nüjie* (Instructions for Women). The significance of her erudition and historical influence, however, is made problematic by her intellectual identification with the elite and male-dominated culture of the Han court. An educated woman who advocated more than elementary lessons for girls, Ban Zhao nonetheless reinforced images of female subordination found in Confucian classics such as the *Odes* and *Book of Rites*. In urging women to take humility as their primary duty, Ban Zhao set forth a notion of "four virtues" (*si de*) integral to proper female conduct—womanly fidelity, physical charm, propriety in speech, and efficiency in work—that subordinated women to patriarchal ritual needs and to the desire for patrilineal continuity. It is a great and sad irony that the woman once dubbed "the foremost woman scholar in China" should have fostered the subjection of women to the doctrine of "thrice following" (*san cong*), i.e., following the dictates of father, husband, and eldest son over the course of life.[20]

The present study is not intended to be an historical overview of women in Confucianism; the focus of the volume is on women's roles and the construction of femininity in light of fundamentalist movements.[21] The nettlesome problem, however, is that twentieth-century Confucian traditions are neither easily nor precisely classified as fundamentalist; that designation may more fully, if anachronistically, describe the religious and philosophical renaissance of Confucianism that occurred almost a thousand years ago.

"Fundamentalist" Confucianism

For the sake of the present argument, "Confucian fundamentalism" shall loosely refer to "Neo-Confucianism," the historical revitalization movement that first gained momentum in the Song dynasty (960–1279 CE). Neo-Confucianism was an intellectual and spiritual response to the challenge of Buddhism and, to a lesser degree, sectarian Taoism. By the beginning of the Song, these two religions had all but eclipsed Confucianism. Buddhism, for example, provided specific techniques, notably meditation, for advancing religious self-cultivation; it provided a vastly expanded conceptual world in its sophisticated appreciation of the psychology of suffering and in its rich cosmology; its traditions of monasticism and celibacy threatened the family, the very foundation of Chinese society; and various sects often enjoyed imperial patronage, tax exemptions, and other forms of financial support from wealthy individuals, thereby siphoning funds from state coffers. In all these ways, Buddhism loomed large as a threat to the received Confucian tradition, attacking and gaining ground on the triple fronts of faith, family, and state.

The Song Neo-Confucian response was advanced in the eleventh century by the brothers Cheng Yi and Cheng Hao, and reached its zenith a century later in the works of Zhu Xi (1130–1200), a charismatic and articulate scholar who seems uncannily, if anachronistically, "fundamentalist." Using Marty and Appleby's definitional terms, Neo-Confucians such as Zhu Xi can be seen as having *fought with* a carefully chosen repertoire of resources: they reached back to real and imagined pasts, and selected what they regarded as fundamental.[22] They issued a clear call to return to the fundamentals of ritual, virtue, and self-cultivation. They demonstrated the foundational role of these concepts through painstakingly circular exegesis in countless commentaries and collectanea, augmented by an almost obsessive attention to matters of lineage and origin. Meticulously re-creating a new orthodoxy, the Neo-Confucians all but fetishized several of the classical treatises they now proclaimed to be the canonical core, especially the *Great Learning* and the *Doctrine of the Mean*. Words were not only their call to arms but also their weapons, enabling them to incorporate techniques appropriated from rival traditions. Buddhist meditation now became Confucian "quiet sitting," an activity practiced by the scholar as a means of muting the noise of a turbulent era, and classical Confucian textual study was now transformed into "embodied reading."[23]

The Neo-Confucians *fought against* perceived "others," both external and internal. Externally, Buddhism was a worthy opponent. Internally, pitched battles were waged among inheritors of the Confucian tradition for both ideological superiority and lineage authority.[24] The Neo-Confucians also *fought under the sign of some transcendent reference*, in this case, an inclusive Heaven (*tian*) that, through the person of the sage, could metaphysically unite all people as siblings. The churlish critic might see here a strong resemblance to Mahayana Buddhist doctrines of the compassionate bodhisattva and universal Buddha-nature, but to the Neo-Confucian, such images were but extensions of classical Confucian formulations of the unity of Heaven, Earth, and humanity. They were not "new" at all.

The above discussion is deliberately provocative in framing the construction of Neo-Confucian orthodoxy in terms of fundamentalism. For Song Neo-Confucians, the threat to tradition was certainly not "modernity"; rather, the greatest threats were monasticism and the dismantling of traditional patterns of patronage, i.e., incursions into the inner circles of family and state, the sacred precincts of Confucian religiosity. Alienated and under siege, the architects of Neo-Confucianism were clearly "caught off balance." It is not surprising, therefore, that their response to perceived external threats encompassed a heightened sensitivity to internal threats as well.

Even a cursory survey of Neo-Confucian texts confirms that women were seen to hinder male religious practice. Historian Theresa Kelleher has made the link between enhanced Neo-Confucian concerns for spiritual interiority and a renewed drive to control women's sexuality: desire was seen as a formidable obstacle to the cultivation of sageliness, and the solution, predictably, was to rein in women rather than condemn male vulnerability.[25] The Neo-Confucian moral code for women, largely a continuation of the classical Han paradigm, became focused to an almost obsessive degree on chastity, with widows singled out for particular attention. Zhu Xi not only repeated the earlier master Cheng Yi's dictum that widows should never remarry but ensured that the chaste widow model was inculcated early in the future arbiters of womanly virtue—boys. The *Elementary Learning* (*Xiaoxue*), an influential primer compiled by Zhu Xi, promotes this ideal through stories of women who mutilate themselves to forestall remarriage or who resist rape by hurling themselves off cliffs or onto rocks.[26] Idealized female virtues were also represented in the Neo-Confucian masters' compilations of extensive manuals for family instruction (*jiaxun*), in which women, as essentialized representations of *yin*, were regarded with wary ambivalence. On the one hand, women were to be educated so as to partake in a family's higher culture, but on the other, their sexuality was a matter of grave concern.[27]

The Song period was a watershed in Confucian history. The Neo-Confucian masters advocated tighter control over women's autonomy, and once Song Neo-Confucianism was established as state orthodoxy in the later Yuan and Ming dynasties (1280–1368–1644), their hopes came to fruition. In the public realm, Confucian texts and precepts formed the basis for the imperial civil service examination system, thereby becoming the common currency of intellectuals and scholar-officials. In the private realm, control of womanly virtue, constructed in terms of chastity, advanced through the Ming dynasty, eventually filtering down all the way to the commoner class. Printing made possible the cheap production of illustrated morality books and, as functional literacy rates rose, elementary texts for women were broadly disseminated. As the work of many scholars has shown, these didactic works uniformly stressed female receptivity to regulation; by the Ming-Qing dynastic transition (mid-seventeenth century), the ideal wife was described as one who complemented her husband "like a shadow or an echo."[28]

Sociologist of religion Winston Davis has observed that fundamentalism manifests itself both religiously and politically, and that religious and political fundamentalisms are structurally related.[29] In the Chinese case, the relation of Confucian political and religious institutions and agendas could hardly be closer than in the late imperial period; thus was Neo-Confucianism's "fundamentalist" agenda for women successfully enacted. The history of political control over women/females in China is well documented: on the level of the family, mechanisms to properly "educate" women accelerated during periods of social stress and cultural upheaval; on the level of the state, government manipulation of cults of female goddesses intensified during these same periods, most blatantly in the imperial elevation of Tianhou/Mazu within the state cult.[30] To be sure, individual women flourished in eras and areas of greater permissiveness, but their numbers were small and their significance lies in being the remarkable exceptions to the rule of an ideology oppressive to women.[31]

In the waning years of the nineteenth century, the visionary Confucian scholar Kang Yuwei (1858–1927) persuaded the emperor to undertake what was later called the Hundred Days' Reform. Kang advocated peace and equality for all people, the latter fully inclusive of women, whom he felt should be free to marry for love, move into the public sphere, and engage in life's activities in every way equal to men. The Reform was quickly quashed—by the empress dowager—but it provides a useful reminder that not all Confucian scholars were unfeeling toward women's plight.[32]

The adoption of Neo-Confucian principles in Korea and, to lesser extent, in Japan further illustrate the tradition's "fundamentalist" impulse to control women. During the Koryo dynasty (918–1392), the indigenous female shamanic tradition combined with the influence of Buddhism to allow Korean women relative freedom to publicly interact with men; it was a time when females could be acknowledged heads of households, had equal inheritance rights with men, and remarriage was widely practiced and socially accepted. The situation changed in the early Choson dynasty (1392–1910) when Confucianism was promoted by the new rulers to justify their control and regulate the state. Examination in Confucian texts now determined the selection of officials, and the discriminatory effects of Neo-Confucian philosophy—in the Korean case heavily colored by *yin-yang* theory—gradually established themselves in Korean society. Initially, the Confucian moral code and its legal enforcement were directed to royal and upper-class women; eventually, Neo-Confucian images of obedient, chaste, and quietly dedicated woman became deeply and universally entrenched Korean ideals. As this process advanced, women's freedoms were restricted, their roles strictly defined, and their status diminished. Exemplary biographies of virtuous women, didactic texts for women, and books of family instruction proliferated and promoted the Confucian vision of women. By the early twentieth-century, Confucianism permeated every aspect of Korean society.[33]

Similarly but more slowly, when Neo-Confucianism was officially embraced by the Tokugawa rulers (1603–1868) as the ideological basis for their rule, the vision of women as little more than "heir providers" gradually percolated down through the Japanese social strata. Although the subsequent Meiji Restoration formally ended feudalism, the new code continued Confucian practices of male domination, often referring explicitly to texts such as *The Great Learning for Women*. Men were awarded rights and privileges, but women were generally accorded duties and obligations. In those instances where women were granted rights, e.g., the 1872 mandate for women's education, such privileges were still determined by Confucian priorities, i.e., in order for them to become *ryusai kembo*, or "good wives and mothers."[34]

In sum, despite occasional protests and calls for reform, the male-dominance of fundamentalist Neo-Confucian ideology remained largely uncontested in East Asia until the twentieth-century dissolution of imperial rule, the rise of republicanism, and the multiple challenges wrought by modernity and by contact with Western Enlightenment-influenced notions of individual autonomy and democracy.

The People's Republic of China (PRC)

In China, the late nineteenth and twentieth centuries witnessed the fall of the Qing, the last dynasty, and its replacement by a republican government; the incursion of Western imperialism; colonial and wartime occupation by the Japanese; the rise and revision of Mao Zedong's "Communism with a Chinese face"; the pendulum swings of vilification and rehabilitation of Confucius; the push toward limited capitalism; and, most recently, the call for "socialist spiritual civilization." Throughout the disarray and dislocations of this "post-fundamentalist" era, the social status of women and the cultural construction of gender have remained focal sites of contention, with tensions most obvious when deep cultural expectations are directly and visibly challenged, i.e., in transgressions of the Confucian boundary between public and private spheres of action. The present examination is limited to the realms of education and the workforce, areas in which women have begun to cross the private-public divide in increasing, if not necessarily significant, numbers.[35]

Beginning in the 1910s and 1920s, social reformers rallied against the degradation of women, typified for them by foot binding, widespread female infanticide, and the wholesale trade in women as brides, concubines, and slaves. None of these practices was inherently Confucian, but together they were emblematic of the subordination of women endemic to the Neo-Confucian system. Unfortunately, in what would prove to be a common pattern, many such calls for the liberation of women fell into disarray or were co-opted into some larger ideal.

The case of the idealistic Communist Party founders proves instructive. Despite their early commitment to gender transformation, numerous contradictions emerge to demonstrate their reinscription of central aspects of the existing "feudal" gender system, ironically predicated upon intrinsically Confucian values. Historian Christina Gilmartin's research shows that the Communist Party's attitudes and practices concerning women's status and roles have long been contradictory and in the service of goals quite unrelated to women's issues. Even in the early years of the party, she concludes, the liberation of women had more symbolic than actual import: those women who did become important leaders either sent their children off to relatives to raise, were childless, or else found themselves cast in supportive, nurturing, or organizational roles compatible with "mothering" experiences.[36]

Gilmartin's study, along with numerous others undertaken since the mid-1970s, attest to the reproduction of certain patriarchal structures under socialism—the unchallenged male-domination of the political hierarchy, the sexual division of labor in political life at all levels, and the often great resentment against women in the political realm. Anthropologist Ann Anagnost has concluded that it is undoubtedly the case that "the socialist state assumed that once private property was collectivized, 'feudal ideology' would disappear through education."[37]

But how can "feudal ideology" disappear if its creator does not? In the PRC, state policy toward Confucius and the tradition bearing his name has shifted wildly according to political circumstance. After 1949, all public ceremonials in honor of Confucius disappeared, and most local temples were turned into schools, cultural centers, or museums. The transformation was easy without an organized clergy to have to sweep away, and local people did not oppose the idea of using a temple for community purposes. The Communist regime attacked Confucianism as an autocratic expression of an old, feudal culture that had enslaved the Chinese for centuries; yet Mao Zedong also advised the Chinese to "sum up everything from Confucius to Sun Yat-sen and inherit this valuable legacy."[38]

By the time of the Cultural Revolution in the mid-1960s, the Confucian legacy no longer had value. Confucius was reviled as the "number one criminal of feudal teaching," and Kong family relics and the temple at Confucius's birthplace in Qufu were destroyed. In the early 1970s, anti-Confucius activities were coupled to a major ideological campaign to discredit Mao's former associate, Lin Piao, for his alleged failure to eradicate his feudal habits despite the state's best efforts at revolutionary transformation. This was the last official attempt to orchestrate an anti-Confucius campaign, and the late 1970s and the early 1980s brought yet another reappraisal of the role of Confucius, with Jiang Qing and the Gang of Four blamed for the excesses of the anti-Confucius campaigns. As explained in a 1979 volume of the *Beijing Review*, "The teachings of Confucius were distorted by political opportunists who criticized him in order to gain advancement for themselves."[39] These sorts of pronouncements set the stage for a guided revival of the past, reinterpreted within the framework of Marxist-Leninist-Maoist-Socialist thought.

Confucius's grave and temple at Qufu were restored in 1979 and opened to the public; classical Confucian works were again printed and widely circulated.

The last twenty years have ushered in a new appreciation of Confucius and new appropriations of Confucianism. Jin Guantao, one of China's most articulate Westernizers, has gone so far as to characterize Chinese Communism, as sinicized by Mao Zedong and Liu Shaoqi, as a "thoroughly Confucianized Marxism."[40] In 1984, the state-supported China Confucius Foundation was established to promote "Confucius, the Confucian School, China's traditional cultural ideas, [and] Oriental cultural ideas with China's traditional ideas as source of radiation."[41] A major conference was held at Qufu in 1987, and an international conference on Confucius was held in Beijing in October 1989 during which prominent government officials repeatedly appealed to Confucian teachers and traditions as models for modern conduct.[42]

The resurgence of interest in Confucianism in the PRC can be attributed in part to government fears of declining morals in the face of rising capitalist tendencies; in part to long-suppressed scholarly desire for study *sans* political correctness; in part to the recognition that Confucianism is very much on the minds of China's immediate neighbors and trade partners, Japan and South Korea, and thus could link countries harboring formidable distrust of each others' nationalism; and in part to a cynical bid to boost tourism and investment dollars from overseas Chinese, for whom the Confucian tradition is presumed to be of more than passing historical interest.

It is true that Chinese women have made significant progress over their pre-Revolutionary status, but today, fifty years after the Revolution, they still endure educational, economic, political, and cultural inequalities that are standard features of women's secondary status worldwide. A major contributing factor has been the subordination of discussions of women's issues and gender equality—although declared objectives of the party and state—to questions of class. In the pre–market reform era, any program designed to improve the status of a group defined entirely by their sex rather than class, came under attack by definition as bourgeois liberalism in its capacity to weaken social solidarity. Even the valorization of the now-despised "Iron Girl" model of the Cultural Revolution had little to do with women and everything to do with the state's need to create categories of its own, as well as the rampant yet empty iconoclasm of that time. More recently, in the continuing wake of post-Mao economic reforms, the strengthening of the family as not only a viable but a vital economic unit has resulted in the resurrection of the traditional model of ideal wife and mother, transformed slightly into a consumer-oriented one with "knowledge, skills, and ideas of her own."[43]

"Woman" still is not truly a category of analysis, as Marilyn Young and Tani Barlow have shown,[44] but in those instances where the government has made women the independent subjects of inquiry, policy decisions evince assumptions that, to an important extent, biology is destiny. Women, not men, are restricted from some occupations for fear that such work might damage their reproductive capacity.[45] Provisions of the state's "One Child" family planning policies are far from benign. Women, not men, are punished for out-of-quota births, and women are subjected to the "three surgeries" (abortion, IUD insertion, and sterilization), while male contraceptive use lags far behind. State policy has done little, therefore, to dismantle traditional attitudes that women are responsible for reproduction.[46]

In the realm of education, 70 percent of secondary school dropouts in the countryside are female, and 70 percent of China's 200 million illiterate or subliterate individuals are female.[47] Men have routinely been admitted to university with lower scores on entrance exams than their female counterparts, and successful female graduates are not always accorded the respect of their male peers or rewarded for their intellectual achievements to the same degree.[48] By 1990, almost 30 percent of university faculty in China were women (an increase from the 11 percent recorded in 1950), but a full two-thirds of them occupied less lucrative, low status positions as lecturers, research assistants, or teaching associates.[49] Moreover, female faculty, like women in all professions, are expected to retire at age fifty-five, whereas men may continue on until age sixty, or even longer in academe if they are funded by grants.[50]

Beyond the universities, there is ample evidence that recent moves toward privatization, the influx of multinational corporations, and the dismantling of collectives in rural areas have increased disparities between men and women. Chinese employers now watch their production levels and profit margins carefully; they are often reluctant to hire women, who may require maternity leave or child care. Foreign factories simply keep their eye on the bottom line, with resultant and familiar labor abuses falling hardest on unskilled women. In rural areas, agriculture is reorganizing along family lines, with women once again subjected to patriarchal control.[51]

Lastly, no discussion of the "position of women" in the "post-fundamentalist" PRC would be complete without some mention of the deadly combination of traditional son-preference and modern "One Child" family planning regulations, which have produced the phenomenon of "missing girls," i.e., the thousands of Chinese girls whose births ought to have been registered, but who—based on normal male-to-female birth ratios—seem not to have been born at all. A normal ratio would be 105–106 boys born for every 100 girls, reflecting a natural imbalance that compensates for higher male mortality rates. In China, the births of 113.8 boys are reported for every 100 girls, and in some provinces, the ratio is well over 115 to 100. In short, some 12 percent of baby girls are unaccounted for each year. Many of these are doubtless aborted female fetuses, their sex having been determined (illegally) via ultrasound exam[52]; others were likely abandoned; a few are those taken into orphanages and commodified for the Western adoption market; some are murdered by families desperate for a son; and some are possibly unreported but shielded by parents who are still hoping for the birth of a boy. In provinces where the sex ratio has been out of balance for years, the need for young women of marriageable age has occasioned reports of bride auctions; other reports point to increased affluence as fostering the return of pre-Communist practices such as the abduction and sale of women for prostitution, marriage, or slavery—some of the very same practices that prompted calls for revolution nearly a century ago.[53]

The Republic of China (ROC) on Taiwan

The Communist victory in the mainland forced the retreat to Taiwan of the Nationalist government, run by the Kuomintang political party (KMT). The government-in-exile of the Republic of China enshrined itself as the guardian of traditional Chinese culture and actively sought to inculcate virtues of filiality and loyalty. The 1947 constitution declared women's status to be equal to that of men, but in actuality, women's roles until recently were seen to be complementary to, rather than equal to, that of men. As part of the ROC plan for "national reconstruction," women were expected to contribute to the stability, progress, and prosperity of Taiwanese society in their capacities as wives, mothers, and volunteer workers.[54]

In the 1960s, female elementary and junior high graduates were urged to enter the work force, helping fuel economic expansion but curtailing their higher education.[55] During the 1970s, the growth of a new urban middle class, born of economic prosperity, led government rhetoricians to once again raise high the traditional model of "virtuous wife and good mother," now properly understood as women's appropriate contribution to national development.[56] No matter how responsible the position held by female civil servants, for example, they were expected to report to the Chinese Women's Anti-(Communist) Aggression League office each month to sew pants for soldiers. As the '70s progressed, local politics were complexifying due to increasing discontent with the restrictions of martial law and the suppression of native Taiwanese political participation. Hoping to forestall trouble, the ROC government stressed preservation of Chinese tradition, expressed through the paternalistic "Three Bonds" (*sanbang*) of respect for ruler/state, father, and husband.

Spearheading the revival of traditional Confucian rhetoric was Chen Lifu, a respected but feared political ideologue who was a high-ranking KMT party organizer for decades in China prior to the Communist takeover. After spending twenty years in voluntary exile in the United States, Chen returned to Taiwan. As a former minister of education, Chen's "academic" credentials were sufficient to establish him as a senior spokesman for the promotion of traditional values in general and of Confucian ethics in particular. The content of his message, in the words of Tu Wei-ming, combines:

cultural chauvinism, nationalism, ethnocentrism, anthropocentrism, and political conservatism. Chen believes that the continuous vitality of Chinese culture for more than five thousand years is firm proof that Confucianism, as the predominant intellectual tradition in China, is the superior ideology in human history.[57]

For Chen, Confucianism is the defining characteristic of Chinese civilization, but it is also a rational humanism compatible with science.[58] Moreover, it is arguably a religious enterprise—the key phrase being *rujiao* ("Confucian [religious] teachings") rather than *ruxue* ("Confucian studies") or *rujia sixiang* ("Confucian thought"). Chen's self-assigned tasks were to position Confucianism at the center of national consciousness and to make of Confucian ethics a civil religion.

Part of this campaign entailed the establishment of the Confucius-Mencius Scholarly Society (*Kong-Meng xuehui*) and the revival of rituals honoring Confucius. The government-supported Scholarly Society sponsors lectures and conferences, underwrites numerous publications, holds open discussions on Confucian ethics in public halls, and has been active in public education, but the organization has not had much scholarly credibility. The campaign to reestablish Confucian rituals was broadly successful: each year on September 28 (an inexact translation from lunar dating which regularized observance), the anniversary of the sage's birth is celebrated as Teachers' Day; on that day, major Confucian temples islandwide conduct early morning ceremonies replete with sacrificial offerings, traditional feather dances, and music played on ancient instruments.

Yet even as patriarchal Confucian images and ideology dominated official discourse, the 1970s saw the first stirrings of feminism. In 1974, Lü Hsiu-lien published her pioneering feminist work *Xin nüxingzhuyi* (New feminism), a book whose effect in Taiwan has been likened to that of Betty Friedan's 1963 *Feminine Mystique*. In her work, Lü provided a synopsis of Chinese women's history, and outlined gender inequalities she observed in Taiwan's legal, political, economic, and educational domains. In contrast to visible inequalities such as economic indicators, Lü argued that invisible concepts of patriarchal values continued to control Chinese women's fates. Chief among these patriarchal values were the following: (1) "continuing the family line" (*zhuanzong jiedai*), which generates the phenomenon of "emphasizing the man and slighting the woman" (*zhongnan qingnü*); (2) the concept of "thrice following and four virtues" (*sancong side*), which generates the phenomenon of "man is respected and woman, debased" (*nanzun nübei*); (3) the concept of "one-sided chastity" (*pianmian zhencao*), which generates a double moral standard; and (4) the concept of "men go out, women stay in" (*nanwai nünei*), which generates sex role differentiation (*xingbie jiaose chabie*).[59]

At least three of these four instances of "patriarchal values"—all but the notion of "one-sided chastity"—are directly related to Confucian emphases on the family, reverence for ancestors, and the differentiation of labor as defining the spousal relationship; the double moral standard of "one-sided chastity" is an indirect byproduct of traditional marriage practice coupled with the advantages men can derive from their ability to "go out." Lü called the Confucian tradition to accountability. Its texts were written by men for men; Confucian goals of self-cultivation, regulation of the family, governance of the country, and pacification of all under heaven were impossible for women to pursue.[60] It was a daring challenge to a society whose political culture was defined by the Confucian discourse promulgated by both Chen Lifu and the academic philosophers of the New Confucianism movement (discussed below).

Lü was accused of "encouraging promiscuity"; her criticism of "one-sided chastity" was read, perversely, not as a condemnation of male behavior but as incitement to female wantonness. She was further accused of wanting to destabilize society, a task she planned to accomplish by "encouraging disputes between husbands and wives of high-ranking officials so as to break up their marriages."[61] Eventually, her dual involvement in feminist activism and Taiwan independence politics led to her imprisonment. After her release, she was instrumental in the founding of the New Awakening Foundation (*Funü xinzhi jijinhui*), the first feminist organization in Taiwan; from this platform, she rallied women to political campaigns on behalf of abused women and against child prostitution. In 1993, Lü—a member of the opposition Democratic Progressive Party—was elected to the Executive Yuan (legislature), where, she has noted wryly, she was the section chief of the Commission on Law and Regulation but still had to recess from her work a half day each month to sew pants for soldiers.[62] Finally, in March 2000, Lü was elected vice president and was able to put aside her seamstress duties.

Today, although women in Taiwanese society participate in extra-domestic life in increasing numbers and over a longer period of their life cycles, the rationale for that participation remains different from men's participation in public life. That is, women are typically seen as earning supplemental rather than essential wages—a formulation that denies any sense of career or meaningful identity for women outside the home.[63] Middle-class men have increasingly but selectively taken on domestic duties: they will feed but not diaper the baby, prepare light meals but not do laundry. The climate for public expression and pluralism in public discourse is more open today than virtually anyone could have guessed even a decade ago, and yet, despite women's higher levels of education, greater economic power, and a measure of social and legal recognition, feminist Taiwanese scholars see "traditional social norms and cultural values" as "a ceiling on further improvement" in women's status.[64] Women workers have made significant gains in commerce and service industries at all levels, but recent studies indicate that vertical integration into the core of the Taiwanese economic system is poor: the majority of women are still located in the lower end of the production relationship and the dominance of men in the employer class and women in the unpaid category persists over time.[65] In other words, socioeconomic changes appear to be a necessary but insufficient condition for improvement in women's status—in both the People's Republic and on Taiwan. The Confucian legacy is deeply rooted and tenacious.

The present study thus far has advanced the notion that both Chinas today are "post-fundamentalist" Confucian cultures—fundamentalism having been embodied in the religiopolitical institutions of the late imperial state. A rather different approach is suggested by Winston Davis, who, in his analysis of fundamentalism in Japan, has differentiated institutional and diffuse forms of fundamentalism, the former being that embodied in specific, organized religions or political organizations, and the latter being a "climate of opinion" that is spread less formally throughout the general culture, especially by the mass media.[66]

In posing the question of whether or not a diffuse fundamentalism exists in East Asian Confucian cultures, it is clear that ideals of male superiority and patriarchal custom are pervasive. Educational access and achievements are limited for women, as are employment opportunities. Educated middle- and upper-class women are often idled after marriage, not always by their own design or desire. Women who work outside the home do so out of some economic necessity, generally earn less than 55 percent of male colleagues' salaries for comparable work, and find that their work status only adds to their burden of domestic responsibility. Legislative attempts to redress inequalities are embarrassingly recent (e.g., the 1991 passage of the Family Law of Korea, which outlawed differential inheritance provisions; previously, the bulk of family inheritance was given to the elder son, at the expense of the widow as well as any other children), often insufficient, or else mask alternative agenda that serve to maintain the patriarchal status quo. In Japan, the disingenuously named 1986 Equal Employment Opportunity Law for Men and Women does not in fact prohibit differential treatment of women with respect to recruiting, hiring, assignments, and promotion; its language requires only the "endeavor" to prevent discrimination.[67] A woman has status and honor within the basic social unit of the family but little if any identity beyond its confines. Historically, women in Confucian cultures were prized primarily for their reproductive capacities, and only secondarily for their labor value; today, the perceived need to control women's bodies and female sexuality still underlies and informs public discourse about gender roles.

The experience of Japan and at least three of the "Four Tigers" (or "Four Mini-Dragons") of Hong Kong, Taiwan, Singapore, and South Korea shows that ubiquitous technology and access to the outside world masks the reality that social change advances unevenly. In the public as well as private domain, "women's alternatives are late in coming, limited in scope, and lower in social value."[68] Gender inequalities in education and employment, and disparities in social status reinforce each other, founded as they are upon the bedrock of gendered Neo-Confucian familism and traditional *yin-yang* complementarity. Small wonder that as recently as the late 1980s, a Seoul newspaper quoted a survey in which 60 percent of Korean teenage girls said that they would rather be boys if they could be born again.[69]

New Confucianism

This general "climate of opinion" concerning the fundamental place and value of traditional Confucian notions of family and gender roles is partially yet ironically fueled by proponents of what has been called "New Confucianism," a transnational revitalization movement. Significantly different from Chen Lifu's partisan Confucian revival and the textually and politically conservative Confucius-Mencius Society, the academic "New Confucian" movement emerged at Peking University in the 1920s with Xiong Shili and developed at New Asia College in Hong Kong in the 1940s under Tang Junyi; further refinements came in the 1960s at Tunghai University in Taiwan under Mou Zongsan and Xu Fuguan. Currently, among Confucians in diasporic "cultural China," Liu Shu-hsien, Cheng Chung-ying, and the "Boston Confucians" around Tu Wei-ming at Harvard University continue to shape the movement.[70] Lee Sang-eun (South Korea) and Okada Takehiko (Japan) have also contributed to the New Confucian dialogue with modernity, adding their respective and distinctive calls for the true Confucian as servant of the people rather than the state, and for the preservation of meditational practices as part of New Confucian self-cultivation.[71]

New Confucians argue for contemporary engagement with tradition on the basis that the strategies of relegating Confucianism to a residual category or denouncing it as a dispensable psychopathological burden have not brought fruitful results. Among New Confucians, Mou Zongsan and Tu Wei-ming have asserted the essentially religious nature of the Confucian tradition, implying that the tradition's deep roots will naturally continue to surface even if temporarily plowed under by the rhetoric of Marxism, science, or Enlightenment rationality. Theirs is a strong belief that the spiritual resources of the Confucian tradition can and must be mobilized to critique the unintended negative consequences of industrialization, urbanization, bureaucratization, and the widespread influence of mass communication. According to Tu,

> Confucian humanism, premised on an anthropocosmic vision which advocates harmony with nature and union with Heaven, is in a better position than the Enlightenment mentality to cope with issues in ecology, environment, and resources.... Underlying this mode of thought is a communal critical awareness that tradition can assume a variety of cultural forms.... The significance of Confucian humanism, in light of this awareness, is not confined to its historicity. The Confucian form of life, to the extent that it locates ultimate human concerns in ordinary day-to-day existence, can continue to provide spiritual resources and standards of inspiration for the future.[72]

The New Confucian movement's primary concern is the transformation of Confucian humanism as a creative response to the impact of modernity and the West. In this view, the retention of traditional ideals is not inimical to the advancement of science or to the embrasure of a universal democratic impulse.

New Confucianism fails to fit the fundamentalist mold in other important ways: it knows the limitations of its past and it lacks any real sense of militancy—due not to any pacifist orientation but from a conviction of victory-assured. New Confucians actually do "fight" the threat of Western-defined modernity, but they do so by declaring that any such battle would be a nonevent. At least in theory, Confucianism already possesses the conceptual framework necessary to inaugurate its "Third Epoch," its modern flourishing for the benefit of all humanity.[73] As Tu has optimistically and expansively declared, "As a common heritage of East Asian humanism, the form of life [Confucianism] embodies allows the coexistence of a variety of cultural expressions; as a result, conflict in ethnicity, language, territoriality, class, gender, and religion is minimized, if not resolved."[74]

It is true that Confucianism ranged far beyond its Shandong origins over the centuries to coexist with Buddhism, Taoism, Shinto, and indigenous shamanic and folk traditions for people of every social stratum across East and Southeast Asia; in this way, the historical Confucian tradition successfully blurred many distinctions of ethnicity, language, territoriality, religion, and, to some degree, class. Contemporary New Confucianism strongly affirms the transnational character of the tradition, referring to it as a distinctively "East Asian" spirituality. Yet from the Song to the present, Confucianism has tended to maintain sharp distinctions between the sexes, presuming the virtual identity of sex and gender. That is, there is a seemingly "natural" divide between men and women wherein the former are perceived as superior to the latter, no matter what the geographic, ethnic, linguistic, or temporal setting. All men are Confucian, and all women should be "good wives and virtuous mothers."

New Confucians are not insensitive to these issues; awareness of the symbolic resources of the canonical Confucian tradition as overwhelmingly male and masculinist has stirred interest in the recovery of women's history and in devising language that might address the problem of exclusivist male imagery.[75] Nonetheless, attention to "feminist issues" has yet to satisfactorily reconcile the gendered and sexualized embodied nature of the self with the traditional focus on the human "heart-mind." Within the Confucian tradition, heart and mind—the affective and the cognitive—cannot be separated. To know something, one has to embody it. New Confucian theorists are, with few exceptions, male academics, many of whom are supported by institutions that are not only unsupportive of women but also remarkably resistant to change. Perhaps for these reasons, New Confucianism has hardly considered female embodiment—and then only in ironically cerebral terms.[76] Whether the transformative Confucian experience of realizing and participating fully in human existence can be known in a woman's body, whether the tradition can come to terms with new models of family structure, male-female relationality, or a full range of female sexuality—complex questions such as these remain unanswered and, often, unasked.

It would be misleading to suggest that New Confucians represent the views of the general populace; even though the academic leaders of the movement often enjoy governmental support of their ideals and activities, it is not clear that they have an identifiable following. In particular, the New Confucians' reference to Confucianism as a world religion distances them from the overwhelming majority of people in East Asia, even those who share these "traditional" values and moral vision. A recent study by Byong-ik Koh regarding the identification of Confucianism in Korea proves instructive. According to a government census released in 1984, only 2 percent of the population identified themselves as Confucian, and a subsequent Korea Gallup poll revealed that less than 1 percent declared themselves Confucian. However, accompanying in-depth interviews designed to measure the respondents' degree of adherence to specific convictions and practices, e.g., filial piety and loyalty, veneration of sages, and the inviolability of tradition, revealed that nearly 92 percent were "found to be Confucianized."[77]

Apparent rejection of Confucian identity thus belies a significant adherence to Confucian ideals and norms, and the amorphous or diffuse nature of current belief and practice provides no safeguard against the rise of a more coherent fundamentalist Confucianism in the future. Throughout Confucian East Asia, the goal of the state has always been to create a culturally united and morally efficient family-state.[78] That goal persists today but is pursued in the face of new urban, industrial, and capitalist modalities; the shrinkage, dispersal, and weakening of multigenerational families; and the concomitant loosening of traditional patriarchal control over social structures.

Academic New Confucians see the discourse of "the Confucian project" rising to meet these challenges on its own terms; they are sure Confucian values can be embodied in ways appropriate to the times. Once again, however, the crux of the problem may lie in defining this notion of embodiment. Confucians employ the term in reference to a deeply transformative experience wherein the Cartesian duality of mind and body is overcome through realizing the inseparable nature of heart and mind; self-cultivation results in the individual forming "a single body with Heaven and Earth." In this schema, sex and gender distinctions associated with physical bodies can be diminished to reveal bio-cosmological processes of change, interchange, and evolution; viewed on the grand scale, *yang* yields to *yin*, *yang* overcomes *yin*, and so on, in endlessly alternating and self-altering complementary configurations suffusing all realms—individual, social, and cosmic.

Yet recent studies of fundamentalism suggest a different, more prosaic approach to understanding the traditional interpersonal dynamic of male authority and female obedience, namely, to appreciate that it is inextricably connected to an entire fabric of feelings and moral entitlements that constitute a way of life based on male supremacy. These include the pleasures of protecting the weak, of placing trust in the strong, of giving and receiving the gratitude, admiration, and deference that properly belongs to those who have the responsibility for the survival and well-being of others.[79]

Historically Confucian societies now harbor an array of nascent cultural movements, primarily focused on issues of gender, sexuality, and human rights—all of which threaten the everyday sentiments, expectations, and emotional rewards enjoyed by Confucian rulers, fathers, and husbands for centuries. These are precisely the circumstances—articulated as threats to "traditional" values—that might well trigger the growth of a political-religious Confucian fundamentalism. In this way, the diffuse East Asian "climate of opinion" draws near to fundamentalisms elsewhere in the world through its predilection for "symbolic regression," a tendency described by Winston Davis as a means of coping with complex sociopolitical realities by withdrawing symbolically to the imagined simplicities of the past—a tendency that can be called fundamentalist.[80]

Communism, capitalism, and global consciousness notwithstanding, the persistent sentiment in Confucian cultures continues to idealize women primarily as self-sacrificing wives and mothers in need of personal, cultural, and legal protection. Industrialization and modernization have brought demonstrable changes to women's lives: they have access to education, work in an increasing variety of enterprises, and appear to move freely in the public realm; nevertheless, it remains true that Confucian patriarchalism continues to define the kind and degree of change permissible in the operative sex-gender system. The social acceptance of single working women, women who return to the workforce despite childcare or eldercare demands, deliberately childless couples, or same-sex unions—such challenges to traditional norms are the fault lines that threaten to break open, exposing latent religio-political fundamentalist attitudes and behaviors below the secular civil surface. As Hawley and Proudfoot note, "When 'secular humanism' and those who struggle for women's rights assert that a woman's deepest identity may be found in something other than her connection to her family … the challenge to fundamentalism is profound."[81]

The present study has suggested that contemporary East Asian Confucian cultures can be seen as "post-fundamentalist," moving perhaps toward a Third Epoch of Confucian humanism. Alternatively, we may discern in East Asia a diffuse fundamentalism, an ongoing process of symbolic regression, resistant to reconfigurations of female identity, that may yet provoke organized fundamentalist reaction. Whether such fundamentalism will arise in East Asia remains to be seen, but the future is sure to be determined in large measure by contemporary Confucian responses to conflicting demands for both the liberation and control of women.

Notes

* The present essay draws in part on a draft manuscript on the history of Confucianism and feminism in cultural China, portions of which have been presented at Columbia University, Hamilton College, Harvard University, Syracuse University, the Claremont Colleges, and the University of California, Riverside. Appreciation is due the many individuals whose comments have proven catalytic to my continued research; I am particularly grateful to Douglas Oliver for our conversations about the nature of fundamentalism, and to Savita Bal, Matt Center, and Jonathan H. X. Lee for their research and editorial assistance.

1. For the origins of fundamentalism, see George Marsden, *Fundamentalism and American Culture: The Shaping of Twentieth-Century Evangelicalism: 1870–1925* (New York: Oxford University Press, 1980).

2. The term "neo-traditionalism" has been used as an alternative to "Islamic fundamentalism" by Bruce B. Lawrence, *Defenders of God: Fundamentalist Revolt Against the Modern Age* (San Francisco: Harper and Row, 1989), 163. Particularly in the case of Islam, the alternate designation works to offset the popular orientalist characterization of the tradition as extremist—or even fanatical—thereby comfortably distancing Muslim fundamentalism from the presumed superiority of "Western" Enlightenment rationality and moderation. On this last point, see also Edward Said, *Culture and Imperialism* (New York: Vintage Books, 1994), 375–77.

3. Martin E. Marty and R. Scott Appleby, coordinators of the American Academy of Arts and Sciences' Fundamentalism Project, also describe a necessary tension with the dominant tradition, and a grounding in metaphysical distinctions between good and evil; see their introduction to *Fundamentalisms Observed* (Chicago: University of Chicago Press, 1991), the initial volume of the Fundamentalism Project series.

4. Karen McCarthy Brown, "Fundamentalism and the Control of Women," in *Fundamentalism and Gender*, ed. John Stratton Hawley (New York: Oxford University Press, 1994), 190.

5. John Stratton Hawley and Wayne Proudfoot, "Introduction," in *Fundamentalism and Gender* (New York: Oxford University Press, 1994), 12.

6. Martin E. Marty and R. Scott Appleby, "The Fundamentalism Project: A User's Guide," in Marty and Appleby, *Fundamentalisms Observed*, ix.

7. Shahin Gerami, *Women and Fundamentalism: Islam and Christianity* (New York: Garland, 1996), 31.

8. Lionel Caplan, ed., *Studies in Religious Fundamentalism* (Albany, NY: State University of New York Press, 1987), 19.

9. Hawley and Proudfoot, "Introduction," 27.

10. Brown, "Fundamentalism and the Control of Women," 188, citing Simone de Beauvoir's *The Second Sex.*

11. Hawley and Proudfoot, "Introduction," 30.

12. Summarized by Hawley and Proudfoot, "Introduction," 31.

13. Despite the widespread Western identification of Confucianism with China, and its more recent association with Japanese management systems, it is arguable that the Confucian tradition has exerted a stronger hold on Korea than on any other nation in the world. Prior to the adoption of Confucian ideology, however, Korean society, as in Japan, exhibited remarkably egalitarian attitudes and practices with respect to gender issues. The Confucian tradition had significant influence in Vietnamese culture and history as well, but, for reasons of space, the Vietnamese case will not be taken up in this study.

14. See Lionel M. Jensen, *Manufacturing Confucianism: Chinese Traditions and Universal Civilization* (Durham, NC: Duke University Press, 1997).

15. Historically, Confucians used the terms *daoxue* ("the study of the *dao*, or way"), *lixue* ("the study of principle"), or *daotong* ("orthodox transmission of the *dao*, or way")—all of which have been subsumed under the rubric of "Confucianism."

16. Wei-ming Tu, "The Search for Roots in Industrial East Asia: The Case of the Confucian Revival," in Marty and Appleby, *Fundamentalisms Observed*, 773.

17. See Richard W. Guisso, "Thunder Over the Lake: The Five Classics and the Perception of Woman in Early China," in *Women in China: Current Directions in Historical Scholarship*, ed. Richard W. Guisso and Stanley Johannesen (Youngstown, OH: Philo Press, 1981), 47–61; Theresa Kelleher, "Confucianism," in *Women in World Religions*, ed. Arvind Sharma (Albany, NY: State University of New York Press, 1987), 135–59; and Vivian-Lee Nyitray, "Treacherous Terrain: Mapping Feminine Spirituality in Confucian Worlds," in *Confucian Spirituality*, vol. II, ed. Wei-ming Tu and Mary Evelyn Tucker (New York: Crossroad, 2004).

18. For illustration of the complexity of the Han synthesis, see Terry Woo, "Confucianism and Feminism," in *Feminism and World Religions*, ed. Arvind Sharma and Katherine K. Young (Albany: State University of New York Press, 1999), 120–32.

19. The "Skilled in Debate" (*bian tong*) chapter of the *Biographies* contains the story of the incident at Agu: coming upon a young woman washing at the river, Confucius repeatedly sends his student Zigong to induce her to violate propriety, even to the point of attempting to seduce her. Her resistance takes the form of moral instruction, leading Confucius to declare her to be one who truly understands propriety. For extended treatments of the *lienü* tradition, see Marina H. Sung, "The Chinese Lieh-nü Tradition," in *Women in China: New Directions in Historical Scholarship*, ed. Richard W. Guisso and Stanley Johannesen (Youngstown, OH: Philo Press, 1981), 63–74; and Lisa Raphals, *Sharing the Light: Representations of Women and Virtue in Early China* (Albany, NY: State University of New York Press, 1998). For a brilliant and disturbing analysis of later appropriations of the *lienü* tradition, see Katherine Carlitz, "Desire, Danger, and the Body: Stories of Women's Virtue in Late Ming China," in *Engendering China: Women, Culture, and the State*, ed. Christina K. Gilmartin et al. (Cambridge, MA: Harvard University Press, 1994), 101–24.

20. See Nancy Lee Swann, *Pan Chao: Foremost Woman Scholar of China* (New York: Russell and Russell, 1968). Regarding *san cong*, the general import of the original text in the *Book of Rites* I:441, is that females were to "follow," i.e., to be socially ranked at the level of the male head of their household for ritual purposes (most likely style of dress or processional

order). Later interpretations extended the notion of *cong* (the etymology of which implies "following") from social signifier to a submission to authority; the term *sancong* is therefore frequently translated as "three obediences." Arguing that such models of total dependence oversimplifies the relation between Chinese gender systems and Confucian ethics, Dorothy Ko advocates the translation "thrice following," which I have adopted here; see *Teachers of the Inner Chambers: Women and Culture in Seventeenth-Century China* (Stanford, CA: Stanford University Press, 1994), 6f.

21. For the history of women within the Chinese Confucian tradition, see Theresa Kelleher's overview; for a broader insights into women in premodern Confucian cultures, see *Women and Confucian Cultures in Premodern China, Korea, and Japan*, ed. Dorothy Y. Ko, JyaHun Kim Haboush, and Joan Piggott (Berkeley: University of California Press, 2003). Translations of relevant primary texts are provided in Deborah Sommer, ed., *Chinese Religion: An Anthology of Sources* (New York: Oxford University Press, 1995), and Serinity Young, ed., *An Anthology of Sacred Texts by and About Women* (New York: Crossroad, 1993).

22. Marty and Appleby, "The Fundamentalism Project: A User's Guide," ixf.

23. See Daniel Gardiner's essay on this subject in Tu and Tucker, *Confucian Spirituality*.

24. See Thomas Wilson, *Genealogy of the Way: The Construction and Uses of the Confucian Tradition in Late Imperial China* (Stanford, CA: Stanford University Press, 1995).

25. Kelleher, "Confucianism," 155.

26. For more detail in English translation, see Kelleher, "Confucianism," 156.

27. For a comprehensive overview, see Patricia Buckley Ebrey, *The Inner Quarters: Marriage and the Lives of Chinese Women in the Sung Period* (Berkeley: University of California Press, 1993).

28. For discussion of popular didactic works, see Carlitz, "Desire, Danger, and the Body," and Tienchi Martin-Liao, "Traditional Handbooks of Women's Education," in *Woman and Literature in China*, ed. Anna Gerstlacher, Ruth Keen, et al. (Bochum, Germany: Studienverlag Brockmeyer, 1985). The quote is from the *Nüxian*, as cited in R. H. van Gulik, *Sexual Life in Ancient China* (Leiden: E.J. Brill, 1961), 101n8.

29. Winston B. Davis, "Fundamentalism in Japan: Religious and Political," in Marty and Appleby, *Fundamentalisms Observed*, 785.

30. See James L. Watson, "Standardizing the Gods: The Promotion of T'ien Hou ('Empress of Heaven') Along the South China Coast, 960–1960," in *Popular Culture in Late Imperial China*, ed. David Johnson, Andrew J. Nathan, and Evelyn S. Rawski (Berkeley: University of California Press, 1985); and Nyitray, "Becoming the Empress of Heaven: The Life and Bureaucratic Career of Tianhou/Mazu," in *Goddesses Who Rule*, ed. Elisabeth Benard and Beverly Moon (New York: Oxford University Press, 2000).

31. Historian Susan Mann once estimated that the "talented women" (*cainü*) she has studied never represented more than one-thousandth of 1 percent of the women in the Lower Yangtze Basin during the Ming and Qing era (UCLA Center for Chinese Studies presentation, November 1993).

32. See Joanna F. Handlin, "Lü K'un's New Audience: The Influence of Women's Literacy on Sixteenth-Century Thought," in *Women in Chinese Society*, ed. Margery Wolf and Roxane Witke (Stanford, CA: Stanford University Press, 1975).

33. See Elizabeth Choi, "Status of Motherhood and the Family for Korean Women," in *Women of Japan and Korea: Continuity and Change*, ed. Joyce Gelb and Marian Lief Palley (Philadelphia: Temple University Press, 1994); and Yu Eui Young, "Women in Traditional and Modern Korea," in *Korean Women in Transition: At Home and Abroad*, ed. Young and Earl H. Phillips (Los Angeles: California State University Press, 1987).

34. See Joyce Lebra, Joy Paulson, and Elizabeth Powers, *Women in Changing Japan* (Boulder, CO: Westview Press, 1976), 13; and Joyce Gelb and Marian Lief Pally, "Introduction," in Gelb and Palley, *Women of Japan and Korea*.

35. Other potential areas of investigation would be the political arena and the formation of women's organizations. See, for example, Kimiko Kubo and Joyce Gelb, "Obstacles and Opportunities: Women and Political Participation in Japan," Lisa Kim Davis, "Korean Women's Groups Organize for Change," and Sohn Bong Scuk, "Agenda for Social Reform: Women's Political Participation in South Korea," in Gelb and Palley, *Women of Japan and Korea*; Yoko Sato, "From the Home to the Political Arena," Naoko Sasakura, "Aokage Takaka: Housewife Turned Political Representative from Seikatsu Club Seikyo," and Emiko Kaya, "Mitsui Mariko: An Avowed Feminist Assemblywoman," in *Japanese Women: New Feminist Perspectives on the Past, Present, and Future*, ed. Kumiko Fujimura-Fanselow and Atsuko Kameda (New York: The Feminist Press, 1995).

36. Christina Kelley Gilmartin, *Engendering the Chinese Revolution: Radical Women, Communist Politics, and Mass Movements in the 1920s* (Berkeley: University of California Press, 1995).

37. Ann Anagnost, "Transformation of Gender in Modern China," in *Gender and Anthropology: Critical Reviews for Research and Teaching*, ed. Sandra Morgan (Washington, DC: American Anthropological Association, 1989), 314.

38. Raymond Pong and Carlo Caldarola, "China: Religion in a Revolutionary Society," in *Religions and Societies: Asia and the Middle East*, ed. Carlo Caldarola (New York: Mouton, 1982), 567.

39. Pong and Caldarola, "China: Religion in a Revolutionary Society," 567f, quoting *Beijing Review* 14 (1979): 19f.

40. Tu, "Search for Roots in Industrial East Asia," 771.

41. From the English language version of "A Brief Introduction to the China Confucius Foundation," quoted in William Theodore de Bary, "The New Confucianism in Beijing," *The American Scholar* 64, no. 2 (Spring 1995): 180.

42. My colleague Ron Guey Chu observed that the Qufu conference was marked by the complete absence of discussion about feminism or women's issues relative to the tradition. He noted too that there were few women participants, a situation in keeping with women's minimal presence at higher, more visible levels of both academic and public administration. (Personal communication.)

43. Emily Honig and Gail Hershatter, *Personal Voices: Chinese Women in the 1980s* (Stanford, CA: Stanford University Press, 1988), 175.

44. See Marilyn Young, "Chicken Little in China: Some Reflections on Women," in *Marxism and the Chinese Experience: Issues of Socialism in a Third World Socialist Society*, ed. Arif Dirlik and Maurice Meisner (Armonk, NY: ME Sharpe, 1989); see also Tani E. Barlow, "Theorizing Woman: *Funü, Guojia, Jiating* (Chinese Woman, Chinese State, Chinese Family)," in *Body, Subject, and Power in China*, ed. Angela Zito and Tani E. Barlow (Chicago: University of Chicago Press, 1994), 253–89.

45. China is not alone in having devised such "protections" for women. In Japan, for example, until 1985, the Labor Standards Law was built on the assumption that women, like minors, require special consideration for health reasons and that it is incumbent upon a democratic state to establishing protective provisions for them, e.g., women couldn't be made to work too much overtime, or to work on holidays, or to work late-night (10 p.m.– 5 a.m.), or six weeks before or after childbirth. Moreover, employers could not force a woman to work during menstruation if it presented a hardship for her to do so, and if she requested "menstrual leave." In 1985, the Equal Employment Opportunity for Men and Women Law removed the phrase "menstrual leave" from the law, but a special "menstrual hardship" measure remains in effect, enabling women to request such leave. The EEOMW Law also removed restrictions on overtime, holidays, etc. from women in managerial positions or whose work falls into specific categories related to technical or other specialized knowledge skills; even with this change, however, less than 10 percent of the female labor force is accorded equal treatment with their male colleagues. Male-dominated unions continue to champion protective clauses, thereby unnecessarily problematizing women's reproductive functions in ways that limit the perception of women's capacity to participate in the work force. Measures seeking to expand the range of protection, e.g., to include paid time for breast-feeding, ostensibly shield women from exploitation but would effectively restrict them to jobs based on homework, piecework, or short shifts where such "protection" would not be necessary. See Eiko Shinotsuka, "Women Workers in Japan: Past, Present, and Future," 105ff., and Sandra Buckley, "A Short History of the Feminist Movement in Japan," 161, 175, in Gelb and Palley, *Women of Japan and Korea* Gelb and Palley.

46. Nancy E. Riley, "Chinese Women's Lives: Rhetoric and Reality," *Asia Pacific Issues* 25 (September 1995): 5ff., wherein she cites Greenhalgh.

47. Judith Stacey, *Patriarchy and Socialist Revolution in China* (Berkeley: University of California Press, 1983), 4; Zhao Hung, *The Role of Chinese Women in Today's Family and Society* (Ann Arbor: University of Michigan Center for Chinese Studies Occasional Papers, 1989), 9.

48. Clear evidence of gender bias in educational expectation and access abounds as well for Japan and Korea. A 1988 NHK (Japan Broadcasting Corporation) survey indicated that roughly 80 percent of Japanese parents wanted to give their son four years of college, whereas only 33 percent wanted the same for a daughter, most wanting two years of junior college for them instead. In 1990, 40 percent of those women who undertook postsecondary education enrolled in four-year universities, with the other 60 percent enrolling in junior

colleges; the comparable figures for men show that nearly all of them (95 percent) enroll in universities. Even among women who do attend a university, a large portion are enrolled in women's colleges and few attend the prestigious national universities that provide access to career mobility; at Japan's premier institution, Tokyo University, female representation is especially small, with just 10 percent of the students being women. Finally, at all postsecondary institutions, women are likely to major in such traditional fields as home economics, literature, or education, a pattern similar to that found in Korea, where most female college graduates who are found in corporate offices are there as secretaries. See Gelb and Palley's "Introduction" to *Women of Japan and Korea*, 8ff.; in the same volume, see also Kumiko Fujimura-Fanselow and Atsuko Kameda, "Women's Education and Gender Roles in Japan," 46ff., and Chizuko Ueno, "Women and the Family in Transition in Postindustrial Japan," 30.

49. In general, the higher the professional rank, the lower the representation of women. In Japan, women make up approximately 10 percent of university faculty but only 5 percent of full professorial, graduate-level faculty. At the most prestigious institutions such as Tokyo and Kyoto Universities, representation of women falls to less than 2 percent overall. See Fujimura-Fanselow and Kameda, "Women's Education and Gender Roles," 59, and also Takako Michii, "The Chosen Few: Women Academics in Japan" (PhD dissertation, State University of New York at Buffalo, 1982).

50. Carol Sun, personal communication. Nancy Riley notes that the five-year differential in retirement age is common throughout the labor force; see "Chinese Women's Lives," 4.

51. Riley, "Chinese Women's Lives," passim.

52. South Korea is also cited as a country with a reversed male-to-female birth ratio in consequence of strong son-preference leading women to elect ultrasound scanning and abortion of female fetuses. See Elizabeth Choi, "Status of Motherhood and the Family for Korean Women," in Gelb and Palley, *Women of Japan and Korea*, 194, citing "Discarding the Females," *World Press Review* 34 (March 1989): 5. Choi also relates the traditional Korean belief that women born in the Year of the Horse "make bad wives," leading some observers to surmise that even more female fetuses than usual were aborted in 1990, a Horse Year.

53. Riley, "Chinese Women's Lives," especially 1 and 6–7.

54. An instructive comparison can be drawn with Japan during this period. The 1950s and early 1960s witnessed an increasingly polarized debate on work vs. motherhood as women's vocation. Governmental strategies for postwar recovery and rapid economic growth were predicated from the start on the encouragement of cheap female labor, and the post-Occupation constitution guaranteed women a broad array of rights; however, by 1963, a government White Paper on Child Welfare stated that "a deficiency in the level of nurturing [was] creating a risk for the children of this generation," and it drew a direct connection between "the decline of child welfare" and "women's increased penetration of the work force." This and other documents, including "Image of the Ideal Japanese" (1966) and "Toward a Better Family Life" (1967) officially reinforced the traditional and dominant

assumption that women's primary role was wife-and-mother. See Buckley, "A Short History of the Feminist Movement in Japan," 155.

55. Rita S. Gallin, "The Entry of Chinese Women into the Rural Labor Market: A Case Study from Taiwan," *Signs* 9, no. 3 (1984): 383–98.

56. Norma Diamond, "The Status of Women in Taiwan: One Step Forward, Two Steps Back," in *Women in China*, ed. Marilyn Young (Ann Arbor: University of Michigan Press, 1973), and "Women Under Kuomintang Rule: Variations on the Feminine Mystique," *Modern China* 1, no.1 (1975): 3–45.

57. Tu, "The Search for Roots in Industrial East Asia," 768f.

58. During the 1960s, liberal democrats attacked Confucianism as a stifling impediment to scientific progress, a charge that subsequent Confucian defenders have taken pains to counter.

59. Lü Hsiu-lien, *Xin nüxingzhuyi* (New Feminism), (Taibei: China Yushi yüekan, 1974), 105–28. For an English-language introduction to her thought, see Barbara Reed, "Women and Chinese Religion in Contemporary Taiwan," in *Today's Woman in World Religions*, ed. Arvind Sharma (Albany, NY: State University of New York Press, 1994), 227–32.

60. Lü, *Xin nüxingzhuyi*, 154f.

61. Hsiu-Lien Annette Lü, "Women's Liberation: The Taiwanese Experience," in *The Other Taiwan: 1945 to the Present*, ed. Murray A. Rubinstein (Armonk, NY: ME Sharpe, 1994), 303n16.

62. Ibid., 303n17.

63. Catherine S. Farris, "The Social Discourse on Women's Roles in Taiwan: A Textual Analysis," in Rubinstein, *The Other Taiwan*, 312. Noted feminist Chizuko Ueno has observed that more than half of all Japanese women work outside the home; Japan lacks a pool of foreign guest workers, so women's participation in the labor force fills a crucial need for laborers who will take on tasks Japanese men disdain. The reality of the majority of working women's lives is dismal: they carry the dual burden of maintaining domestic responsibilities as well as engaging in marginalized labor for little money under poor working conditions. In such circumstances, being a full-time housewife becomes an attractive proof of economic sufficiency, even for women possessing an advanced educational background. See Ueno, "Women and the Family in Transition," passim.

64. Catherine S. Farris, "The Social Discourse on Women's Roles in Taiwan: A Textual Analysis," *Michigan Discussions in Anthropology* (Spring 1990): 93.

65. Bi-erh Chou, "Changing Patterns of Women's Employment in Taiwan, 1966–1986," in Rubinstein, *The Other Taiwan*, 352.

66. Davis, "Fundamentalism in Japan," 785.

67. According to Chizuko Ueno, the Equal Employment Opportunity Law "was promulgated hastily in 1985 to meet the requirements for ratification of the United Nations treaty for women, which the Japanese government unwilling signed in Copenhagen in 1980" ("Women and the Family in Transition," 34). She notes that "equal opportunity" applies only to individuals with identical academic credentials, thus permitting

discrimination on the basis of educational background against women graduates of junior colleges; age discrimination is also prevalent. Japanese and Korean women tend to have discontinuous participation in the labor force—although women can no longer be forced to leave their jobs after the birth of their child(ren), many choose to do so, only to find later that there are few jobs open to women over forty. The most egregious violations of the spirit if not the letter of the Law are manifest in companies that immediately introduced two-track personnel advancement systems consisting of a career track and a noncareer track, changing gender discrimination into "personal choice," even though less than 1 percent of newly hired women graduates enter the career track (34ff.). See also Shinotsuka, "Women Workers in Japan," 116.

68. Gerami, *Women and Fundamentalism*, 35.

69. Ben Kremenak, "Women's Progress in Korea: Promise, Progress, and Frustration," *Asia Foundation Quarterly* 2 (Summer 1988): 1, cited in Gelb and Palley, "Introduction," *Women of Japan and Korea*, 4n10.

70. Tu is too modest to place himself in any such listing, but his status as student of Mou Zongsan and his prodigious publication record on the religious vitality of the Confucian tradition force his inclusion. One might also include on this list Julia Ching, the bulk of whose work has been on Confucian-Christian dialogue.

71. On Lee Sang-eun, see Tu, "The Search for Roots in Industrial East Asia," 766; on Okada, see Rodney L. Taylor, *The Confucian Way of Contemplation: Okada Takehiko and the Tradition of Quiet Sitting* (Columbia: University of South Carolina Press, 1988).

72. Tu, "The Search for Roots in Industrial East Asia," 770f. The present discussion of the Confucian dialogue with modernity owes much of its shape to Tu's public and private observations over the past ten years.

73. Reference to the "Third Epoch" is to the hoped-for flourishing of tradition; the First and Second Epochs refer to the Zhou dynasty origins and the Song-Ming revival of Neo-Confucianism. Wei-Ming Tu, "Towards a Third Epoch of Confucian Humanism: A Background Understanding," in *Confucianism: The Dynamics of Tradition*, ed. Irene Eber (New York: Macmillan, 1986), 3–21.

74. Tu, "The Search for Roots in Industrial East Asia," 770.

75. See John H. Berthrong, *Transformations of the Confucian Way* (Boulder, CO: Westview Press, 1998), especially 181f. and 192f. Writing in English, Wei-ming Tu has long offered an inclusive-language rendition of the traditional ideal of the "gentleman," translating the Chinese *junzi* into "perfected person."

76. Wei-ming Tu has initiated the discussion of embodiment, but his analysis remains incomplete. The gendered nature of subjective awareness provides both opportunities and obstacles along the path of self-cultivation, but these factors have yet to be analyzed to the degree to which the problem of mind-body dualism has been investigated. See "A Confucian Perspective on Embodiment," in *The Body in Medical Thought and Practice*, ed. Drew Leder (Netherlands: Kluwer Academic Publishers, 1992), 87–100. In an earlier discussion of the topic, Tu is quoted as saying that the subject of "embodiment" is not the body understood in the physical sense at all; see "Concluding Session" in *The Psycho-Cultural Dynamics of the*

Confucian Family: Past and Present, ed. Walter H. Slote (Seoul: International Cultural Society of Korea, 1986), 408.

77. Koh, "Confucianism in Contemporary Korea," in *Confucian Traditions in East Asian Modernity: Moral Education and Economic Culture in Japan and the Four Mini-Dragons*, ed. Wei-ming Tu (Cambridge, MA: Harvard University Press, 1996), 191ff; see also Tu et al., eds., *The Confucian World Observed: A Contemporary Discussion of Confucian Humanism in East Asia* (Honolulu: East-West Center, 1992), 127.

78. The language of moral efficiency in this regard is drawn from Winston Davis's work on modern Japanese society; see "Fundamentalism in Japan," 807.

79. John Exdell, "Feminism, Fundamentalism, and Liberal Legitimacy," *Canadian Journal of Philosophy* 24, no. 3 (September 1994): 448.

80. Davis, "Fundamentalism in Japan," especially 784 and 804f.

81. Hawley and Proudfoot, "Introduction," 4.

CHAPTER 4

Reading from Right to Left: Fundamentalism, Feminism, and Women's Changing Roles in Jewish Societies*

Sylvia Barack Fishman

Introduction: Fundamentalism and Feminism as Conflicting Contemporary Influences

This chapter explores the transformation of contemporary Jewish life by fundamentalism, feminism, and other social movements. The goal of this chapter is to illuminate the broader intersection of Jewish traditionalism, Western humanistic values, and feminist critiques of society, paying special attention to the tension between fundamentalism and feminism as bimodal influences shaping recent developments in several Jewish societies. Rather than studying one particular group in isolation, this chapter considers Jewish intergroup relationships, noting new developments in the symbiosis between American and Israeli feminists; bridges between Orthodox and non-Orthodox Jewish feminists, and the ways the various streams of liberal and traditionalist Judaism have influenced each other. Occasional reference is made to parallel or contrasting changes in other religious groups. This chapter compares contemporary emancipated Jewish life to more traditionalist milieus and attitudes, paying special attention to pathways through which the significance of women's issues acquired a symbolic valence in Jewish life, and places sociological transformations into several overlapping contexts, including the pervasive framework of bourgeois Western culture in which most Jews make their homes. The impact of these two conflicting movements is considered not only in relationship to women's lives, but also in relationship to their families, communities, synagogues, and organizations.

Demographers estimated the global Jewish population at a little over 13 million in the year 2000, compared to an international Christian population of about 2 billion and Muslim population of about 1.1 billion. The world's two largest Jewish communities are located in the United States and in Israel, with Jewish populations of approximately 5.7 million and 4.9 million, respectively. The third largest Jewish community is located in France, which had 520,000 Jews, and other diaspora communities (other European countries, South, Central, and Latin America, Russia and the FSU, North and South Africa), had much lower Jewish populations.[1] It is not surprising, then, that the Jewish communities of each country have a distinctive and in many ways idiosyncratic profile. In America and Israel there are enough Jews of many different religious and secular persuasion to create diverse critical masses, and thus the possibility for vibrantly diverse cultural centers and approaches to Judaism. America and Israel are home to the two influential centers of fundamentalist influence and also two interrelated but distinctive centers of Jewish feminist ferment.

The vast majority of Jews who live in the two largest communities—North America and Israel—lead Westernized lives. Most of these Westernized Jews acquire secular education in academic or professional settings, and live and work in middle class neighborhoods. Most Jews today appear indistinguishable from non-Jewish citizens in terms of their external lifestyles and deportments. In the United States, Orthodox Jews comprise well under 10 percent of the Jewish community, and over half of these Orthodox Jews fall into the category of "Modern" Orthodox, rather than fundamentalist Ultra-Orthodox. Like other Orthodox Jews, Modern Orthodox Jews observe a complex network of religious rituals and/or their involvement in Judaic cultural, intellectual, organizational and social networks, but like the more liberal Conservative Reconstuctionist, Reform, and completely secular Jews, most Modern Orthodox Jews are not isolated and obtain high levels of secular education and live basically Western lives.

Nevertheless, despite the Westernization of most Jewish populations, fundamentalism has been a potent force in contemporary Jewish societies. As we shall see, women's roles are a profound symbol of the extent to which Jewish societies accept—or reject—modernity and Westernization.

The reason that fundamentalism has salience within some Jewish societies is closely related to the definition of fundamentalism itself. As Joan Mencher suggests, fundamentalism means different things within different religious societies, but

> Almost all the definitions of fundamentalism seem to refer to a kind of return to a former "golden age" when life was more harmonious, when people knew their proper roles, and in which people are envisaged as being happy and content. Many of course refer to periods of time when women were much more completely controlled by the men in their families than they are today.[2]

For fundamentalist—in Hebrew, *haredi*—Jews, the golden age of Jewish life is the premodern European environment in which Jews comprised coherent, self-enclosed societies. Clustered in primarily Jewish enclaves, Jews spoke their own languages, answered to their own religious and communal authorities, were immersed in their own cultural heritages, and lived according to their own societal norms. Although Jewish isolation from surrounding cultures was far from complete, and diverse cultural elements were actually shared and borrowed between Jews and the non-Jews around them, widespread (often government-sanctioned) anti-Semitism from without and xenophobia from within kept most Jews enclosed within coherent social networks.

During the eighteenth and nineteenth centuries, the Emancipation of the Jews, the Jewish Enlightenment (*Haskalah*), and succeeding waves of secular ideologies and social trends eroded significant barriers separating Jew from non-Jew. Many Jews eagerly embraced the opportunity to become part of liberal Western societies.[3] However, rather than celebrating the release of Europe's Jews from their pariah status, *haredi* Jews glorify premodern Jewish societies and their norms. They remember the anti-Semitic religious persecutions that frequently cemented the (often literal) fences between Jew and non-Jew as yet another manifestation of the wickedness of the outside world—an alien world that they believe to be basically unchanged, and to be avoided at all costs.

The most fundamentalist Jewish societies aim to replicate historical conditions by creating similarly isolated living conditions and by rejecting many of the premises of modern life. Jewish fundamentalists make a point of behaving as contrary as they can to the norms of their surrounding societies, deliberately courting extremism in their rejection of modernity. Their stance is one of principled opposition, as ethnographer Samuel Heilman notes. "'If there is no extremism, there is no completeness,' wrote Rabbi Abraham Karelitz (1878–1953), the Hazon Ish":

> The haredi essence is to offer extreme and opposing alternative Jewish values and perspectives…. Whatever the others do is what the haredim must not do; whatever they value or believe is what haredim disdain and doubt; what is normal to them is abnormal for haredim. If it does not thus contest the other realities, haredi society risks tacitly conceding the attractions of the contemporary world. And if that is possible, it is also possible to be morally enticed by those attractions. Ironically, and in spite of themselves, haredim have become increasingly concerned with tracing every new fall from grace that occurs in Jewish life and which they must counter.[4]

In *haredi* eyes many of the most egregious "falls from grace" have concerned the changing roles of Jewish women. Thus, those Jewish societies that perceive themselves to be fully modernized and Westernized take pride in the ways in which they have emancipated their women and tried to give them equal roles in religious and communal settings. They often describe themselves as "feminist" or egalitarian. In contrast, those Jewish societies that think of themselves as rejecting modernity and Western values have frequently rejected "feminism" by name with great fanfare, declaring this modern movement to be akin to "licentiousness."

In addition to devotedly insular, self-consciously fundamentalist Jewish societies, right wing but not completely insular Jewish traditionalist Jewish societies,
including non-hasidic (*mitnagdic*) groups affiliated with the *Agudat Yisrael*, often
become increasingly fundamentalist in regard to women's status—but not fundamentalist to the same extent in other areas of life. By rejecting female emancipation—
while participating in other aspects of Westernization—traditionalist Jewish
societies are enabled to think of themselves as faithful to the authentic Jewish values
and behaviors of the past. However, from a psychosocial standpoint, even the rejection of a movement demands engagement with it. A self-consciously fundamentalist society that focuses much of its reactionary energy on women is very
different from the unselfconscious premodern Jewish communities that comprised
Jewish life before the impact of the Emancipation and the Enlightenment on Jewish
populations.

Recent research on Jewish fundamentalism has grown along with global scholarly interest in fundamentalism. Some of these studies are general historical and/
or ethnographic essays, such as David Landau's colorful panorama of *Piety and
Power: The World of Jewish Fundamentalism*[5] and Shahak and Mezvinsky's overview
of the varieties of *Jewish Fundamentalism in Israel*.[6] Some focus on specific religious
groups, such as Samuel Heilman's brilliant ethnography *Defenders of the Faith*,[7]
and his article distinguishing between "Quiescent and Active Fundamentalisms:
The Jewish Cases."[8] A few have located gender as one of the critical keys to understanding the role of fundamentalism in contemporary Jewish life: Fundamentalism
and male identity construction are explored by Warren Rosenberg in his *Legacy of
Rage: Jewish Masculinity, Violence and Culture*[9]; the impact of biblical and rabbinical thinking on Jewish conceptions of maleness are the subject of Daniel Boyarin,
*Unheroic Conduct: The Rise of Heterosexuality and the Invention of the Jewish
Man*.[10] The impact of fundamentalism on Jewish female identity construction,
Jewish culture, and Jewish women's lives gets close anthropological examination
by Tamar El-Or in *Educated and Ignorant* and *Next Year I Will Know More*,[11] Susan
Sered in *What Makes Women Sick*,[12] and others. In addition, much can be learned
from looking at primary materials such as "educational" propaganda put out by a
particular social group for its own women, such as the Lubavitch Women's Organization publication *Aura: A Reader on Jewish Womanhood*.[13] This chapter builds
on this important literature, and differs from previous studies in its consideration
of fundamentalism and feminism in tandem, analyzing their mutual impact on the
lives of Jewish women and the societies in which they live.

Fundamentalists and Contemporary Jewish Communities

Israel and American Jewish norms differ from each other in significant ways. One
of the most profound differences is related to the fact that Jews in the United States
are in fact a tiny religious minority, making up well under 3 percent of the population. In contrast, Jews comprise an overwhelming majority of the population in

Israel. Even more significant, in America the separation of church and state prevents any religion from exercising true authority over the lives of its adherents. In Israel, however, the *haredi* population has acquired significant political power, making it intensely resented by the rest of the population. Thus, in the United States Ultra-Orthodox communities are often regarded as charmingly quaint by their coreligionists, whereas in Israel the fundamentalist stance of the *haredi* population means that it is often regarded as the political enemy by secular Jews.

In the United States, one of fundamentalist Judaism's most compelling arguments is related to the relatively small number of Jews around the world, compared to the number of Christians and Muslims. While traditionally Judaism tended to emphasize Jewish commitment to the commandments, as explained and elaborated in rabbinic law (*halakhah*), only Jews were obligated in the observance of these laws, and Jewish texts teach that "the righteous of all nations have a share in the world to come," provided that non-Jews observe the seen Noahide laws. In other words, one did not need to be a Jew to be eligible for salvation, thus removing one of the common religious rationales for evangelical activity.

Because Judaism has not been a proselytizing faith for most of its history, Jews do not look to the conversion of non-Jews as a way of promoting religious vitality and/or greater numbers. Instead, Jewish religious and communal leaders have tended to emphasize the maintaining of Jews as committed members of Jewish communities. It is more difficult for young adults to "defect" from the relatively insular communities created by Jewish fundamentalists, than it is to leave more liberal forms of Judaism. As a result, children raised in fundamentalist Jewish communities are less likely to assimilate into Western culture, becoming secular or drifting toward another religious group.

Fundamentalist Jews both in Israel and the United States argue that their form of Jewish expression is not only more historically "authentic" than more liberal forms of Judaism, but also a better strategy for dealing with the challenges of modernity—essentially by shutting modernity out, and closing the next generation in. The curtailing of women's and girls' activities in fundamentalist Jewish communities thus becomes part of a communal strategy for guaranteeing the loyalty of the next generation. And, because participation in Jewish life today is voluntary, fundamentalist ability to seal out the external world has become, if anything, even more symbolically important to practitioners than it was in less open times and places.

Rabbinic Prescriptions for Sexual and Gender Roles

Contemporary social scientists assume that while certain aspects of sexuality are biologically determined, gender roles are constructed by societies. While biology provides male and female reproductive organs, enabling men to father children and women to gestate and lactate, societies construct elaborate prescriptions for gender roles that are often only tangentially related to differences between the sexes. These gender roles can differ considerably from culture to culture, while seeming "natural" to each culture's vision of the nature of maleness and femaleness.

Historical rabbinic Judaism had much to say about both sexual and gender differences. Most modern Jews are only vaguely acquainted with the complexity of Judaic approaches to sexuality, but the intricacies of rabbinic law are significant in the lives of observant Jews, and comprise a very important element in fundamentalist Jewish societies. Rabbinic law builds gender role prescriptions based on assumptions about male and female sexuality. Males are perceived as easy to arouse sexually, and many restrictions on women's access to public Jewish venues are designed to keep women—with their potential for arousing men—away from men. Additionally, prescriptions and biblical taboos against cohabiting with a menstrual woman are elaborated by rabbinic law, which required married couples to avoid sexual intercourse during menstruation and during a "white" or "clean" period following menstruation, for a minimum of twelve days. The demarcation between a woman's unavailable and available times of the month is marked by her immersion in a carefully supervised ritual bath.

Not surprisingly, fundamentalist Jews legislate in each of these areas according to the most stringent interpretations of the law, in ways that tend to control and limit woman's activities. While fundamentalist Jews believe their interpretations of sexual prescriptions are completely faithful to the spirit as well as the letter of Jewish law and tradition, observant Jews within more modernized streams of Jewish thought often find fundamentalist attitudes considerably more narrow than those of the centuries of rabbinic thinkers who wrote the Talmud and its commentaries. Halakhic texts, which calmly and dispassionately discuss a broad spectrum of sexual activities, often differ from one passage to another as to the optimum form of acceptable behavior. However, despite rabbinic differences of opinion, the *halakhah* consistently prescribes that adult Jewish men and women should live in marital unions in which male-female genital sexual activity occurs on a regular basis. Most Jewish societies had little interest in—and considerable suspicion of—celibate lifestyles, and communities were cautioned not to hire unmarried males to teach their young children. Judaic texts describe sexuality as a good and sacred aspect of life within the marital framework and at prescribed times and places. For example, according to most Jewish interpretations of the Hebrew Bible, sexuality did not cause the "fall." Adam and Eve correctly cohabited together on the first Sabbath eve after their creation; it was their disobedience to the divine decree regarding the tree(s), not their sexual activity, that displeased God. As a result, partially in memory of the first couple enjoying their paradisical Sabbath, observant Jews regard Sabbath eve (Friday night) as a most auspicious and sacred opportunity for sexual congress.

Rabbinic law recognizes women's sexual rights within marriage. First, a married woman has the right to sexual fulfillment. Rabbinic texts assume that women desire but are shy about initiating sexual encounters; minimum frequency with which husbands should offer their wives sexual satisfaction are stipulated in order to prevent distracted husbands from neglecting their wives' emotional well-being.[14] Second, within Jewish law every women had the right to refuse sexual advances that did not please her. Jewish law recognized the reality of marital rape and forbade it. The author of *Iggeret HaKodesh*, for example, advises husbands:

> You ought to engage her first in matters which please her heart and mind and cheer her.... And you should say such things some of which will urge her to passion and intercourse, to affection, desire and lovemaking.... And you shall not possess her against her will nor force her because in that kind of a union there is no divine presence [*shekhinah*] because your intentions are opposite to hers and her wish does not agree with yours. And do not quarrel with her nor beat her for the sake of having intercourse.[15]

In fundamentalist communities, however, the gentle, idealized eroticism of the *Iggeret HaKodesh* may be less important to practitioners than enabling young men to maintain control over their boyhood lusts. Heilman's compelling ethnography of fundamentalist Hasidic Jews revealed young men utterly ignorant of either male or female physiology and disdainful of erotic pleasure as a marital goal. One informant remembered being told for the first time about sexual intercourse the night before his wedding, "I was sure it was something that goyim [non-Jews] (and people who wanted to be like goyim) did. I could never imagine that anything so animal-like and coarse would be done by erlicher [refined, authentic] Yidn [Jews]." The counselor assigned to explain sexuality encouraged him by telling him that

> Adam, the first man, had done it. He told me that our patriarch Abraham did it, and so too Isaac and Jacob.... He told me my father did it and that he himself did it. And then he told me that even the rebbe, may he live long years, amen, did it.
>
> And when he said this, I knew I too would have to do it. Still, I wasn't really sure what it was. But I'll tell you, when he finally told me what it was that I would have to do, I was in shock."

Another informant recalled:

> Until he comes to the actual act, the boy who sits in the yeshiva knows nothing. Those who know something are *prostakim* [louts]. Look, when I was a *bochur* [boy], I also knew that we had these desires. I controlled them, buried them. But when they sat with me a few hours before my wedding and told me everything, I thought they were taking a knife to me and

cutting off my legs. I was in total shock. Tomorrow night with a stranger? It couldn't be.[16]

In addition to the shock of sexual initiation (which is, however traumatic, a one-time event), the sexual lives of fundamentalist women are profoundly affected by an elaborate rabbinic complex of laws of menstrual purity, called in Hebrew *taharat hamishpakhah*. Fundamentalist observance of these laws, which prohibit intercourse while a wife has the ritual status of *niddah* (a woman who has not yet visited the *mikvah* and become "clean" for sexual activity), discourage any physical contact between husband and wife. Elaborate precautions—not passing keys or cups or a child to one another, using different placemats than usual, not wearing cosmetics or jewelry—aim to prevent the husband from experiencing an unfulfil-lable and thus inappropriate sexual urge toward his wife. Within the context of the way Jewish law approaches all appetites, this preoccupation with detail—and control—is not unusual. However, human beings internalize feelings about sexu-ality in a mode more intense and complicated than those they use to deal with other areas of life. Ideas about what women are, what they want and need, and what should be expected from them in fundamentalist Jewish societies is deeply grounded in the sexualization of rabbinic concepts of women's intellects and emotions, as well as their bodies.

Historical Judaism considers individuals within hierarchies of social, familial, and communal group categories. Rabbinic experts or decisors (*poskim*) living in each community made decisions about which behaviors fell into the categories of being obligatory, on one end of the spectrum, or forbidden, at the other end of the spectrum. In between came a broad continuum of behaviors that were permissible, but might or might not be desirable.

The reason that women's roles are so vulnerable to reactionary shifts in rabbinic pronouncements is that many women's issues fall into the category of permissibility but indeterminate desirability. To some extent, these behaviors have come to seem controversial precisely because human judgment is such an important factor in how they are viewed: whether or not a given behavior is judged to be desirable depends on the evaluation of individual rabbinic *poskim*. Most of the decision-making vis-à-vis women's lives falls into that middle grouping, neither forbidden nor obligatory, but rather dependent on rabbinic decisions about whether a given permissible behavior is or is not appropriate for women. This decentralized system gives the individual rabbi-*posek* a great deal of power, since he decides what com-prises Jewish law for his community. However, it is difficult for one rabbi to break the mold and act independently when his professional social network of other rabbinic authorities takes a stringent attitude, or *khumrah*. The communal thresh-old tips, and frequently in the fundamentalist Jewish community stringent attitudes on women's issues have carried some categories of behavior that once were con-sidered extreme into the normative mode.

Although recent research by Bernadette Brooten and others has revealed that in ancient Jewish communities powerful, wealthy women probably played significant nonreligious leadership roles as public Jews,[17] rabbinic decisors systematically constricted women's roles as the centuries passed. The rabbinic Judaism of mainstream postmedieval European communities restricted women's roles, using halakhic proclamations that overtly prohibited females as a group from functioning as leaders.

Women's roles were separated by rabbinic Judaism in great part because of the fear of male sexual response, with its commensurate loss of control, leading to inappropriate sexual behavior. This reason is frequently given in rabbinic literature discussing laws that separate men from women in public religious and communal settings. Women are not, by and large, pictured within classical rabbinic texts as deliberate temptresses, as they are in some other religious cultures. Rather, in the rabbinic imagination, men have extremely low sexual flashpoints. Male sexuality is viewed as an extremely volatile element. Given visual or aural stimulation, and given opportunity, the assumption is that men will pursue inappropriate sexual liaisons. Fascinatingly, the rabbis of the Talmud seemed to include themselves in this observation. Many anecdotes that illustrate the strength and involuntary nature of male sexual response feature prominent rabbis trying to outwit their own powerful sexual impulses. One way of dealing with men's capacity for inappropriate sexual activity was simply to prevent interaction between men and women, except under the most controlled conditions. One might say that rabbinic law prevented sexual intercourse by prohibiting social intercourse.

Thus, women were shunted away from a visible role or voice in public Judaism because men might fell ashamed or do something shameful. The side effect of these halakhic prohibitions—largely ignored by the rabbis who promulgated them—was the isolation of women from the center of public Jewish life. Today, for those Jewish women and men who chose to live in an environment of rigorous Orthodox culture, change takes place slowly. Jews with a more liberal interpretive framework relegate the halakhic system to flexible guideline, rather than a strict boundary for behavior. It should be noted, however, that even in the more liberal wings of Judaism where social and religious changes have been dramatically achieved, the process initially precipitated struggle and conflict. Today, within non-Orthodox public Jewish life, women are increasingly sharing ownership with men in a number of key areas, including rabbinic text learning, secular Jewish study, Jewish thought, synagogue life, and communal life cycle rituals. However, in fundamentalist Jewish societies, which are bent on opposing current trends, restrictions on women have in many ways become more stringent than ever. Fundamentalists are especially opposed to the presence of women in leadership roles and public synagogue honors and participation.

One reason given for discouraging women from public leadership roles is *k'vod hatzibbur*, the dignity of the (male) community: the presence of prominent women might signify that no men could be found with similar leadership qualifications. Within this social-psychological framework, the prominence of women signals the diminished competence of men. Female leaders make men feel ashamed.

A second reason for keeping women out of leadership positions in public Jewish spheres is consideration for female modesty. Women who are thrust—or thrust themselves—into the public eye might garner inappropriate male attention to their persons. Interestingly, in most Ashkenazi communities this concern about women in public places has been primarily in public Jewish settings, not in the marketplace. Thus, while women often were occupied in business, they were not found in the *bait midrash*, the sacralized text-study hall, nor were their voices heard in public worship in the synagogue.

Sociologically, a case study deserving of special attention is provided by the recent emphasis in fundamentalist Jewish societies upon a cluster of laws and customs connected to *kol isha*, a rabbinic prohibition against listening to the voice of a woman. Historically, the evolution of the concept of *kol isha* is convoluted, as rabbi Saul Berman traces the law's unlikely history. A brief summary of the evolution of the *kol isha* concept can be summarized as follows. The talmudic axiom: *kol b'isha ervah* [the voice of a woman is naked/sexual/licentious] is twice attributed to the Amora Rabbi Samuel (circa 254 CE). These initial talmudic references to *kol isha* are concerned with the *speaking* voices of women, not their singing voices. In the first, primary text, the sound of women speaking is considered a distraction to men absorbed in sacred tasks: were a man to hear his wife's voice as he recited the pivotal *sh'ma yisrael* prayer, it might distract him in a similar way as her naked body would, and he would lose his devotional intent and intensity (*Berakhot 24a*). Secondly, in a completely different discussion, Rabbi Samuel is quoted by a colleague who insists that talking or communicating via messages or messengers with married women, even to inquire about another man's wife's well-being, might lead to billet-doux and illicit sexual liaisons (*Kiddushin* 70a). A third, entirely separate discussion about banning singing at feasts, comments that when men and women sing together in a festive environment they create an erotic conflagration (*Sotah* 48a). This discussion became the basis for prohibiting female instrumentalists or vocalists at such gatherings, but was not linked to the concept of *kol isha* until much later.

The two separate talmudic principles about the dangers of women's speaking voices (1) in prayer, or (2) in conversation, remained unlinked in rabbinic literature for hundreds of years. Some rabbis focused on *which* women's voices should be prohibited, stipulating that the voice of a woman who is sexually unavailable to a man—that is, another man's wife—is the most important application of *kol b'isha ervah*. It was not until the late medieval period that the contemporary conception of *kol isha* began to jell. By the time of the *Rishonim* in Franco-Germany (eleventh–sixteenth centuries), rabbinic assumptions were usually that *kol isha* refers to women's singing voices, rather than to their speaking voices. Many of these commentators did not consider women's voices to be inherently inappropriate, only situationally inappropriate. Moreover, they articulated the principle that the novelty of exposure makes *kol isha* arousing and problematic, whereas regularity—*regilut*—insulates men from erotic feelings in ordinary situations.[18]

Perhaps counterintuitively, greater stringency developed in the rabbinic definition of *kol isha* as the years passed. With a few important exceptions, rabbinic conceptions in early modern and modern times moved toward considering the voices of postpubescent women as tantamount to nudity. Today, Jewish fundamentalist communities place public emphasis on women and girls not singing out loud in the synagogue, or anywhere else that men can hear their voices. The strict observance of *kol isha* laws thus has the effect of silencing women in public settings.

In a highly significant development, the center-to-right strictly—but not truly fundamentalist—Orthodox community has "discovered" *kol isha* as a way of aligning itself with the *haredi* community, and distancing itself from the modern Orthodox community. In center-to-right synagogues such as many Young Israel synagogues in the United States, where women once unself-consciously chanted the prayers from their side of the fence *mekhitzah* that divides men from women, many women now self-consciously keep their voices to a whisper. In many families, women have now silenced themselves even at the Sabbath table. Especially if there are guests present, women and girls may leave the singing of Sabbath psalms to men.[19]

Fundamentalism in a Demographically Postfeminist Age

These religious restrictions, leading to the silencing of women even in right-to-center Orthodox communities, are especially striking because demographically these communities are very modernized. Indeed, today's Jewish women—the vast majority of whom do not live in fundamentalist communities—can be said to have reached a demographically postfeminist state. During the last quarter of the twentieth century, the lives of Westernized Jews as individuals, in family groups, and in communal settings have undergone sweeping changes vis-à-vis gender role construction. Many of these changes have come to seem so commonplace that their revolutionary status and flavor has been virtually lost. In the United States, most Jewish women attend college, and almost one-third of them also acquire graduate or professional degrees. Although higher education is somewhat less pronounced among Jewish women in other diaspora communities and in Israel, the gender gap has been steadily shrinking in all communities. The vast majority of Jewish women around the world enjoy personal freedoms that must be mentioned only because so many women in the world are denied access to the autonomies afforded by an ability to drive, vote, earn money, have their own bank accounts and safe deposit boxes, and make their own choices about whom they wish to live with and/or marry, where they wish to live, and which friends and activities they wish to espouse. In terms of demographic realities and personal ideals, normative ethnic boundaries have been relocated for contemporary Jewish women.

One major demographic change in contemporary Jewish women's lives concerns family planning and the nearly universal use of birth control in major Jewish communities. In Israel, which has the most pronatalist government and society and the largest general fertility rate of Jewish communities worldwide, birth control is widespread. Westernized Israeli Jews limit their families carefully, although—unlike American Jews—they more than replace themselves. Recently, American Jewish fertility levels have fallen to well under replacement level (generally considered to be 2.1 children per woman). In contrast to today's low birthrates, and following the general American post–World War II pattern, in 1946 more than half of American Jewish women were married by age 22 and over 80 percent were married by age 25, and in 1953 almost two-thirds of Jewish women were married by age 22 and more than three-quarters were married by age 25. In the 1950s and 1960s, American Jews were the most universally married of all American populations. The postwar baby boom facilitated by these early marriages temporarily reversed what had been a century-long trend toward smaller Jewish families. However, even during this family-hungry period, more than any other ethnic group, Jewish couples planned their families carefully, having their children a little later, providing space between siblings, and concluding their childbearing a little earlier than other women—with the result that their families were somewhat smaller. Thus the 1970 national Jewish Population Study revealed that married Jewish women had 2.8 children per family, although their fertility rate still lagged behind the American non-Jewish average of 3.5.

American Jewish women are currently most likely to have their children during the 15-year period between ages 27 to 42; their mothers were most likely to have their children during the 15-year period between ages 20 to 35. For women currently ages 55 to 64, the average age of marriage was 22 and the average age of first childbirth was 24. In contrast, among married, fertile 1990 NJPS respondents ages 35 to 44, the average age of marriage was 25 and the average age of first childbirth was 27.[20] (Women who have not yet married and had children were excluded from these percentages.)

Today, while modern and centrist Orthodox women postpone marriage and childbearing less than other American Jewish women and have more children than any other group, they too are affected by changing American mores in regard to family formation. Fundamentalist Jewish women have by far the highest levels of fertility. Most have no fewer than five children, and it is not unheard of for fundamentalist couples to have ten or more. Nevertheless, studies indicate that the vast majority of Orthodox women—including fundamentalist women—engage in some form of family planning. When fundamentalist women use birth control, however, they do not always tell their husbands, and they usually explain this usage to themselves and others as "medical" rather than "personal" in origin.[21]

Nonfundamentalist Orthodox women are far more likely than other Jewish women to marry in their early twenties, and to begin their families by their mid-twenties, and yet they are not less likely than other Jewish women to attain advanced degrees and to pursue high status careers. They often accomplish their educational/professional goals while accommodating Orthodox marriage patterns by juggling roles earlier than non-Orthodox women. Their fertility rates are higher than those of their non-Orthodox sisters, with younger Orthodox women averaging three to four children, while non-Orthodox women average fewer than two children per family—below replacement rate.

Another great demographic change in the lives of Jewish women centers around women working outside their homes for pay—labor force participation. Dual career Jewish households have become the new normative Jewish family; well over half of American Jewish women with children under six years old are employed outside the home. The readiness of contemporary American Jewish women to pursue higher education and high-powered careers may be seen as an extremely complicated kind of coalescence, which is built on a rejection of earlier coalescence. In the 1950s American Jewish women stayed home and took care of their families not because this was originally a Jewish value, but because it was originally an American value. However, American Jewish women came to believe that they avoided workforce participation because it was a Jewish value for married women to stay home. Indeed, when they left their homes to go to work, many felt that they were disobeying Jewish norms. Since the late 1960s, Jewish women have been at the forefront of feminist striving, almost universally acquiring higher education and pursuing career goals. Educational accomplishment for women because a coalesced American-Jewish value decades ago, and now occupational accomplishment for women is becoming a coalesced American-Jewish value as well.

Religious but nonfundamentalist (Modern Orthodox) Jews do not substantially differ from the educational patterns characteristic of other Jews in their cohort. Indeed, as Moshe and Harriet Hartman have painstakingly demonstrated in their recent monograph, "the more involved in formal and informal Jewish social circles, the collective celebration of Jewish identity, and the closer to Orthodox affiliation, the higher is the educational achievement." Not only does modern Orthodox affiliation indicate normative Jewish secular educational levels, but even within individual households, "contrary to popular opinion, Orthodoxy is not associated with more spousal inequality: educational differences are even smaller than among the Conservatives, Reforms, and Reconstructionists." When the narrowed gender gap and the positive relationship between secular education and Jewish connections are considered together, secular education for women emerges as associated with stronger, not weaker, Jewish bonds. As the Hartmans note, "The relationship between Jewishness and education is slightly stronger for women than for men."[22]

When comparing female roles in Orthodox Judaism with those in fundamentalist Christian communities, one striking area of difference revolves around the dynamic between male and female spouse in the family setting. To Christian fundamentalists, aspirations to higher education and high-powered careers are often viewed as antithetical to God's law and human normalcy. As Brasher describes the Christian fundamentalist antifeminist narrative: "In this story, disheveled gender expectations, fragmented marriages, economic instability, and widespread cultural malaise figure prominently, for fundamentalist women describe these societal factors as the cultural fuel that propelled them on a spiritual search."[23] While many Christian fundamentalist women do work outside the home, their employment is viewed as a regrettable economic necessity, rather than a source of liberation or fulfillment. For Jews, including Orthodox Jews, however, women's secular education and career trajectories cause fewer ideological ripples.

Publications underscore the extent to which changes in the family dynamic have transformed American Jewish family life throughout mainstream populations and across denominational lines, including many segments of the seemingly fundamentalist, strictly orthodox community. For example, one recent issue of *The Jewish Parent Connection*, a publication of the Orthodox Torah Umesorah National Society for Hebrew Day Schools, features articles such as "Babysitter or Day Care Center: That Is the Question"—making the assumption that "due to today's high cost of living ... it is frequently necessary for both Jewish parents to pursue careers." The pediatrician/author considers the "pros and cons" of "nanny, au pair, babysitter, or day care center," without ever once trying to instill guilt in the working mother or assuming that she should remain at home until her children are in school all day long.[24] Two other articles consider ways for women with small children to find time for their spiritual lives. These articles suggest a proactive approach, including studying the High Holiday liturgy well before the holidays, determining which prayers are most meaningful and important, and hiring a babysitter or negotiating with family members who can facilitate participation during those parts of the service. During this process, the authors urge mothers to establish "channels for communication without recrimination" with the children's father, with the suggestion that he enable spiritual time for his wife.[25]

Women and girls who live in fundamentalist Jewish communities thus have often been influenced by Western mores and feminism, even though the details of quotidian life and major life cycle decisions are determined by fundamentalist norms and expectations, as we shall see. Even nonfundamentalist Jewish women, who comprise the great majority of Jewish women today, are affected in some ways by the influence of fundamentalist Jewish authorities and communities. However, the obverse is also true: fundamentalist Jewish communities, and the girls and women within them, are affected by the transformed lives of nonfundamentalist Jewish societies as well.

The social psychology of today's Jews is conditioned by movement to the left through assimilation and intermarriage, and to the right by "centrist" Orthodox institutions and authorities as well as frankly fundamentalist groups. The tension from left to right is partially a tension between fundamentalism and feminism, which in turn affects relationship between differing Jewish subgroups, their leadership, and their communities of belief.

Sacred Study as a Tool of Oppression—and Liberation

In Judaism, with its scholarly hierarchy, religious education has and continues to occupy a uniquely privileged and important position. Only the most elite of initiates are considered erudite enough to interpret biblical and rabbinic law and to make halakhic decisions. Recognizing the extent to which a rigorous education in rabbinic texts has led to social power, the ability to make or influence decisions, and communal status in traditional Jewish societies, is key to understanding why contemporary Jewish women's scholarship comprises a true revolution.

Jewish emphasis on study and articulation as a means of primarily male cultural transmission has deep historical roots. The ubiquitousness of the educational enterprise is expressed in the biblical prayer *Shema Yisrael* (Hear, oh Israel), adapted since ancient times as the central prayer of Jewish liturgy. In its powerful passages, worshipping Jews repeatedly voiced their commitment to provide their children with Jewish education, promising to speak about divine commandments when active or resting, residing at home or walking outside. The prayer presents Jewish education not primarily in an elite or formal classroom situation; rather, ordinary parents are enjoined to be involved in religious matters with passionate intensity, heart and soul, so that these subjects virtually never depart from their lips.

Rabbinical interpretation of these passages focused on the teaching of the oral law and defined the responsibility to teach as applying to fathers and sons. Additionally, assuming that many fathers might not feel themselves capable of fulfilling these educational injunctions, rabbinical law permitted delegation: fathers who cannot teach their sons themselves are expected to hire appropriate teachers. Nevertheless, the expectation was that much education would also take place in the home and other settings. Historical Jewish societies took quite seriously the responsibility to provide Jewish education for boys and to encourage lifelong Judaic study for men. In historical Jewish communities, the aura of talmudic learning hovered palpably over communal life. Judaism has been different from many other religious/ethnic identity construction modes because intellectualism defines male excellence. The legal decision and text-based discussions of Jewish scholars had widespread influence on the normative behaviors of both male and female members of Jewish folk classes.

Most rabbinic commentaries interpreted the Shema passage restrictively as referring to "sons and not daughters." Indeed, some talmudic views discourage fathers from providing rigorous text study to their daughters, arguing that they may bring dishonor both to their daughters and to the texts they study. As a consequence, female Jews have until recently experienced the world of intensive Judaic study vicariously or at one remove. Girls were usually taught practical religious fundamentals at home by their mothers. Many girls were taught to read in their Jewish vernacular but not to read Hebrew; others were taught to read basic Hebrew liturgy in the prayer book. In some families knowledgeable fathers or mothers provided their daughters with text study opportunities or hired tutors for them, and in a few communities young girls also attended school. A limited number of wives and daughters in elite families received impressive rabbinic text education at home from their fathers, brothers, or husbands, although the world of talmudic study was largely closed to females. Some of these women made names for themselves as scholars, and some are cited by name or by relationship in rabbinic literature. Moreover, in European communities women and less educated men commonly read Yiddish translations of biblical text and rabbinic commentaries, and participated through these texts in the liturgical activity of ongoing education.[26]

Women's new role in Jewish schooling can be traced back to the Bais Yaakov movement, begun a century ago by Sara Schnirer, a pious Eastern European woman, in a daring response to the challenges of secular modernity. Observing that in enlightened German communities Jewish women who lacked deep knowledge of Judaic texts might more easily drift away from Jewish lifestyles, Schnirer opened a school in 1917 with 25 girls; the school expanded rapidly and new branches were established. In 1937–38, 35,585 girls were enrolled in 248 Bais Yaakov schools in Poland alone. Although the original Bais Yaakov movement's vitality in Europe was brutally cut off during World War II, along with millions of lives and an irreplaceable, richly diverse cultural heritage, the basic assumptions underlying the formation of the Bais Yaakov schools revolutionized attitudes toward Jewish education for girls. Today, across the denominational spectrum, providing girls with a Jewish education has become a communal norm.[27]

Girls' and women's increased access to public study followed different but mutually reinforcing paths in the United States and Israel. In the United States, girls began to have access to intensive day school education with the exponential increase in American Jewish day schools after the emigration of pious Jews in the immediate post–World War II years. Within these twelve-year day schools, girls and boys began to acquire similar levels of Jewish education long before other educational setting (such as the afternoon Talmud Torah or Hebrew School) experienced equal levels of enrollment for girls and boys. Among a non–day school attending population, young boys were far more likely to acquire an afternoon school education than were girls, because of the influence of synagogue educational requirements for Bar Mitzvah. As Bat Mitzvah celebrations gained in popularity, parents of girls were required to send their daughters to afternoon schools in the same proportion as their sons, and the gender gap in Jewish education narrowed.

Jewish feminism played a role in the growing ubiquitousness of the Bat Mitzvah celebration in the United States, where second-wave feminism began to gather popular forced following the publication of Betty Friedan's critique of *The Feminine Mystique* in 1963.[28] Jewishly focused feminism emerged among Reform, Reconstructionist, and Conservative activist women's groups in the early 1970s. Not much later, the first Orthodox women's *tefillah* groups were initiated in 1973 in St. Louis, Missouri, and Cambridge, Massachusetts, followed a few years later by better known groups in Riverdale, New York, Baltimore, Maryland, and elsewhere. Thus, Orthodox Jewish women from the beginning were influenced by broader feminist social movements, as well as by revolutions in the more liberal Jewish denominations.

The 1990 National Jewish Population Survey data show that Orthodox girls as a group attend Jewish schools at approximately the same number of hours and years as their brothers. Perhaps counterintuitively, the gender gap in length and intensity of Jewish education is lower among Orthodox Jewish youth than among any other group, although curricula vary by gender. This growing cadre of highly educated Jewish women has been enhanced by the creation of women's *yeshivot* in Israel, accompanied by the expectation among American Jewish day school administrators that their female graduates, like their male graduates, will spend a year of intensive study in Israel before they proceeded to college.

Haredi schools, including Lubavitch schools, for example, do not teach talmudic texts to girls. Ironically, the late Lubavitcher Rebbe stated that women should be taught the Gemara in order to preserve the quality of Jewish life, and in order that the tradition should be passed down from generation to generation. In a Hebrew article, he urges that women be taught in oral Torah so that they, who provide the most consistent presence in the home, can supervise and guide their children's religious studies. These study sessions are necessary, says Rabbi Schneerson, because without them women can easily be seduced by the charms of secular studies. Rabbi Schneerson asserted that women should study with their husbands subjects even including the "fine, dialectical" points of law that most previous rabbis posited as being inappropriate for women. He wrote: "It is human nature for male and female to delight in their kind of study. Through this there will develop in them (the women) the proper sensitivities and talents in the spirit of our Holy Torah."[29] Despite his statement, in fundamentalist communities in the United States and especially in Israel, girls are taught information but not given the intellectual skills to confront text study on their own.[30]

As day schools have become more and more available in medium-sized communities across the United States, rather than only in the major metropolitan areas, a commitment to day school education has become a normative marker within committed families. Today the majority of Orthodox families, along with a growing core of committed Conservative and some Reform families, provide both daughters and sons with day school education, many of them continuing through the high school years.

In addition to the now normative year of Israeli *yeshiva* study for modern Orthodox girls between high school and college, women now have the opportunity to do serious text study throughout their adult lives. Women's text study is offered in settings as diverse as the Orthodox Stern College for Women, an undergraduate school of Yeshiva University, and secular universities with strong Judaic studies programs, such as Brandeis, Columbia, University of Pennsylvania, and others. Some women endeavor to gain language and cultural skills necessary for the understanding of the Talmud and other rabbinic texts in independent schools in Israel, such as Jerusalem's *Pardes*, or in the United States in schools such as New York's *Drisha* and *Shalhevet* and Boston's *Ma'ayan*. Some of these schools are for women only, and some are coeducational, but all share a fairly traditional religious orientation.

Women's study of Judaic texts is taking place both on a widespread, grassroots form, and on the most elite and esoteric levels. The expanding world of women's scholarship has given rise to a new generation of female notables. These "stars" of women's Torah learning, many of them Israelis, are having a great impact on the status of learning for Orthodox women in the United States. For decades, one of the few female Torah scholars who was well known enough to be frequently quoted was the brilliant Nechama Leibowitz, whose insightful, accessible books discussing biblical portions of the week and their commentaries appealed to scholars and novices alike. Today, a group of dynamic Orthodox scholars and educators such as Rabbanit Chana Henkin, director of the *Nishmat* school for women, Malka Bina, director of the *Matan* school for women, and Dr. Aviva Zorenberg, who lectures regularly in a variety of venues, are famous both inside and outside the Orthodox world, and travel frequently to the United States on lecture tours and fund-raising trips for their educational institutions. In part because these scholars have refrained from identifying themselves as feminists, their activities have by and large avoided controversy.

Within Modern Orthodox environments, a few rabbis and institutions have created new credentialed positions for scholarly Jewish women. In several New York–area Jewish synagogues, young women have been appointed Inters, who serve the congregational community in numerous para-rabbinic responsibilities. In Israel, Rabbi Shlomo Riskin, who left the American rabbinate of the Lincoln Square Synagogue to found and administer a variety of Jewish educational institutions for boys and girls, men and women, from his Israeli home in Efrat, has been training *toanot*, female para-rabbinic lawyers who serve as advocates for women locked in difficult Israeli divorce situations.

Perhaps the most revolutionary development in this area has recently taken place in Modern Orthodox settings in Israel. For years, a variety of American and Israeli individuals and institutions seriously discussed finding a way to credential women to function as *yoatzot halakhah*, halakhic advisors, a new name that is given to rabbinic adjudicators who can answer religious ritual questions. In the fall of 1999, eight women who began a program at Rabanit Chana Henkin's *Nishmat* school in Jerusalem two years earlier, were credentialed to answer religious questions posed by other women about prescriptive behaviors connected to sexuality and reproduction, *hilkhot niddah* (the laws of the menstrual state). While the program has deliberately been launched quietly and discretely, Orthodox authorities and laypersons both recognize the momentous nature of the change it represents. Indeed, it has been argued that some of the most dynamic innovations in the Orthodox world today, including, but not limited to the roles of women, are occurring in Israel rather than in the United States.

Women Who Embrace Jewish Fundamentalism

Arguably the most antifeminist stance is occupied by women who have internalized the fundamentalist stance of their communities and collaborate in the reproduction of fundamentalist attitudes, rejecting many aspects of modernity. The Agudath Israel of America, for example, frequently makes use of conference platforms and movement publications to blast personalities and particular issues associated with modern Orthodoxy and Conservative Judaism. Sarah Blustain reports that one right-wing newspaper serving the Spring Valley, New York, community referred to Orthodox feminism as "a movement whose poison, if left unchecked, may seep into the minds of some unaware of its essence," which challenges the "root distinctions" between the sexes, and the different roles required of them putatively by divine preference. Some women within these groups have taken up the banner of antifeminism in their own enterprises. For example, the Manhattan Jewish Renaissance Center has sponsored rallies designed to expose what they feel is the true nature of Orthodox feminism—a lack of understanding and feminine self-esteem.[31] As Blu Greenberg notes, the Ultra-Orthodox rejection of Orthodox feminism spills over into the "centrist" Orthodox world, affecting women in very practical ways:

> Whether a prospective bride fully accepts kol isha—which extends to singing … *zemirot* around the Shabbat dinner table—is a standard question asked by ultra-Orthodox *shadchanim* when they try to match up suitable partners. So nonnegotiable has this become, that is has spilled over into the modern Orthodox community, where kol isha had previously been on the wane.[32]

While modern Orthodox women's lives most often fully reflect demographic changes influenced by Western feminism, younger modern Orthodox women often picture themselves as "not really feminist." Indeed, it is far more common for modern Orthodox women in their teens, twenties, and thirties to explicitly reject what they call "the feminist agendas" of their mothers' cohort. Many areas of proposed feminist change concern behaviors falling into the category of permissibility but indeterminate desirability. To some extent, these behaviors have come to seem controversial precisely because human judgment is such an important factor in how they are viewed: whether or not a given behavior is judged to be desirable depends on the evaluation of individual rabbinic *poskim*. Some examples of activities that rabbinic law neither obligates nor prohibits to women, but which instead fall on the permissible continuum, include: making the blessing over the *lulav* and *etrog* on *Succot*, eating in a *Succah*, reading the scroll of the Book of Esther, *megillat Esther*, for other women, and studying Torah. In Orthodox communities in the United States, for example, women's Succot observance and Torah study have long been normative, while women reading the *megillat Esther* scroll under Orthodox congregational auspices is still relatively rare.

A Case Study in Paradox: The Orthodox Feminist

When looking at the impact of fundamentalism on Jewish women's lives, it is useful to pay special attention to one population who encapsulate the tension between fundamentalism and feminism in their daily lives—Orthodox Jewish feminists. Until recently, only a few serious studies have explored Orthodox feminism. Blu Greenberg's groundbreaking book of essays, *Women and Judaism: A View from Tradition*, discussed numerous topics of relevance to a "mild mannered yeshiva girl … among the feminists,"[33] and observant feminist speakers such as Norma Baumel Joesph and Nessa Rappaport, among others, have contributed thoughtful and provocative approaches to the subject. Important books dealing with particular aspects of rabbinic responses to women's issues include the recently published *Equality Lost* by Yehuda Henkin[34]; a collection, *Jewish Legal Writings by Women*, edited by Micah Halpern and Chana Safrai[35]; *Women and Water: Menstruation in Jewish Life and Law*, edited by Rachel Wasserfall; the volumes *Midrashic Women: Constructing the Female in Rabbinic Literature*, by Judith Basin, and *Eros and Ethics: Jewish Women and Rabbinic Law*, by Rochelle Millen[36]; and such established, influential works as Joel Wolowelsky's *Women, Jewish Law, and Modernity*,[37] Eliezer Berkovits's *Jewish Women in Time and Torah*,[38] and Avraham Weiss's *Women at Prayer: A Halakhic Analysis of Women's Prayer Groups*.[39] Important but scattered information is available in a few qualitative sociological studies, relevant discussion groups in the electronic media, rabbinic response literature, articles such by sociologists such as Aileen Nusbacher[40] and others on members of women's *tefillah* prayer groups, and recent scholarship on traditionalist Jewish and non-Jewish American religious groups.

Jews located within liberal Judaic religious movements or within the secular camp see themselves as rejecting all fundamentalism as morally and religiously repulsive. In contrast, observers both inside and outside contemporary Orthodox communities have claimed that Orthodox Jews are insulated from many adaptive trends that characterize other American Jews. Consequently, most studies of social change in the American Jewish community have focused on Conservative, Reform, and Secular/Unaffiliated Jews. Ethnographies of the Orthodox world have primarily centered on men's activities and lives, with the noteworthy exception of Debra Kaufman's and Lynn Davidman's two studies of newly Orthodox Jewish women. Even these studies of *ba'a lot teshuva* (who comprise about 6 percent of Orthodox Jews and 1 percent of all American Jews) have been interested in the women themselves, rather than their impact on larger segments of the Orthodox community.[41]

Orthodox women living in modern or in fundamentalist communities face special conflicts between modernity and tradition. First, Orthodox Jews have levels of praxis that differ dramatically from the non-Orthodox community. Many of them feel responsible even for laws about which they are lax. This feeling of responsibility for observance can be summed up in the phrase, *ol malkhut shamayim*, "the yoke of the kingdom of heaven." Unlike non-Orthodox Americans, whose primary orienting ideology is often that of personal freedom, Orthodox Jews are oriented to an ideology of religious commandedness to a network of laws, which they may experience as being in direct conflict with personal freedom.

Second, Orthodox Jews are presumed to feel allegiance to some interpretation of the traditional concept of divine revelation of Jewish law, *Torah mi Sinai* (the Torah was revealed at Mt. Sinai), a belief that the complex, prescriptive codes of rabbinic law derive from God's articulated instructions to the Jewish people. A very broad interpretive gamut is reflected as Orthodox Jews of various shades and stripes formulate what *Torah mi Sinai* means to them. However, no matter how liberal an individual Orthodox person's interpretation of divine revelation, daily life is influenced by group of observances that are precisely dictated by written texts.

As a result, religious texts have a level of concreteness, of solidity, especially to well-educated younger Orthodox Jews, which sometimes makes them seem more real than lived experience itself. In the Orthodox map of meaning, rabbinic texts emanate from and reflect an ideal *halakhah* that has a kind of Platonic truthfulness. Many ordinary Jews try repeatedly to upgrade their religious behavior, attempting to come close to ideal *halakhah* through study and observance of rabbinic law. Thus, as indicated in the words of some respondents who struggle with a perceived conflict between Western feminism and rabbinic prescriptions, the Orthodox individual's sociologically analyzable, empirical experience may seem subordinate to the "reality" of the rabbinic page.

Jewish Organization

Like family life, organizational life in Westernized and fundamentalist milieus has been transformed by changing lifestyles. Older Orthodox women, like their non-Orthodox sisters, sometimes complain that women from "the younger generation" are less willing to volunteer time to work for Jewish organizations. Some of them see a relationship between younger orthodox women's greater stress on learning, and declining emphasis on working for Jewish causes. In the eyes of some older activists, women are learning instead of volunteering. However, contrary to this impression, and perhaps surprisingly for women with so many demands on their time, observant working mothers as a group volunteer some time for Jewish organizations, but chose their volunteer activities very carefully. More of them said they are willing to donate money than volunteer time.

This attitude reflects profound shifts in the expectations that women have for themselves and the way they spend their time. For much of the twentieth century, organizational activism provided American Jewish women arenas both for accomplishing Americanization and expressing their Jewishness, analogous in some ways to the public religious roles of groups of Jewish men in the synagogue and parallel to the activism in prestigious church-related activities. For the rank and file of organizational membership—and for most women, including those who have sought out leadership roles, according to anecdotal reports—voluntarism for Jewish organizations has always served a social function, in addition to whatever religious and communal ideals it represented. Jewish organizational life was greatly enhanced by untold millions of hours of free labor and organizational ability. Women's Jewish organizations often developed a cultural ambience that was different than that of male-dominated philanthropies. Within women's organizations, hard work and organizational ability were as important as the ability to donate money if women aspired to leadership positions. This culture of earned progression up a leadership ladder was reportedly very fulfilling for many talented, energetic women.

Today, persons with higher levels of Jewish education are the most likely to volunteer time for Jewish causes, according to data from the 1990 NJPS. Orthodox Jews volunteer more time than non-Orthodox Jews. Some volunteer primarily for Orthodox causes. However, Orthodox women partake fully of the trend to "boutique" voluntarism, which reflects very personalized organizational activism.

Women in the Synagogue

In the United States, where holding office in a synagogue was viewed for decades as prestigious—and a male activity—Reform, Reconstructionist, and Conservative synagogues now often have female officers. On the more liberal edge of the

Orthodox spectrum, many synagogues allow women to hold board positions or serve as officers, and some have female presidents. Many congregations now allow women opportunities to speak in a congregational setting: the more right-wing congregations limit women's speaking to the social hall or lecture contexts that clearly are outside the setting of worship services, while more liberal Orthodox congregations have women speaking from the *bimah* (prayer lectern) after services are over, but before worshipers disband. In Israel, these privileges are enjoyed by women in the small number of Reform and Conservative congregations, and in a few but very vital pioneering Orthodox congregations in Jerusalem and elsewhere.

Fundamentalist backlash sometimes focuses on synagogue architecture. In old-style Orthodox synagogue buildings, women were usually physically distanced from the worship service by being placed in a balcony or behind a substantial *mekhitza*, and in some cases women prayed in a separate room adjoining the men. As a mark of changing times, these extreme separations of women fell out of favor, and for decades the trend in synagogue architecture approached giving women close to equal access to the central activities of the prayer service. Even in some Hasidic circles, concern for women's participation was manifest, as one-way mirrors were installed,[42] which would allow women complete visual access, while preventing the men from looking at them.

In the United States, for decades the construction of balconies for women was on the wane when new congregations were built. These synagogues that did make use of balconies were more likely to build U-shaped, low-slung balconies surrounding the men's section on three sides, from which the ark and reading stand were clearly visible and the service was easily heard. During the past ten years, however, some Orthodox congregations that rebuild have reverted to the older style of high balconies, in which hearing and seeing the service is significantly impeded for female worshippers. This reclamation of the synagogue gallery is an unmistakable sign of fundamentalist pressure.

In European cities, most congregations are still largely a male preserve. Indeed, since Jewish education for women persists at a rudimentary level in Paris, Rome, Prague, and elsewhere, it seems unlikely that Jewish women will occupy synagogue leadership positions anytime soon. In some places it is ironically only the fundamentalists that provide a substantial Jewish education to their girls and women. Thus, in some synagogues in major European cities, only girls connected to fundamentalist communities can navigate with ease through the Hebrew liturgy, while more "liberal" women sit and chat with each other behind the curtains of the women's section. It should be noted, of course, that fundamentalist Jewish women pray far from men's eyes, and generally rely for religious inspiration upon male preachers and teachers of Bible and other sacred texts.

In contrast, within fundamentalist Christian groups, women's sacred study and worship group activities are not viewed as threatening. Brasher describes the host of women's activities attended by fundamentalist Christian women, with the full blessing of the male-dominated church:

> There, the programs that contribute to the formation of the enclave include five women's Bible studies, a biannual women's retreat, a monthly women's outreach luncheon, an ongoing women's prison outreach ministry, a monthly women's breakfast, and various other special programs for women…. At each, the core women's ministry program is the women's Bible study…. At all women's ministry events, women are the speakers, table leaders, musicians, and film/tape crew as well as the attendees. During the Bible studies, detailed examination of biblical texts takes place in a small study/prayer cell cluster of eight to ten women.[43]

Re-evaluating the Fundamentals of Life Cycle Events

In most historical Jewish communities the life cycle events of women were only celebrated when they overlapped with those of men. Thus, when a Jewish woman gave birth to a daughter, her husband was honored on the Sabbath following her childbirth by being called to the Torah; while receiving this honor, he both informed the community of the name of his new daughter, and recited prayers on behalf of his wife's recovery and health. In most communities it was unusual for either mother or daughter to be present at services while this took place, and no further ritual or celebratory events took place to mark the birth of the daughter, or to welcome her into the Jewish community. In contrast, when a woman gave birth to a son, the whole community was often invited to the ritual circumcision (*brit milah*) on the eighth day following birth. The blessings accompanying the circumcision welcome the infant boy into the community of Israel, and the "bris," as it is colloquially called, and the whole event has a celebratory tenor, complete with refreshments. Thus, from the very first moment of a Jewish girl's life, her lack of inclusion into the public ritual community (*kehillah*) of Jews was made apparent.

One of the most profound and sweeping transformations of Jewish communal life, especially in the United States, has been the creation (and in some cases, rediscovery) of ritualized, celebratory treatments of life cycle events. Across Orthodox, Conservative, and Reform/Reconstructionist denominational lines, the birth of Jewish baby girls is now marked by communal events commonly referred to as *shalom bat, brit banot, britah*, or similar other names. Some families hold girls' ceremonies on the eighth day, to parallel the timing—but never the surgical procedure—of the *brit milah*. Other families take advantage of the fact that this celebration has few historical precedents, and schedule it for a time convenient to far-flung family members. What each of these events has in common is that they include the recitation of psalms and other liturgical materials along with an explanation of the infant girl's name. The communal celebration of female children's birth is almost universal in American Modern Orthodox communities, but it is still somewhat controversial in fundamentalist Orthodox communities. As a result, *shalom bat* ceremonies do take place in some fundamentalist Orthodox communities but not in others. Communities that shun the practice cite their resistance to "outside influences" (i.e., feminism) as the reason.

Interestingly, in fundamentalist communities that refuse to have special ceremonies for daughters, it has become completely expected for the parents of the girl to host an elaborate *kiddush* of refreshments for the congregation following a Sabbath service, in honor of the baby girl's birth. Fifty years ago, hosting such a *kiddush* sometimes elicited sarcastic comments ("All this for a girl?"). Thus, in resisting innovations that are perceived as precipitated by outside influences, Jewish fundamentalist communities often devise alterative strategies, which are themselves responses to feminist challenges.

The most sweeping change affecting many fundamentalist Orthodox American communities has been the incorporation of the concept of Bat Mitzvah into the realm of expectations. Jewish boys become responsible for performing all religious rituals and commandments upon their thirteenth birthdays. At that time, Orthodox boys begin to put on phylacteries (*tefilin*) every weekday morning. The Bar Mitzvah boy is typically honored by being called to the Torah for the first time as an adult; it has been customary to mark this honor by the parents hosting a *kiddush* for the community. During the twentieth century, these celebrations have escalated and often become extremely elaborate.

Bat Mitzvah, the parallel celebration for girls, was popularized within the American Conservative movement in the 1950s and 1960s. Although religiously girls are thought to reach their maturation at age twelve, many communities celebrated the Bat Mitzvah when girls reached age thirteen, to maintain the parallel between girls and boys. Despite these common ages, at first most Conservative synagogues did not call girls to the Torah on Shabbat morning. During the early 1970s, as feminists within the Conservative movement were lobbying for change, many Conservative congregations started to treat Bar and Bat Mitvah ceremonies as identical. During this time period as well, most Reform congregations reinstituted Bar Mitzvah (which they had earlier rejected in favor of Confirmation ceremonies) and instituted identical Bat Mitzvah ceremonies at the same time. As a result, Jewish education for girls, which had been of shorter duration and less intense than Jewish education for boys, became equalized in many communities, as girls, like boys, were preparing for a communally expected event. The gender gap in Jewish religious education in America virtually disappeared as a result of the new ubiquitousness of Bat Mitzvah ceremonies for twelve- or thirteen-year-old girls. Additionally, many older women undertook courses of study leading to adult Bat Mitzvah ceremonies and celebrations. Having a Bat Mitzvah became a new rite of passage for American girls and women, leading them to feel that they were valued members of the religious community.

For a time, Orthodox families and congregations resisted marking the religious maturity of girls with a Bat Mitzvah ceremony. However, American Orthodox women were very influenced by the women's movement, and by the 1970s many Orthodox families had begun having some type of Bat Mitzvah event to mark the religious majority of their daughters. Many had open houses, or a nonsynagogue service festive meal with speeches. It became very common for the Bat Mitzvah girl herself to prepare a serious scholarly talk, dealing with some Judaic subject that she had researched for many months with a teacher or parent. After a time, many Orthodox synagogues created protocols to incorporate Bat Mitzvah ceremonies in a formal way, albeit without calling the young woman up to the Torah as a boy would be called. Within communities that had women's *tefillah* groups, however, Bat Mitzvah girls were called to the Torah, and were often responsible for preparing the entire Torah reading from the scroll, just as a boy would be.

This continuum of modes to celebrate Bat Mitzvah still characterizes the American Orthodox community. On the left, some Modern Orthodox families celebrate Bat Mitzvhas within women's *tefillah* groups. On the fundamentalism right, Bat Mitzvah is usually marked with a home open house, or a social event involving just the young woman and her friends and family. What should not be forgotten is that no matter how different the celebrations accorded girls and boys, in the United States it is only the most isolated communities that do not have any type of celebration for girls. In Israel and other fundamentalist communities, in contrast, it is still common for a girl's passage into Bat Mitzvah status to go unmarked.

The Symbolism of Women and Death Rituals

Communal norms are changing not only in the area of happy life cycle celebrations, but also in the area of death-related ceremonies as well. Indeed, the universality of mortality and loss have made women's roles in Orthodox bereavement situations a motif that touches many nonfeminist women. More and more, Orthodox women expect to be involved—to speak at a funeral, to give a class at the *shiva* home, or to say *kaddish* for a departed loved one.

Once rare, the sight of a woman saying *kaddish*, the traditional prayer that mourning children recite at daily prayer services for eleven months following interment has become increasingly familiar in some American Conservative, Reform, and some Orthodox congregations. This transformation, however, has proceeded at a very uneven pace, so that mourning women in an unfamiliar congregation may well run the risk of encountering unreceptive responses. In addition, in Israel, Europe, and other Jewish communities worldwide it is still very unusual for women to take upon themselves the responsibility to recite the *kaddish* each day in the synagogue.

"Three years ago, when I was saying *kaddish* for my mother, most congregations were not used to seeing a woman on weekdays," one woman recalls. "On occasion, men screamed at me. Some ogled. Finally, one old man walked over to me and asked me who I was saying *kaddish* for. I told him, my mother. 'Oh,' he commiserated sadly, 'she had no children?'"

Just as rabbis sometimes inappropriately declare actions off limits when they are halakhically permissible, Orthodox laypersons who fear change may follow suit. As if to illustrate this phenomenon, in a separate e-mail communication, a writer described a recent incident in a private home in Jerusalem. A married couple and four visiting women shared a Shabbat meal. When a female guest asked for the women to participate in *zimmum*, stating that women are encouraged by rabbinic law to recite the group grace together, the male host agitatedly blurted out, *Ani batel et zeh!* ("I revoke the permission!") and prevented the women from praying together.

Confronting Divorce, Abusive Spouses, and Other Social Problems

The situation of the *agunah*, the woman chained to a situation of marital limbo, "remains the most intractable issue in Orthodox life in the United States and Israel," according to Susan Aranoff and other Jewish women's activists (New York, 3/15/99). A woman becomes an *agunah* either when her husband disappears through war, travel, or some other scenario, or when she seeks a religious divorce process, a *get*, but her husband refuses to cooperate. The *get* is a legal proceeding terminating the conditions set forth upon the signing of the *t'nayim* and *ketubah*, the legal contracts entered into at the time of the couple's betrothal and wedding. Jewish divorce proceedings can be initiated by the husband but theoretically should not be performed without the wife's acquiescence. When a couple separates without a *get*, under the terms of Jewish law a husband is free to remarry, while his wife becomes an *agunah*, a chained woman, and may not remarry. If a Jewish woman remarries without a *get*, her children are considered to be *mamzerim*, the illegitimate children of an adulterous union, who cannot marry into the legitimate Jewish community for ten generations; a man who has remarried without a *get*, on the other hand, does not stigmatize the children who come out of the new marriage.

The proliferation of such chained women is in many ways a product of the hyphenated lives of Westernized Jews. The freedom of choice that many American Jews take as their birthright, together with the inequity of Jewish divorce law regarded women, combines to make the position of Jewish women vis-à-vis divorce even more unequal than it has been in historical Jewish communities, because American Jewish men have the option of obtaining a civil divorce and remarrying in a civil ceremony. Divorce has increased in all segments of the Jewish community, although there is an inverse relationship between the traditionalism of the household and the likelihood of divorce, with households strongly connected to Jewish behaviors and community showing lower rates of divorce than those with weak connections. Although divorce is less common in Orthodox communities, rates of divorce have risen here as well, and Orthodox women are far more vulnerable than others to the threat of an *agunah* status.

Some communities have attempted to deal with the problems of women caught in *agunah* situations, either on a systematic or a case-by-case basis. Advocacy organizations for women being denied a *get* have been formed in several cities and on a nationwide basis. Some of the organizations that deal with the issue are G.E.T.—Getting Equitable Treatment, Agunah, Inc., Kayama, and the Israel Women's Network. One of the most recent and controversial Orthodox attempts to deal with the plight of *agunot* has been spearheaded by Rabbi Emanuel Rackman, chancellor of Israel's Bar Ilan University, and long a champion of women's rights within a halakhic framework, and Rabbi Moshe Morgenstern, of the *Bet Din Tzekek Leboyot Agunot*. The *beit din*, rabbinic court, that they sponsor ends the marriages of chained women by using the hypothesis that no women would have entered into a problem marriage had she realized her husband's character flaws from the outset.

> Rabbi Rackman comments on the importance of annulment as a strategy: The annulment accomplishes three things. First, it disempowers extortionist husbands who use the get to obtain financial or custodial concessions to which they would not be entitled. Second, it frees a wife from her captor husband whose pathological need to control her is expressed in statements such as, "You'll die before I ever give you a get," or "If I'm going to rot in jail, you'll rot too." And third, it provides closure for the women who yearn to begin their lives anew.

He concludes, "If for preventing husbands and others from causing pain to Jewish daughters I am impaled on the spikes of rabbinic fundamentalism, it is a relatively small price to pay for living with one's conscience."[44]

Reaction to this rabbinic court has indeed been dramatic on both sides of the spectrum. Those who approve hail the annulment procedure as the first broadly based, humane rabbinic response to a festering human problem. Susan Aranoff, intensely consumed by her constant devotion to the cause, reflects: "In looking back over all my years of activism, the saddest thing I've experienced is rabbis continuing year after year to insist that Jewish law requires that women suffer. Isaiah's compassion for the widow, the orphan, the downtrodden—how can rabbis say that what's happening to *agunot* is halakhic! Judaism is being dragged through the gutter!" (New York, 3/15/99). Activists such as Aranoff and Rifka Haut, Orthodox *agunah* activist and author of articles and books on women in Judaism, continue to express frustration or outrage because thousands of women are trapped in situations in which husbands and lawyers use the obtaining of a Jewish divorce as a tool for unfair bargaining or wreaking vengeance.[45] However, not every activist believes that the annulment approach is halakhically workable. Indeed, even Rifka Haut has regretfully suggested that the *beit din* does not pay enough attention to halakhic protocol, and may thus be inadvertently worsening the situation of the women involved, by making them think they are free, when in the opinion of many they are not.

On the other side of the issue are traditionalists who see the vocal outrage of women like Aranoff and Haut as a brazen attempt to undermine rabbinic authority. When confronted with the tragic cases of actual trapped women, these traditionalists express sorrow that the *agunot* are thus afflicted, but say that the principles of rabbinic authority and halakhic integrity are more important than the situations of individuals.

The non-Jewish press has helped to publicize the extent to which the Orthodox world has had its own specialized problems with divorce. Understanding all too well the desperate need of Orthodox women for a religious divorce, some lawyers servicing traditional communities have allegedly deliberately specialized in "encouraging husbands to extort large settlements from their wives in return for granting a *get*." One male attorney combating a policy of "absolute blackmail" on the part of such colleagues initiated a "Get Project" in the *New York Law Journal* for the purpose of collecting data in the form of cases and complaints—affidavits, bank books, correspondence between litigants—concerning lawyers who encourage *get* extortion.[46]

Not infrequently, agunah-related divorce situations are related to spousal abuse. Dr. Samuel Klagsbrun, executive director of Four Winds Hospital, a private psychiatric hospital in Katonah, New York, has been working with abusive situations in Jewish households for many years, including high-profile situations such as the notorious case of Hedda Nussbaum, who allowed her daughter Lisa to be beaten to death by her husband, Joel Steinberg. Klagsbrun believes that resistance to dealing with violent family dysfunctions has, ironically, been based on attempts to preserve traditional family values such as *shalom bayis*, the Jewish ideal of the serene and orderly household. In addition, loathing of women's liberation makes some in the right-wing Orthodox community skeptical about battered women's assertions and unsympathetic to women who come to them for aid: "These women don't feel safe going to rabbis who will tell them they've been contaminated by women's rights." When women finally work up the courage to leave, husbands frequently response with escalated violence. As Klagsbrun notes: "Seventy-five percent of murders of women who are abused occur at the time of, or shortly after, the time the woman leaves. Their fear is real."[47]

Fundamentalism and the Fear of Slippery Slopes

Rabbinic authorities, both those who perceive themselves as basically friendly to women's issues, and those unconflicted fundamentalists who are outspoken opponents of feminist-induced change, have characteristically responded to women's questions by invoking *halakhah*, rabbinic law. Depending on their positioning on the egalitarian continuum, each rabbi takes a firm (for some, it is firm-but-friendly) stance at the point at which they think "the *halakhah* can bend no farther." As one interviewed rabbi put it, "Sociological concerns are valid and legitimate considerations when making an halakhic decision." It is important to note that this acceptance of extrinsic considerations seems to work only in one direction: it is acceptable to consider social-psychological factors when resisting change, but not when attempting to implement change.

Rabbis who are hostile to change in Orthodox women's lives agree with all or most of the following statements. While not every rabbi agrees that each of these are serious obstacles, with only two exceptions even the "woman-friendly" rabbis interviewed for this study subscribed to at least some of these statements:

- Unaccustomed activities cannot be initiated by women who lack the proper "*motivation.*" Knowledgeable, devout women who are motivated purely by a love of Torah and a love of God might be allowed certain halakhically acceptable activities. However, those women who are motivated by a desire to make a point or to acquire power should expressly not be allowed to initiate atypical activities.
- *Feminism* is a pernicious, impious outside influence. If a suggested change seems to emanate from feminist impulses, it should be rejected even if it is halakhically permitted.
- Many women who lobby for change are actually trying to imitate men. They would be men if they could. Their activities are often referred to as "masculo-feminist" behavior. Their goals are inimicable to the wholesome gender role definitions of historical Judaism.
- Giving women opportunities to change starts them down a *slippery slope* toward liberal varieties of Judaism. If they are given one change, they will not be happy or satisfied, they will just ask for another change. Eventually, they will reach the point where there is no choice but to say, "No." When that time comes, they will be frustrated and angry. Since they are going to be frustrated and angry anyway, there is no reason to upset the Orthodox status quo. Most people like the status quo. Why upset the normal Orthodox Jews to meet the unmeetable demands of the others?
- Women ought to consider the impact that their demands have on the larger community. They cannot elevate their selfish concerns above the greater good of the Jewish people. *Women's inappropriate demands have already brought great grief and schism* to local, national, and international traditional Jewish

communities. Therefore, even if their requests could be justified halakhically, women should show their devotion to the Jewish future by abandoning these troublesome demands.

Jewish Women Bridging Boundaries

"One person can't dance at two weddings," suggests a familiar Yiddish aphorism. However, despite the vigorous efforts against and the denial of change, contemporary Jewish religious life has been transformed by feminism and other social movements. Across the spectrum, despite fundamentalist pressure Jewish societies have undergone deep and multifaceted changes. Many of these changes have occurred as the very natural byproduct of sweeping changes in society at large.

Significantly, bald statements that women should be secluded from public Judaism because of their gender have diminished. Women's access to the Torah has been dramatically expanded in many settings, including fundamentalists settings. The rabbinic principle that women are not halakhically prohibited from being near or touching the Torah has become far more well-known today than it was for hundreds of years. However, many argue for women's continued exclusion because of sexual issues as they affect men and the communal dynamic.

On the other hand, observant women now serve as a living bridge between fundamentalist, modern Orthodox, and other streams of American Judaisms. From data provided by systematic personal interviews, and from other sources on contemporary Jewish societies,[48] it seems clear that women's new leadership and activism in the major wings of Judaism has fostered a level of mutual influence quite different in nature from the competitive, often male-dominated "turf wars" that characterize much of the Jewish organizational world. Although fundamentalist communities still restrict Orthodox women's exponential leap into rabbinic text study, claiming enthusiastically for themselves a cultural value long limited to men, feminism has played an important role in the revitalization of adult education for men and women, non-Orthodox and Orthodox, devout and even secularized Jews. Reform and Reconstructionist women's successful entry into rabbinical and other leadership roles galvanized the social forces that resulted in Conservative ordination of women, and eventually in Orthodox creation of para-rabbinic roles and credentials. Conservative women's liturgical literacy, nurtured by the Ramah camping movement and the elite Leadership Training Fellowship educational youth group cadre, provided a model of women's competency in public prayer that had an impact on the growth of the women's *tefillah* prayer group network. It is fair to say that, as a group, Jewish feminists who are committed to the health and survival of their respective wings of Judaism have created significant paradigms for cooperation, listening, and learning from each other.

The paradoxical case of Orthodox feminists illustrates resistance to both fundamentalism and assimilation. With fully egalitarian worship opportunities literally down the road from their Orthodox synagogues, Orthodox feminists insist that historical, halakhic Jewish behaviors, lifestyles, and values are part of their birthright, belonging to them as well as to their brothers and their more fundamentalist sisters. Rather than leave the spiritual place they call home, they continue to strive to make their home more welcoming and nurturing to their religious needs.

Women's issues continue to be a focal point and potent symbol both for those drawn to liberalism and to fundamentalists who are repelled by them. As this study has demonstrated, some fundamentalist communities respond to external stimuli primarily through negative reaction. More substantial proportions of the Jewish community manage to "dance at both weddings"—whether they acknowledge it or not—by fostering a marriage, or coalescence of American and Judaic values. While many experience the discomfort of confronting overtly conflicting and competing systems, many contemporary Jewish women have created spiritual, intellectual, social, and emotional bridges in their ongoing dialogue.

Conclusion: Jewish Fundamentalism and Gender

Gender role construction in fundamentalist Jewish communities, based on traditional concepts of rabbinic Judaism, do not precisely match those of other religions. Male gender role prescriptions include a cultural ideal of lifelong study of complex sacred texts as well as regular prayer. They also include a number of social tasks that are relegated to women in some other religious traditions: for example, within Judaism men are responsible for visiting the sick, welcoming guests, endowing indigent brides with dowries and other necessities, comforting mourners, and caring for aging parents. Women are also responsible for these tasks, but their responsibility does not relieve men from doing their share. This socialization has resulted in a male gender role construction that might be considered "feminized," when compared with some other religious traditions.

This traditional male gender role construction, with its many womanlike aspects, is premised on the supportive role of Jewish women. Women play subordinate roles, but they are central to the system. One reason for this is logistical: men can only be free to study sacred texts and take care of society's most vulnerable members if women take care of them and their families. In many Jewish fundamentalist societies, women also have breadwinning responsibilities. Thus, Jewish women in fundamentalist societies tend to be less sheltered and cut off than women in some other religious fundamentalist societies. This tendency for women in fundamentalists societies to be breadwinners and out in the marketplace has, if anything, become more pronounced as the proportion of young Jewish men devoting themselves full time to sacred study has increased.

A second reason for the subordinate role of women seems to be psychological: men take their religious responsibilities seriously partially because they are part of the privilege of being a fundamentalist Jewish male. In more liberal wings of Judaism, congregations have become startlingly feminized: with women occupying many of the religious and organization leadership positions, men in many cases no longer seek out these positions. Worshipping congregations are composed largely of women, except when a Bar/Bat Mitzvah or other special events occur. Thus, even in liberal wings of Judaism men seem to respond positively to a males-only, private club kind of atmosphere, and to loose interest when the religious environment becomes egalitarian.

A third reason for women's subordinate role in fundamentalist Jewish societies surely has to do with the need these societies have to control their girls and women in regard to their sexual and social activities. This sexual component is made explicit in much of the Jewish fundamentalist antiliberalization, antifeminist rhetoric, particularly that which focuses on women's modesty. Women who participate in women's prayer groups, for example, are accused of making themselves part of the "licentiousness" of feminism. "Transgressions" of women's traditional roles are read as if they were sexual transgressions, and women rabbis and other Jewish women leaders are spoken of as though they were "brazen" morally loose women, although this presumption might seem far-fetched to persons outside fundamentalist communities. Even women who want to speak publicly at their own family religious festivities are discouraged, because they will be breaching the rules of modesty.

Jewish fundamentalist communities have acquired a cache in some circles, because they seem to be a kind of insurance policy against the disappearance of Judaism as a faith tradition. Although the vast majority of contemporary Jews in communities around the world choose for themselves to participate in the advantages of modern life, some fear that their own Westernized forms of Judaism will not survive the seductions of assimilation. Some wonder whether insulation again the eroding forces of modernity may not in the end prove the more effective strategy in preserving the rich heritage of ancient Jewish civilizations of the past. However, for most contemporary Jews, the subordinate role of women in fundamentalist Jewish societies proves one of the most problematic elements in fundamentalist social and religious norms. Women's roles are symbolic for non-fundamentalist Jews, just as they are for fundamentalist Jews. For Jewish fundamentalists, defining and circumscribing women's roles is a way of resealing boundaries between them and the outside world and symbolically rejecting modernity. For Jewish nonfundamentalists, expanding women's roles—and finding other, more creative ways of re-engaging Jewish men—have become symbolic of meeting the challenges of modernity while remaining in dialogue with historical Judaism.

Notes

   * Hebrew is read from right to left. My thanks to Suzy Klein who assisted me in research tasks under the auspices of the Brandeis University Women's Studies Center Scholar-Student Partnership Program.

   1. Sergio DellaPergola, Uzi Rebhun, and Mark Tolts, "Prospecting the Jewish Future: Population Projections, 2000–2080," in *American Jewish Year Book 2000*, 103–46, 123.

   2. Judy Brink and Joan Mencher, eds., *Mixed Blessings: Gender and Religious Fundamentalism Cross Culturally* (New York and London: Routledge, 1997), 6.

   3. See Jacob Katz, *Out of the Ghetto: The Social Background of the Jewish Emancipation, 1770–1870* (New York: Schocken Books, 1978).

   4. Samuel C. Heilman, *Defenders of the Faith: Inside Ultra-Orthodox Jewry* (New York: Schocken Books, 1992), 38–39.

   5. David Landau, *Piety and Power: The World of Jewish Fundamentalism* (New York: Hill and Wang, 1993).

   6. Israel Shahak and Norton Mezvinsky, *Jewish Fundamentalism in Israel* (Sterling, VA: Pluto Press, 1999).

   7. Heilman, *Defenders of the Faith*.

   8. Samuel C. Heilman, "Quiescent and Active Fundamentalisms: The Jewish Cases," in *Accounting for Fundamentalisms: The Dynamic Character of Movements, ed.* Martin E. Marty and R. Scott Appleby (Chicago: University of Chicago Press, 1994), 173–96.

   9. Warren Rosenberg, *Legacy of Rage: Jewish Masculinity, Violence and Culture* (Amherst: University of Massachusetts Press, 2001).

   10. Daniel Boyarin, *Unheroic Conduct: The Rise of Heterosexuality and the Invention of the Jewish Man* (Berkeley: University of California Press, 1997).

   11. Tamar El-Or, *Educated and Ignorant: Ultraorthodox Jewish Women and Their World* (Boulder, CO: Lynne Rienner Publishers, 1994); and *Next Year I Will Know More: Literacy and Identity among Young Orthodox Women in Israel* (Detroit: Wayne State University Press, 2002).

   12. Susan Sered, *What Makes Women Sick?: Maternity, Modesty, and Militarism in Israeli Society* (Dartmouth, NH: Brandeis University Press Series on Jewish Women, 2000).

   13. Tema Gurary and Zalman Kleinman, *Aura: A Reader on Jewish Womanhood* (New York: Lubavitch Women's Organization, 1984).

   14. *Talmudic tractate Ketubot* 61b, 62b; *Mishnah Torah*, Ishut 14:1. See also Menachem M. Brayer, *The Jewish Woman in Rabbinic Literature: A Psychohistorical Approach* (Hoboken, NJ: Ktav Publishing House, 1986), 1:23–95, 121–86; 2:8–11, 58–59, 131–46.

   15. The *Iggeret HaKodesh*, literally the "Holy Epistle," is an anonymous thirteenth-century cabalistic work that broke ground as the first work to openly apply Jewish mystical

teachings to everyday behavior. It deals extensively with sexual relations between husband and wife.

16. Hielman, *Defenders of the Faith*, 324–235.

17. Bernadette Brooten, *Women Leaders in the Ancient Synagogue* (Chico, CA: Scholars Press, 1982).

18. Saul Berman, "Kol Isha," *Tradition* (Fall 1973): 45–66.

19. The Young Israel movement was founded in 1912 in response to the lack of observance in America at the time, in an attempt to make observant Jewish environments more appealing to Americanized Jews. Many jobs required Jews to work on Shabbat and American-born Jews did not have enough Jewish education or attachment to historical Jewish communal norms to resist assimilation. Young Israel synagogues were marked by their propensity for group participation and lively singing, and were considered a very modern Orthodox movement. Today there are 146 Young Israel affiliated congregations throughout the United States, and as a group these congregations have moved dramatically to the right.

20. Sidney Goldstein, *Profile of American Jewry: Insights from the 1990 National Jewish Population Survey* (New York: Council of Jewish Federations and CUNY Graduate School Occasional Papers No. 6, 1993), 117.

21. Studies indicate that even among Ultra-Orthodox Jewish women, contraceptive usage is the norm; however, women in that environment often do not begin using birth control until after they have had five children, do not always tell their husbands they are using it, and typically describe their motivation as being medical, rather than personal.

22. Moshe Hartman and Harriet Hartman, *Gender Equality and American Jews* (Albany: State University of New York Press, 1996), 219–25.

23. Brenda E. Brasher, *Godly Women: Fundamentalism & Female Power* (New Brunswick, NJ: Rutgers University Press, 1998), 9.

24. David Zigelman, "Babysitter or Day Care Center: That Is the Question," *The Jewish Parent Connection* (September/October 1995): 9, 13.

25. Deena Garber, "Mom and the Machzor: Balancing Spirituality and Maternal Realities," and Sharon First, "8 Ways to Help Make the High Holy Days More Meaningful for the Whole Family," *The Jewish Parent Connection* (September/October 1995): 9, 13.

26. Shoshana Zolty, *And All Your Children Shall Be Learned: Women and the Study of Torah in Jewish Law and History* (Northvale, NJ: Jason Aronson, 1993).

27. For a fuller discussion, see Sylvia Barack Fishman, *A Breath of Life: Feminism in the American Jewish Community* (New York: Free Press, 1993), 181–200.

28. Betty Friedan, *The Feminine Mystique* (New York: Norton, 1963).

29. Rabbi Menachem Schneerson, *Me-Sichat Shabbat Parshat Emor, Erev Lag B'Omer 5771: Al Devar Hiyyuv Neshei Yisrael be'Hinukh Limud haTorah*, May 1990.

30. Tamar El-Or, *Educated and Ignorant: Ultraorthodox Jewish Women and Their World* (Boulder, CO: Lynne Rienner Publishers, 1994) and *New Year I Will Know More* (Detroit: Wayne State University Press, 2002).

31. Sarah Blustain, "Right-Wing Women: Keeping Orthodoxy Safe From Feminists?"

in *Lilith* 23, no. 4 (Winter 1998–99): 8–15, 9.

32. Blu Greenberg, "Ultra-Orthodox Women Confront Feminism," in *Moment* 21, no. 3 (June 1996): 36–37, 63, 36.

33. Blu Greenberg, *Women and Judaism: A View from Tradition* (Philadelphia: The Jewish Publication Society of America, 1981).

34. Rabbi Yehuda Henkin, *Equality Lost: Essays in Torah Commentary, Halacha, and Jewish Thought* (Jerusalem: Urim Publications, 1999).

35. Micah D. Halpern and Chana Safrai, eds., *Jewish Legal Writings by Women* (Jerusalem: Urim Publications, 1998).

36. Rahel Wasserfall, *Women and Water: Menstruation in Jewish Life and Law* (Hanover, MA: University Press of New England, 1999); Judith Baskin, *Midrashic Women: Constructing the Female in Rabbinic Law* (Hanover, MA: University Press of New England, 2002); Rochelle Millen, *Eros and Ethics: Jewish Women and Rabbinic Law* (Hanover, MA: University Press of New England, 2000).

37. Joel B. Wolowelsky, *Women, Jewish Law, and Modernity: New Opportunities in a Post-Feminist Age* (Hoboken, NJ: Ktav Publishing House, 1998).

38. Eliezer Berkovits, *Jewish Women in Time and Torah* (Hoboken, NJ: Ktav Publishing House, 1990).

39. Avraham Weiss, *Women at Prayer: A Halakhic Analysis of Women's Prayer Groups* (Hoboken, NJ: Ktav Publishing House, 1990).

40. Aileen Cohen Nusbacher, "Efforts to Change in a Traditional Denomination: The Case of Orthodox Women's Prayer Groups," in *Nashim* 2 (Spring 1999): 95–113.

41. Lynn Davidman, *Tradition in a Rootless World: Women Turn to Orthodox Judaism* (Berkeley: University of California Press, 1991); and Debra Renee Kaufman, *Rachel's Daughters: Newly Orthodox Jewish Women* (New Brunswick, NJ: Rutgers University Press, 1991).

42. Karla Goldman, *Beyond the Synagogue Gallery* (Cambridge: Harvard University Press, 2000), 3–4.

43. Brasher, *Godly Women*, 14–15.

44. Emanuel Rackman, "For Agunah, Leeway in the Law," *The Jewish Week*, March 5, 1999, 28.

45. See, for example, Nathalie Friedman, "Divorced Parents and the Jewish Community," 53–102, and Eliot Gertel, "Jewish Views on Divorce," 201–30, in *The Jewish Family and Jewish Continuity*, ed. Steven Bayme and Gladys Rosen (New York: Ktav, 1994).

46. Steve Lipman, "Orthodox Wives Are Victims of 'Get Blackmail' Lawyer," *Jewish Week*, November 22, 1985.

47. Debra Darvick, "To Have and to Harm: Waking Up to the Reality that Domestic Violence Happens in Nice Jewish Homes," *Forward*, November 8, 1996, 13.

48. See Fishman, *A Breath of Life*.

CHAPTER 5

Chastening Tale: Figuring Woman across the Christian Fundamentalist/Feminist Divide*

Heidi Epstein

Introduction: Three Objectives and Terminological Clarification

"A fine line cleaves bigotry and critical thought," I once mused to a Pakistani student-friend as we disparaged her parents' old-world marital values. Being "enlightened" rather than racist, we decided, requires a taste for ambiguity.

A similar precariousness attends feminist appraisals of fundamentalist Christian women. In its most global forms, feminism and feminist theology seek to envision, articulate, and facilitate *all* women's full flourishing, more recently with a preferential option for those who are multiplicatively oppressed by race, class, imperialist, and heterosexist discriminatory forces. Diligent integration of such marginalized women's directives is meant to further this goal of radical inclusivity. Despite such vigilant self-critique, feminist dreams of women's global "liberation" will always founder on opposition from fundamentalist Christian women; by their own account, fundamentalist women flourish without (and sometimes in literal spite of) our help. Endorsing a patriarchal status quo, fundamentalist women become part of "the problem." Disowning these "sisters" as duped or warped by androcentrism (often because their bourgeois stability lulls them into "false consciousness")[1] may seem a requisite tradeoff as we promote more "authentic" women's liberation and the wider release of all oppressed peoples. But in my view, the divide between us marks paradoxical confluences that warrant critical scrutiny, precisely to extend feminist values of inclusivity and theoretical probity.

Numerous excellent surveys and case studies of women in Christian fundamentalism already exist.[2] Drawing from these, this paper will be a meta-critical essay; I want to further the project of feminist self-critique by "producing [unlikely] proximities"[3] between Christian feminist and fundamentalist women. I do so to alert students, scholars, and teachers to commonalities that the divide's surface dichotomies obfuscate. My investigation unfolds in three stages. First I shall identify the concrete commonalities between us—our quests for spiritual and economic agency; our strategies of resistance against ecclesial marginalization; our humanitarian initiatives; and, less positively, our shared historical myopia. Second, I shall expose two theoretical fundamentals that drive our divergent definitions of salvation and transcendence: our respective erotics of mastery and sameness. Third, on the basis of these, and enlisting two recent feminist lenses to reframe the divide (tragedy and dispersibility), I shall reconfigure Woman across this impasse in hopes of undermining its intractability, and breaking its polarizing sway over our imaginations. By rereading the divide through these interpretive keys, I shall constrain, *yet precisely because of this refine and thereby strengthen*, our own feminist theological critiques, reconstructions, and justice-making.

An awareness of these shared faultlines may also chasten hasty repudiations of fundamentalist women's "myopia," and encourage a double hermeneutic of suspicion and generosity toward our fundamentalist "sisters." In teasing out these proximities, however, I in no way condone Christian fundamentalists' demonization of, for example, homosexuality and abortion. Still, the morally desirable hermeneutic "cleavage" invoked above—that taste for ambiguity—can only be acquired and sustained (as scholars Jacqueline Rose and Linda Kintz wisely insist) through "a rigorous, thoughtful process of *unknowing*," not through unilateral pontifications.[4] Were I to flout the ambivalence endemic to critiques of our fundamentalist sisters by claiming higher moral ground, I would stoke the "violence" that feeds "grand symbolic and abstract certainties."[5] Instead, like Rose and Kintz whose work I discuss below, I want to help revalorize ambiguity and "unknowing" as difficult yet necessary preconditions for "ethical behavior."[6]

In *Changing the Subject: Women's Discourse and Feminist Theology* (1994), Mary McClintock Fulkerson has already identified unacknowledged elements of women's agency and resistance to patriarchy within both conservative, American, upper-class Presbyterian and working-class Pentecostal churches. Using discourse analysis,[7] she trenchantly deconstructs feminist notions of women's experience and liberation, ultimately to demonstrate that many conservative Christian women still "remake their subject positions" in liberating ways that "refuse" their otherwise "patriarchal capitalist" subordination.[8] As examples, financially dependent Presbyterian women have much to teach us about a globally accountable neighbor-love; poor Pentecostal women's rhetorics of submission and self-deprecation mediate transgressive worship, preaching, and dress practices that need to be reread as "countersignifying processes to the demure, dependent, eroticized body that feminists also resist."[9] I shall engage some of her field work and insights below (and in my notes), but a detailed dialogue with her groundbreaking work exceeds the mandate of this chapter. Still, three points of contact and divergence between us merit discussion before I proceed:

(1)   The specific commonality that Fulkerson exposes and elaborates is a post-structural discursivity that determines every woman's subject formation—a messy, complex terrain that reified feminist notions of "women's experience" occludes, and that subsequently produces flawed theological models "grounded" therein. While Fulkerson deconstructs both terms in the concept of women's experience via discourse analysis, I shall anatomize the concept of Woman in different terms, hoping thereby to expand our sense of its discursivity even more; broadening the conversation, as it were, about the tangled maze of Us and Them such that it will include two other North American religionists (Kathleen Sands and Ellen Armour) and French deconstructionists (Jacques Derrida and Luce Irigaray);

(2)   I also highlight a different discursive commonality—a questionable historical trajectory that feminist/fundamentalist women share, and which the scope of Fulkerson's work (understandably) did not encompass;

(3)   In my view, Fulkerson glosses over a haunting material consequence of this (fundamentalist) discursivity that begs attention (though no resolution). She is right that feminist academicians must not decontextualise conservative Christian women's beliefs from the "discursive networks" that compose their subjectivity, and, conversely, that whatever portraits of them I create below remain just that: products of a very privileged social location whose "certifying discourses" define hegemonic knowledges, values, and "realities."[10] Eschewing such professional elitism as much as possible, Fulkerson skillfully reframes Pentecostal and Presbyterian women's rhetorics of submission-dependence and ministries as paradoxically "emancipatory openings" and "liberating possibilities" that are actually not so "alien" to liberation feminist ideals.[11] And yet, within fundamentalist/Pentecostal (and many Presbyterian) families and communities, gay sons and lesbian daughters are often violently ostracized such that I would be less inclined to conclude that, for example, Pentecostal circles constitute "place[s] of God-sustained integrity."[12] While conservative Christian women do exercise some resistance within their respective "discourses of self-production," effecting exemplary "world transformation or "joyful speaking for God,"[13] daughters', sisters', and mothers' sexual orientation remains coercively heterosexual. "Rules" are not "transgressed" in this "register"—"faith performances" seem more destructive than "graciously productive."[14] The political, juridical, and legislative clout of today's Religious Right, moreover, intensifies my nagging concern for what might otherwise be understood as localized clashes between resistant and canonical scriptural reading regimes and the sexual ethics that they inform.

This is why tragedy is such a crucial interpretive lens. Estrangements, the "otherings" of sister from sister are not solely extramural; family values excoriate family ties, internecine Others are created and expelled, in the name of a purer, more godly flourishing. This is also "the work that belief does."[15] And thus, I identify another correlative elision in Fulkerson's portraits that my own paper expounds: while she would chide feminist theologians to recognize that we always produce the Others whom we assess, and hence these others and our evaluations of them will always be flawed and perniciously "domesticated," it must be acknowledged that the Others' "otherings" of us equally distort, domesticate, even demonize.[16] If feminist discourses produce fundamentalists, theirs produce "us." Fulkerson's prescribed double hermeneutic of generosity toward the Other and suspicion toward our own canonical discourses begs reciprocation. (Indeed, I suspect that she would not disagree here, for she consistently attends to the steady tension between Pentecostal and Presbyterian women's simultaneous "resistance yet repetition"[17] of an oppressively gendered status quo.)

In sum, where Fulkerson's guiding theo-ethical thematic is feminist theology's "liberating commitment to the other," mine is the doggedly tragic nature thereof.[18] This complement serves merely to create even more complex understandings of why our originary dreams of radical inclusivity remain just that. I want to tune even more finely our sense "that we have no access to the real [or to some 'real' other] outside of our power-laden constructions."[19] I seek not to criticize but to further the realization of her objectives by treating more dystopic intersections between feminists and fundamentalists. Persons-as-texts commit intertextual brutalities that scar, haunt, and traumatize; actual lives, however discursively produced, are maimed. We need even more sophisticated interpretive grids to accommodate these side effects of godly desire. In this paper then I simply supply a few more conversation partners' analytical tools with which to minimize "the possibilities of will-to-power in any concrete practice" that is allegedly motivated by agape,[20] a project that Fulkerson's superb reappraisals have already initiated. To do so (after a brief yet necessary definitional excursus on the slippery term "fundamentalism"), I shall enter this hermeneutic circle at the particularly equivocal site mentioned above: ambiguous vignettes of women flourishing within fundamentalist congregations.

Terminological Excursus

According to Brenda Brasher, more recent scholars find it helpful to classify fundamentalists chronologically, making distinctions between an originally separatist form of "first-wave" fundamentalism, and a second, more culturally integrative wave.[21] Despite this newer defensive/offensive categorization, second-wave fundamentalists still subscribe to the classic, five "fundamentals" (est. 1895) that distinguish this brand of Christian conservatism from others, namely: (1) biblical inerrancy, (2) the virgin birth, (3) the doctrine of substitutionary atonement, (4) the bodily resurrection, and (5) physical return of Christ.[22] Despite the perdurance of these canonical rubrics in second-wave fundamentalism, the specific theological content and relative value of these five tenets varies from individual to individual and congregation to congregation. Such variety makes previously clear distinctions between fundamentalists and conservative evangelical Protestants more difficult to establish. The second wave still rides the first in its members' widespread insistence upon compulsory heterosexuality, sex-segregated ministries within churches, and a mistrust of public education systems. (Fundamentalists prefer instead to homeschool or send their children to private Christian schools.[23])

Further terminological confusion arises from recent classificatory hybrids; unlike their predecessors, researchers today apply the fundamentalist rubric more broadly by grouping together previously separate conservative Protestant denominations—Pentecostals, Fundamentalists, Baptists—for research purposes. Latitude is in fact warranted here precisely because second-wave fundamentalist religiosity is often an amalgam of fundamentalist beliefs and previously taboo Pentecostal "threads."[24] I have adopted this broader application of the term because extant analyses of *women* in Christian fundamentalism similarly draw and pool research findings from Pentecostal and Baptist congregations.[25] Adoption of this more generic, second-wave definition within a feminist re-vision of Christian fundamentalist women can be further defended because there exists a noticeable cross-denominational uniformity within conservative evangelicalism in not only the androcentric roles imposed upon conservative evangelical women, but also in fundamentalist/Baptist/Pentecostal women's own self-perceptions.[26]

Along with its assimilation of Pentecostal elements, second-wave fundamentalists (unlike their more reactionary antecedents) have adapted modern musical, psychological, and political trends and popular media to minister and proselytize more effectively.[27] Today's fundamentalists have harnessed, for example, rhetoric and techniques from the secular "self-help" movement. The latter's tamer brands of self-transformation have catalyzed a new, improved "relationship Christianity," alternately dubbed an "experiential" fundamentalism (a type of personal religiosity that of course has more mainstream *theological* roots within evangelical Protestantism).[28] Also in response to wider cultural trends, more culturally conversant second-wave fundamentalists fund and mount expensive political and legal campaigns to oppose (among other things) perceived threats to the nuclear family (e.g., gay rights and abortion laws). These engagements with mainstream secular trends have even led some ethnographers to categorize many of the new fundamentalist churches springing up across North America as new religious/Christian movements, indicating here again that such current assimilative strains should not be treated unilaterally as "direct descendants" of first-wave fundamentalism.[29]

It is precisely this second-wave's positive and negative dialogue with secular society that has produced some of the more *concrete* proximities between fundamentalist and feminist women discussed below. Ironically, fundamentalist women's domestic and public power has grown and diversified (in ways inconceivable to their first-wave forebears) due to ripple effects from the Women's Movement.[30] That said, fundamentalists transhistorically regard men and women as two ontologically distinct groups with different, divinely ordained life purposes.[31] It is to this paradox of fundamentalist women's 'liberation' and the feminist/fundamentalist commonalities that it produces, that I now turn.

Part One
Actual Agency and Questionable Histories: Unlikely Common Ground

A recent volume on *Women in 20ᵗʰ Century Protestantism* offers ample evidence of fundamentalist women's: (1) spiritual authority, (2) financial clout, (3) tactical rebelliousness, (4) administrative expertise, and (5) humanitarian leadership. For example:

1. **Spiritual Authority:** Nationwide within the Pentecostal Assemblies of God, both Latina and Anglo-American women can be ordained. This is also the case within the even more conservative Apostolic Assembly, at least its Afro- and Anglo-American (though *not* Latino) districts. (Women's tenure of higher administrative and pastoral offices, however, remains almost entirely forbidden.[32]) Should certain Pentecostal churches still refuse to hire these women ministers, the latter simply found their own churches.[33] Determined, resourceful, and thwarting sexist opposition, these spiritual leaders realize their vocations in ways that prompt some scholars to question not only the usefulness of normative theoretical distinctions between "subversive" and "co-opted" female subjectivity,[34] but also the cogency of institutional distinctions between, for example, "liberal mainline" and "conservative evangelical" denominations).[35] Religionist Gastòn Espinosa prefers to reframe these ministries of Latina, Afro- and Anglo-American preachers as forms of "paradoxical domesticity" in which women are "end-times prophetesses in the public sphere and devoted mothers and good wives in the private sphere of the home."[36] Analyzing the "faith performances" of women within Church of God Pentecostal communities in the mountains of Virginia, Fulkerson reaches similar conclusions. The "calls stories" that authorize Pentecostal women to minister, testify, and preach are characterized by a "discourse of submission and dependence, [with which] paradoxically, they construct a place of honour outside the home for themselves.... To have a call story is to resist criticism by claiming the ultimate authority for one's practices—God. It is also ... to 'rescript' one's life in a radical way. It is to craft a calling that allows a woman the freedom to travel and lead and to be the object of holy envy."[37] At the same time, these Pentecostal women still affirm "women's place" as that of nurturing "children and husbands," and they endorse the canonical discursive tradition of their milieu that chides women to be "passive and meek homebodies who keep silent and powerless." (Fulkerson

observes the same contradictions permeating the "affective performances" of preaching and testifying that these women's preliminary call stories generate.[38])

2. Financial Clout: While forbidden ordination, in the sex-segregated missionary organizations of both Latino Pentecostal and Southern Baptist churches, women nevertheless wield enormous financial power. For example, the Latina Ladies' Auxiliary is the church's "main fund-raising organization," without which both their wider missionary coalitions and the church's expansion through new "plantings" would collapse.[39] In this "paradoxical space," *and* in that of the Southern Baptist Women's Missionary Union (WMU), fundamentalist women's "organizational acumen" creates financial systems "that put to shame the haphazard ways in which men manage denominational funds."[40] Like the fundamentalist women-preachers above, these financial wizards defy analytical categories by being "evangelical in theology, implicitly feminist in some of their actions, yet also accepting of the self-sacrificial rhetoric of their foremothers."[41] Moreover, because the WMU women actively but subtly oppose the "stridently fundamentalist leadership" that now characterizes the Southern Baptist Executive, historian Paul Harvey concludes that they occupy an analytical terrain somewhere *between* fundamentalist and feminist.[42]

Despite such evidence of "feminist" tendencies, Espinosa and Harvey observe that no women preachers or missionary executives regard the feminist movement as a desirable source of inspiration or solidarity when they choose to initiate changes in their particular patriarchal status quo. Here, reverse stereotyping surfaces; the Pentecostal women whom Espinosa interviewed found feminism "too radical, pushy, tied to the gay movement, and a luxury that their working class schedules could not afford."[43] To these and other fundamentalist women, a more rudimentary liberation from private sin, coupled with currently authorized ministerial freedoms, provide a fullness of life imperceptible to "patronizing and condescending" feminists.[44] Espinosa therefore urges feminists to redefine liberation in more generous, respectful terms: "If we take seriously how most Latina Pentecostal women perceive themselves, then they are by their own account 'liberated' and 'empowered.' There are clear limitations to their 'freedom in Christ,' but the stories of Latina clergy ... and many others challenge conventional interpretations of women and religion, historical agency, and what it means to be a truly liberated woman."[45]

3. Strategies of Resistance: Evoking another confusing hybrid of fundamentalist/feminist ideals, a former director of the WMU defended the "controversial" ties that the WMU has established with the Southern Baptist women's ordination coalition (SBWIM) in words that evoke an ethos similar to Sharon Welch's feminist "ethic of risk," the latter an alternative that Welch proposes to those ethical models that promote absolute, permanent resolutions of moral dilemmas and social injustices: in a parallel strategy, rather than seeking total control over their vocational options, Southern Baptist women choose to forge what Welch (in other contexts) would term "matrices of further resistance"—building long-term countervailing future reserves that will ensure subsequent Baptist women's continued vocational growth.[46] Through the WMU's quiet support of and contact with the SBWIM, these women "till the ground for future generations of theologically trained women" even as they safeguard "the continued existence of a variety of ministries for women."[47] In this gently defiant capacity they regard themselves as "effectual ministers" even though they are not ordained. Seconding this ethical preference of risk over that of definitive control, WMU member Alma Hunt argues: "Don't think we're not progressive. We're just not militant."[48] This quasi-ethic of risk, however, remains problematic to feminists in that it is exerted predominantly by affluent, first-world women whose social formation leads them to stay in a sexist regime within an otherwise democratic political system; Welch by contrast emphasizes that an ethic of risk is a long-term strategy indigenously developed by the *oppressed* (and perhaps by some foreigner-activists who *follow* their lead) as a gradual means of undermining the despotism and Western imperialism that plague the two-thirds world.[49] (Here Fulkerson's study of conservative Presbyterian women is helpful in that it explains first-world women's seemingly passive acceptance of subordination within a sexist regime as the result of their lifelong, "learned" (and rewarded) behavior of financial dependence.[50]) Feminists would be inclined to celebrate the more thoroughly marginalized risk-takers in the two-thirds world, and, of course, the myriad *historical* forms of a similar "creativity within constraint"[51] —the politicking, for example, of Hildegard of Bingen, Teresa of Avila, Margery Kempe, or our other anonymous forebears. These historical and contemporary examples diverge significantly from the resistance efforts mounted by that of relatively free, first-world Christian fundamentalist women. Feminists are discouraged that in far more comfortable, democratic settings, such "paradoxical domesticity" is still so necessary for (not to mention attractive to) certain women; such allegiances preempt deeper structural and theological transformations within the Christian church. Indeed, Harvey is forced to concede that: "The WMU's successes have barely nudged upward the mobility of women in the nation's largest Protestant denomination."[52] Here I must further qualify that Welch conceptualized any first-world engagement in an ethic of risk as entailing a set of renunciatory practices for those who—materially comfortable—might languish in the "luxury" of despair. (This passive resignation sets in when grandiose agendas for sociopolitical change both at home and abroad fail.) Moreover, the primary social ills that this ethic of risk targets differ substantially as well—the far more pressing worldwide threats of nuclear war, mass starvation/poverty, and ecological disasters, all of which Western men and women's rapacious consumption have caused.[53]

4. **Administrative Leadership**: In contradistinction to the above, matrices of resistance are not preconditions that fundamentalist American women need before they can occupy central positions of power in one globally influential "parachurch" empire, namely, Focus on Family; as religionist Colleen McDannell

documents, strong, media-savvy, college-educated women already constitute the main editors, writers, and administrators of the communications division within James Dobson's conservative Christian organization. The magazines, books, pamphlets, video/audiotapes, helplines, and broadcasts that these women produce offer concerned audience members a seemingly sage blend of spiritual inspiration, practical information, and troubleshooting advice about a variety of private and public dilemmas. Their offerings are in fact very close in tone and content to similar secular fare. The crucial difference, of course, lies in a noticeable absence of open discussions of controversial topics such as sexual orientation, abortion, family planning, or women's ordination (polemical aversions, moreover, that strategically ensure the broadest possible Christian subscription base).[54] Yet despite such subtly oppressive censorship, McDannell's study of "Dobsonite" media content, its women administrators' corporate ethos, and its (mostly female) audience responses, leads her to challenge the conventional theory that fundamentalism appeals to women because it promises "'clarity, certitude, and control.'"[55] McDannell foregrounds instead the abundant resources for "relationship and empathy" that this organization's producers and audiences clearly value, desire, and cultivate (qualities, not incidentally that feminism consistently promotes.) For example, rather than responding to the moral dilemmas that Focus on Family's multimedia address with simplistically clear, spiritual panaceas, its programs and publications are careful to acknowledge the long-term persistence, complexity, even unavoidability, that characterize the myriad dysfunctions that fundamentalists and other Christians will suffer.

5. **Humanitarian Initiatives**: The patriarchal divide separating fundamentalist and feminist women can eclipse the common humanitarian causes we initiate. Theologian Anne Gilson identifies mutual fundamentalist/feminist struggles against (though antipodal solutions to): violence in all its forms, drug abuse, unemployment, divorce, the destitution ravaging inner cities, the attendant crises of meaning that all the above provoke, and, most urgently, the devastating effects of these ills upon children's values and comportment.[56] Historically in fact, first-wave fundamentalist women's adherence to their narrowly "proper" places at home and in church actually afforded them more time and energy to devote to social activism (e.g., abolishing racism and improving the welfare of women and children).[57] Similarly, religious ethnographer Brenda Brasher's recent congregational studies attest to second-wave fundamentalist women's continued interest in such first-wave causes. However, in keeping with the fundamentalist "matrices of resistance" discussed above, fundamentalist women and men proselytize the universal efficacy of personal salvation as the most powerful means of social rehabilitation, whereas feminists generally advocate structural reform to mitigate human suffering. The former remain convinced that social ills will slowly diminish as one by one, people the world over submit to God and assume their place in "His" right order (a vital stratum of which is heterosexual family life); this gradual conversion

process, moreover, will evolve through fundamentalists' own structural alternatives—their well-established media, parachurch, and missionary organizations. (With the erosion of church-state separation evidenced in George W. Bush's Faith-Based and Community Initiatives [2001], the promotion of "relationship Christianity" as a remedy to social ills of all kinds has become a mainstream "structural" curative.[58])

I conclude these polyvalent, concrete examples of fundamentalist women's flourishing with additional findings from Brasher's research. Her microanalyses of two fundamentalist congregations in California offer composite portraits of women cultivating all five modes of empowerment, the latter due in large part to the churches' sex-segregated ministries. While these enclaves can be read as suppressing women's wider emancipation, Brasher rereads them as *increasing* many kinds of women's power.[59] Each all-female sphere composes a "church within a church"[60] where women become powerful preachers, financial administrators, and pastoral counselors to each other. Interestingly, Brasher continually noticed that these women's preeminent commitment to a "relationship Christianity" preserves this wide range of agency, precisely because it *effectively limits* the power that their husbands, their male pastors, and a collectively androcentric ecclesiology might otherwise wield over them.[61] (The women members whom Brasher interviews constantly insist that they are invested "in a relationship, not a religion."[62]) Thus to Brasher, an all-female environment combined with a privatistic, christocentric soteriology, in fact substantially "undercuts [the] acquiescence" that scholars typically ascribe to fundamentalist women's religiosity.[63]

Similarly generous in her (re-)appraisal, Brasher reminds her readers that such all-female advocacy groups have been crucial to the feminist movement and its lobbies for institutional change. By their members' own accounts, all-female fundamentalist enclaves both symbolize and physically provide "a haven where [women] … momentarily escape from the dynamics of gender and family life."[64] Brasher even notes that, for some members, these spheres offer welcome refuge from abusive male partners (because of whom women are drawn to fundamentalist family values in the first place); for these women, the combination of relationship-style Christianity and abundant all-female oases, constitute a "safe harbor for the self."[65] Sex-segregated ministries provide rich gynocentric sources of emotional, psychological, and material support such as: "intense religiosity, free child care, free counseling, readily available community, lively music, emotive singing, affordable continuing education and inexpensive weekend retreats."[66] Furthermore, the activities that women animate and enjoy together also maximize women's "freedom" to interpret their individual and collective religious experiences. Like other women's advocacy groups, sex-segregated ministries allow women "to differentiate their interests from men," and "to enhance their strength within their institution" (though Brasher acknowledges that fundamentalist women's power remains "incremental" in the wider benefits that it can precipitate. Nor is the agency that Brasher documents consolidated to effectuate deeper, institutional changes).[67]

As another possible example of fundamentalist/sectarian tactical resistance (#4 above), Brasher observes that, when contentious issues arise, all-female enclaves exert a collective pressure on their wider congregations that constitutes "oppositional opportunities" for women such that they effect intra-congregational reforms.[68] Finally, Brasher's findings confirm that second-wave women's groups also pursue humanitarian goals; the women in these Californian churches are socially active in a variety of missions to orphanages, prisons, and the two-thirds world. In sum, despite her liberal Protestant, feminist roots, Brasher accepts the ineradicable paradox that women within sex-segregated ministries/congregations simultaneously "build and discover" power even as membership therein disempowers them in other ways. As an ethnographer, moreover, she takes these women's own assessments of their strength and initiative/autonomy seriously, and consequently reframes these enclaves as counterevidence that illustrates fundamentalist women's "institutional power" and their own self-fashioned "religious alterity."[69] (Fulkerson's research culminates in similarly humbling "contradictions."[70])

Sins of Omission: Dubious Fundamentalist/Feminist Histories

The above counterexamples of fundamentalist women's agency and flourishing lead scholars to emphasize the more variegated, "diffuse" nature of female activism, and to ask whether, within the history of feminism, we should include, for example, conservative Christian women who reject the feminist "label" yet, from an analytical point of view, continue "acting and thinking in feminist ways."[71] *However*, when these examples are read in light of fundamentalism's history, more specifically, its sociopolitical genesis as a form of patriarchal control, feminism's *historically informed* ethos would recast such positive examples of women's flourishing as a betrayal of our Christian foresisters' struggle for social equality and church reform. And yet, as we shall see, we participate with fundamentalists in an equally troubling historical collusion.

While the rise of Christian fundamentalism in the early twentieth century has been variously framed as a reactionary response to theological and/or cultural changes,[72] historian Betty DeBerg counters that it was more precisely the collapse of Victorian *gender* ideology that fuelled fundamentalism's widespread appeal. Fundamentalist Christianity preserved traditional gender roles for men and women during a time of turbulent, fast-paced societal change. DeBerg assembles a persuasive compendium of graphically patriarchal rhetoric from "popular [fundamentalist] religious press," e.g., "periodical literature and addresses and sermons to large lay audiences," all of which were penned and endorsed by religious leaders, and disseminated within a variety of holiness, revivalist, and evangelical organizations.[73] Seemingly indifferent to these questionable sexist roots, second-wave fundamentalist women perpetuate a form of Protestantism in which, historically, clergy strove to "masculinize" Christianity over against its deleterious "feminization" during the nineteenth century. To do so, church leaders not only used misogynist rhetoric, but also curtailed women's range of public and ecclesial activities. (DeBerg is careful to nuance this claim by acknowledging similar sexist trajectories—though divergent rhetorico-theological strategies—at work within the Social Gospel and other liberal protestant denominations.)[74] When positive changes for women via divorce law and dress code reforms, and the rise of women's activism for temperance and suffrage, not to mention the later advent of birth control, shook the gendered status quo, fundamentalists even joined ranks with Roman Catholics to promote a newly "divinized home"[75] a so-called "church within a church" maintained by a parental "priesthood." The nuclear family was thus reconsecrated as the Church's very backbone.[76] Despite the interdenominational tenor of this backlash, the fact remains that, among its allies, fundamentalism was the "most widely accessible" and "unusually popular" countermovement to women's liberation, be it inside or outside the church.[77]

Resituating fundamentalism in this historical critical context, Christian fundamentalist women's current sense of liberation and agency seems at best a deracinated, hence withering blessing. If solidarity is historical—rooted in, indebted to, and honoring our foresisters' dangerous memories—feminists wince when "sisters" endorse a strain of Christianity whose founders demonized not only the *Women's Bible* itself—"that miserable abortion … that is only the impudent utterance of infidelity," but also any brave woman who followed Cady Stanton; the latter, "an awful creature … a reeking lepress." (Any such lepers, it was held, would have "to be washed, and for three weeks to be soaked in carbolic acid, and for a whole year fumigated, before [being] … fit for decent society."[78]) Of course, today's second-wave fundamentalist women might replace their forebears' vitriol with more enlightened adjudications—hating the sin while loving the sinner; or, simply dismiss feminists' *historical* "fundamentalism" as an academic digression from the real-world urgencies of both global evangelism and saving the nuclear family from extinction. This camp's preferred historical foundations lie elsewhere—in biblical revelations tightly framed by five fundamentals, and these canonical discourses invite no parsing of androcentric silences, no critique of the bastardized love-patriarchalism so central to their immaculate domestic and cosmic orders. Indeed, the feminist/fundamentalist impasse can be read as the bilateral continuation of Christian origins and distortions; fundamentalist women support the Greco-Roman household code prescriptions that Christianity absorbed—a trajectory that gained strength then as now precisely by preserving and conforming to wider socio-hierarchical structures. By contrast, feminist Christians seek to restore the Jesus movement's discipleship of equals.[79]

Ironically, it can even be argued that such fundamentalist ahistoricism, with its suppression of women's dangerous memories is *anti*traditionalist as it constitutes a breach of Christianity's originarily self-critical ethos; Rosemary Radford Ruether elaborates the latter in her response to Daphne Hampson's rejection of the entire project of feminist theology. Ruether insists upon Christianity's assertion of an essentially living, *revisionary* tradition: "from its beginnings, [Christianity] has gone about manufacturing new interpretations of its message that responded to new exigencies and world views and which had only very partial justification in Scripture."[80] *Contra* Christian fundamentalists, revelation was never conceptualized as static, past, and, therefore, unreformable. Rather, "the closed canon of the rabbinic authorities" was disputed, and an attentiveness to the Spirit's ongoing revelations in "contemporary religious experience" was promoted.[81] Here, Ruether argues, the Bible itself constitutes a revelatory prototype: "What Christians inherit as the Bible is two libraries of writings which testify to a process of continual revision in which past ideas and norms are challenged and revised."[82]

This historicist objection to fundamentalist women's myopia, however, can backfire; African-American womanist scholars (as well as feminist theorists like Elizabeth Spelman and Ellen Armour) have shown that a shared *racist* history indicts both feminist and fundamentalist concepts of Woman.[83] On the one hand, the nineteenth-century cult of true womanhood that fundamentalist women keep alive perpetuates a form of femininity that was defined in conscious opposition to black "non-women" who were simply property—instinct-driven (sex) slaves or workhorse Mammies.[84] On the other hand, *feminist* "emancipatory" notions of woman have not escaped these racist tenets, not even the more recent, sophisticated configurations of woman in terms of "multiplicity" and "embodiment"; while obviously critical of the cult of true womanhood, and diverging sharply from it, feminist theory rarely if ever denounces Victorian ideology's *racist* undertow. It remains uncritical therefore of this cult's *doubly* oppressive effects upon women of color. Through its own racial (in)difference, whitefeminism actually perpetuates this Victorian cult's tacit legacy. "The subject of whitefeminism is [reprehensibly] inscribed by the history of raced woman."[85] Despite this complicity, and contra feminists' radically inclusive mandate, whitefeminist reflections seldom begin with expositions of feminism's own genesis within this tangled, racist double bind. Nor do feminists prescribe a hyper-vigilance toward this twofold aporia as the prerequisite and working litmus test for constructing any notions of Woman and her full-flourishing. In its sins of omission, feminism shares more with Victorian gender ideology (and its fundamentalist champions) than it realizes.

Having produced jarring proximities between fundamentalist and feminist Christian women—sketching the former's quasi-feminist tendencies, and both camps' racist "apostasy"—I turn now to their common *theoretical*, and equally questionable, roots, namely, their variant logics of mastery and identity-thinking. I begin with an essentializing fundamentalist pattern of thought and then proceed to feminists' similarly erroneous ideals.

Part Two
Shared Theoretical Fundamentals: Erotics of Mastery and Sameness

Fundamentalist Ideological Clarity and Mastery

Undergirding fundamentalist biblicism and ahistoricism lies what sociologist Linda Kintz terms "an ideology of clarity." Sustaining this common-sense ideology, and particularly relevant to this exploration of the fundamentalist/feminist divide, is the prominence within this meaning system of the icon of Woman as Mother. The latter occupies a central place in both fundamentalists' "Russian Doll logic" and its resultant cosmology. Thus Kintz describes the latter as follows:

> Nested within each other like Russian dolls … elements of this [religio-] symbolic structure rise from the womb to the heavens, uniting God as Creator, the family, a divinely inspired Declaration of Independence and U.S. Constitution, a nation defined as God's unique experiment in human history, a belief that the unregulated free market is inherent in human nature, and a claim that the United States has a God-given responsibility to spread free-market democratic capitalism to the rest of the world. At both the beginning and the end of this clear narrative, God's judgment seals a circular logic of *God, family, mother, nation, and global duty* within a Judeo-Christian Book of the World made coherent from top to bottom, from beginning to end.[86]

Kintz's symptomatic reading of the maternal rhetoric central to this "Judeo-Christian Book of the World" is in fact a vivid illustration of the reductionism that such a worldview engenders. Within a rhetorical trajectory that starts with Phyllis Schlafly's 1964 homology of communism, moral degeneracy, and government spending,[87] and which continues up to Beverley LaHaye's 1984 baptism of American (and Brazilian) mothers as emblematic, anticommunist warriors, Kintz chronicles the Religious Right's reduction of complex socioeconomic problems to basic wars between Christian goods and secular evils. More specifically, Kintz foregrounds the "maternal" instrumentality that produces and anchors such ideological clarity. For example, in LaHaye's assessment of the rise of communism in 1960s Brazil, she concludes that, if a group of outraged Christian mothers managed to derail this left-wing onslaught and thus rescue their families from eternal perdition, these mothers raised the bar for later generations of American mothers, who, like them, must defeat, not only communism, but also its demonic offspring—humanism and feminism. (Humanism, according to LaHaye "is really nothing else but Marxism.")[88] This maternal rhetorical trajectory peaks in both Schlafly and LaHaye's attacks upon the ("obviously" communist-inspired) ERA. Both women vilify the ERA's diverse mandate for social reforms as inviting totalistariansim; LaHaye, for example, calls the November 1977 National Women's Conference a "Marxist/lesbian circus ... manipulated and controlled from the beginning by a dissident group of feminists who were demanding federal intervention into our lives."[89] In each case, these politically active right-wing women enlist maternal/ anticommunist rhetoric to sanctify via a literally and figuratively "proper motherly face" the Religious Right's political crusades against such heathen "invasions." Additionally, argues Kintz, motherhood's powerful "symbolic resonance" sanctions an otherwise suspect entry of Christian homemakers into the public sphere as protestors and activists; these forays are positively framed as public displays of riled maternal instincts. (LaHaye invokes "lionesses fighting to the death," and "docile mother dogs" who naturally turn vicious when the safety of their respective prides and litters are threatened.[90]) Milking a collective affinity for such symbolic, maternal charms, LaHaye and Schlafly erase the complexities of American and/or Brazilian political landscapes for their Christian audiences, the latter openly receptive to such domino causalities and the no-nonsense solutions that these female critics provide.[91] Odd, however, that such mandatory clarity rests on a maze of contradictions. So Kintz: "Femininity is here both appealed to and denied ... in a double and contradictory configuration whose instability helps feed the machinery of paranoia. In this configuration, strong conservative women have the capacity to embody the omnipotent mother while at the same time denying feminist claims to female agency. They can, in other words, act exactly like a feminist while condemning feminism."[92]

Contradictions also beset fundamentalists' well-known acts and exhortations of complete surrender to God. These classic tropes and conversion tales veil idolizations of absolute power and mastery. In developing her feminist ethic of risk, Sharon Welch has observed that "doctrines of the sovereignty and omnipotence of God are meant to relativise human claims to power" by reminding human beings of their finitude and "dependence on God." However, beneath such divine-human distinctions lies the tacit assumption that "absolute power can be a good." This Christian tradition contradicts itself therefore by claiming that "one does not attribute demonic or destructive traits to Deity," yet simultaneously ascribing to God an absolute power which "*is* a destructive trait."[93] Here then, the drive for clarity that Kintz illustrates finds its corollary in the worship of power-as-dominion that Welch identifies. This symbiosis allows people in positions of power to legitimate abuses thereof by rationalizing them as simply the fulfillment of commands by devout "slaves to the Lord" or "agents of a higher power."[94]

I have enlisted Kintz and Welch's rhetorical studies, and their attendant illumination of idolatrous, theological, and political love affairs with power-as-domination to expose toxic, gendered "structural necessities" at work in fundamentalist theology and fundamentalist women's self-perception: fundamentalists' ideology of clarity, and the maternal rhetoric sustaining it, are fuelled by a decidedly nonfeminist "erotics of domination."[95] This erotics of power and mastery—so central to fundamentalist discourse—arguably (perhaps definitively) belies any reading of fundamentalist women's incremental acts of resistance and reform as exempla of "risk ethics" in action. And yet, feminist ideals exhibit symptoms of similar erotics.

Feminist Desires for Resolution and Mastery

While feminist thea/ologians may have discarded both fundamentalist and liberal images of an almighty ruler God, revalorizing instead embodied finitude and interdependence, subtler absolutes still preside over feminist theo/alogical meaning systems. Religionist Kathleen Sands elucidates these in her *Escape from Paradise: Evil and Tragedy in Feminist Theology*. Feminists still appeal to transcendent notions of "Justice," or radically immanent ideals of humanity's originary "primal wholeness," and they envision parousial restorations thereof.[96] Sands objects, however, that these (albeit more concrete) ultimate truths and concerns deny, and therefore inadequately respond to, our current, irredeemably tragic context: "At heart, tragedy is the moral paradox that beings who want goodness cannot remain uncontaminated by evil, that even faultedness belongs to the enigma of suffering.... The religious and moral risk of tragic consciousness ... is to encounter elemental power/truth in its radical plurality, unmooring the good from any metaphysical anchor, so that it becomes an entirely human, entirely fragile creation."[97] Sands asks feminist thea/ologians to portray more honestly this terminally *unclear*, "messy" reality: "In this tangled world [of conflicting truths and goods] the religious reflection of women, like that of men, can draw more wisdom from the living functions and clashes of community than from pure Ideas or Ideals."[98]

To illustrate, Sands challenges the ideological clear-cutting of Rosemary Radford Ruether and Carol Christ. On the one hand, much like her masculinist antecedents, Ruether still conceptualizes evil and sin as privative forms of injustice; evil is "nothing more than alienation from authentic being."[99] This worldview reflects an "anti-tragic" ideology of clarity that still relies upon an absolute transcendent Good, now in the form of Justice. Thus in Ruether's *Gaia and God*, Justice becomes "the ground and potential of life."[100] Ruether asserts an indestructible "depth of our being" that may be "distorted and suppressed but never corrupted."[101] Sands questions the credibility of this quintessential universal in our postmodern world, because Sands has observed that within the myriad injustices that women may suffer, there remains the very real possibility (and actuality) that some of them will be so severely brutalized that no salvageable, life-affirming "essence" survives. (Sands cites *Sophie's Choice* as an illustration of such "extreme circumstances," and as one depiction of our ineradicable, "tragic vulnerability."[102])

Turning to the thought of thealogian Carol Christ (who again shares more with her masculinist antecedents than she recognizes), Sands points out that the latter constructs a dualistic worldview in which clear and present Truths remain perceptible within a cosmic arena of good and bad elemental energies; here, however, Christ replaces a masculinist, metaphysical Good with a radically immanent Eros. Meaning- and "world"-construction emerge out of a basic perception of Goddess-nature: conflating Goddess, Woman, and Nature, Christ defines "true eros" as "good" and "inherently creative."[103] (Goddess-nature signifies "an immanent unity of the real and the good."[104]) Though Eros as a life force can, Christ admits, be volatile and terrifying, usually this is because its originary goodness is perverted when our "true desires" are repressed.[105] For example, the "patriarchal eros of war" (mirrored and condoned by a biblical God) "numbs the soldier's sense of connection with those he kills, rapes, and enslaves."[106] Sands objects, however, that in a pluralistic, tragic world of densely entwined and contradictory truths and goods, one person's erotic distortion is another's authentication: "Can this idealized eros speak to the obvious plasticity of sexuality, which can mold and harden around war, violence, and domination quite as well as around mutuality?"[107] Sands is further troubled by any drive for ideological clarity that would reduce privileged women's complicity in social oppressions to misguided "obstructions of our true desires," or that would "explain" these travesties as simply "the hardened shell of psychic repression."[108] (Sands even detects traces of metaphysical a prioris in Sharon Welch's work, though the latter makes no obvious appeals to "a bank of transcendent Truths."[109])

Following Sands, Kathleen Roberts Skerrett also documents how feminist "Eros theologians" similarly idealize this "power in relation" to such a degree that they ultimately construe some women's legitimate needs to "dis-connect" from each other as sisterly betrayals. In response to such distancing acts, the supposedly more erotically-attuned sister can sanctify her own, forceful violation of such "misguided" disconnections as a practice of "compassion."[110] In sum, this brief engagement of Sands and Skerrett is meant to expose the humbling irony that feminists, albeit in the name of all women's flourishing, are not immune to the erotics of mastery and coerced/coercive lucidities that seemed exclusive to fundamentalist logic and theologizing.

I perceive another thematic variation on such erotics of domination in feminist polemics: we often relinquish our "lost" fundamentalist sisters to focus collective energies on those in dire need. While this may indeed be a necessary "evil" (symptomatic, moreover, of our tragic context), the by-product of such triage is an objectification of these women as mere analytical curiosities, a dehumanization antithetical to feminist goals of radical inclusivity and respect for difference. Here Fulkerson's meticulous, poststructural anatomy of humanity's ineluctable, often misleading discursive production of the self and its Others is invaluable. So too is Jessica Benjamin's now classic psychoanalytic portraits of intersubjective drives for mastery, as it chastens any dismissive cynicism toward fundamentalist women (and vice versa). In her analysis, Benjamin targets the reciprocal erotics in which a "false differentiation" between self and other prevails—where "the other" is always constructed "as object."[111] Admittedly, within the fundamaentalist/feminist impasse that I am addressing, the "othering" erotics of domination takes the parochial form of dueling superiority complexes. Nonetheless, this feud fuels the broader, more dangerous erasure of that ethically constructive ambiguity that, for Kintz and Rose we recall, is so vital to actualizing democratic, egalitarian goals. Given these graver repercussions, therefore, I maintain that Benjamin's critique of domination, and to be sure, that of Welch above, can be extended to include a hyper-vigilance over even these more minor battles for moral high ground. (Again I must qualify that Welch's exposure of Christian glorifications of mastery are meant to support her global concern for the poor, *not* to referee the bourgeois in-fighting I am raising here.)

In short, feminist quests for clarity and mastery via theoretical absolutes, along with cynical dismissals of the Other (by both parties) belie seal-tight distinctions between Christian fundamentalist and feminist women. Kintz on the one hand takes seriously "the yearning for solace" that engenders the Religious Right's ideology of clarity, but insists that human aversion to ambiguity, and "superrational" resolutions of the same, actually impede democratic processes (even though such simplistic logic is meant to secure fundamentalist versions thereof).[112] On the other hand, in her reassessment of *feminist* theologians' methods and ideals, Sands remains sympathetic to the latter's passion for justice and holistic reconciliations, yet she ultimately opts for those "non-ideal" lifelines that our limited, because tragically ambiguous, meaning systems can proffer. She directs those who dare "to stand over the cracks of intelligibility and there to think, to position oneself where values collide and there to discern."[113] It is precisely this discomfiting position that the reflections herein are meant to endorse. It would thus be helpful in my view to reframe the fundamentalist/feminist divide as a tragic locus of reflection—an option I shall explore more fully in my conclusion. Before further engagement of Sands' tragic heuristic, however, I would like to straddle another theoretical fault-line uniting fundamentalist/feminist women. To do so, I enlist a recent critique of feminist thea/ologies by Ellen Armour.

The Shared Fundamentalist/Feminist Economy of Sameness

Here the hermeneutic circle turns vicious. In *Deconstruction, Feminist Theology, and the Problem of Difference: Subverting the Race/Gender Divide*, Armour maps in detail feminist theory's "ungrounded ground" to explain how—even when theorists reconstruct Woman in terms of multiplicity and difference—the originary shaping of gender identity by *race* is still ignored. Engaging the critical insights of Jacques Derrida, Luce Irigaray, and African American womanist scholars, Armour locates the deeper roots of this methodological aporia in "the structural necessities that shape ... lines of investigation and argumentation" throughout Western discourses.[114] Armour adopts and adapts key insights from Derrida and Irigaray, then chastens these with African American critiques of Western thinkers' racial blindness, in order to problematize the reified interpretive filter that the race/gender divide has become; Armour then exposes the flawed models of female subjectivity that this divide produces. Her destabilization of this dichotomy, and the positive and negative conceptual grist that issues from such deconstruction, model conceptual, and interpretive strategies for rereading the fundamentalist/feminist divide with similar depth, nuance, and precision. (Armour's clear and careful expositions of Derrida and Irigaray's thought further expedite such revisions.) A very modest summary of Armour's "derridean" solicitations, I submit, will unearth shared bedrock assumptions supporting both fundamentalist and feminist meaning systems. Additionally, Armour's supplementation of Derrida, with critical counterpoints from Irigaray, will exhume a very eccentric Woman inhabiting *both* sides of the divide, despite her repeated burial beneath the divergent interpretive frameworks that both fundamentalist and feminist camps construct.

First and foremost, Armour enlists Derrida's retrieval of the ungrounded ground upon which Western meaning systems build coherent, noncontradictory, quintessential Truths.[115] Their foundations are in fact highly unstable. Such truths are composed of webs of interlocking texts and contexts. The fleeting, shape-shifting, momentary interconnections made within this web are erroneously reframed as metaphysical essences, presences, and meaning-full disclosures.[116] Use of the basic Western binary epistemological divisions—identity and difference—that institute a hegemonic logic and economy of sameness thus eclipse an otherwise messy, intransigent *différance*. This "economy of sameness" is bolstered by a metaphorical set of mirrors. For example: philosophy and theology purport to "reflect" reality; human nature (as *imago dei*) reflects the divine (albeit imperfectly); the material "mirrors" the ideal; finally, and by literal contrast, *negative* mirror images (woman as not-man, other as not-self) also reflect sameness in light of difference.

Mistrustful of these "smooth surfaces,"[117] Derrida demonstrates that meaning and identity are really produced out of constantly unfolding, deeply interdependent chains of texts and contexts. Hard and fast, absolute truths are really evanescent, perceptual sums—fleeting "trace" compositions and decompositions that evaporate, much like (purportedly "soul-ful") melodies spun through space and time. As such, and contrary to Western assertions of meaning's plenitude, these "fundamentals" are by their very nature neither present nor absent. This common "ether" (Armour's metaphor) from which truths and goods emerge boasts no plenary origin or fulfillment. In actuality, the "general text" exudes a thoroughgoing "undecidability" that our inevitable and constant interpretive decision-making channels in not so neutral or objective directions. Consequently, an economy of sameness and full presence is a misnomer; for its hidden "DNA"—*différance*—"does not exist, properly speaking," as Armour explains: "we 'know' it only through the traces it leaves in the effects it produces. It is never fully present to itself (How can difference as such be fully present?), and its (non)presence defers the full presence of what it originates."[118] Any *a prioris* that we assert paper over this "non-originary origin."[119] The facticity of such primal ambiguities need not be bleak, however. That *"il n'y a pas de hors-texte"* does not destroy meaning itself. The economy of *différance* does not destroy these meaning-making "mainframes." Contrary to popular belief, this deconstructive quest for more honest foundations "does not result in a collapse into a [nihilistic] black hole," as Armour elucidates: "Undecidability is not indeterminacy.... *Stable* meaning is differed/deferred. This situation is hardly synonymous with saying meaning is impossible. While this instability can seem to be an affliction, one must recognize that it is also definitive and productive. Without instability, there would be no truth or meaning."[120] Derrida and those who enlist his strategies appreciate the great irony haunting his textual interventions within Western metaphysics and psychoanalysis; he accepts the necessity of theorizing (however counterintuitively) within a "metaphysics of presence." Within these constraints, however, he strives to imagine other economies or at least some intimations of a "radical alterity."[121] Indeed, his "solicitations" are precisely meant to identify, and thereby undermine to some degree, the daunting obstacles that prevent metaphysics from thinking critically about itself.[122]

Applying this self-critique allows Armour to dismantle the theoretical hegemony of the race/gender divide, and, on the basis of the derridean nonfoundations that she uncovers, she argues for their *concurrent* trace compositions of female (and male) subjectivity. I submit that the same diagnostics that Armour uses to understand and correct feminist theory's racial (in)difference elucidates the infrastructure common to fundamentalist/feminist notions of Woman. The most basic example of these specular dynamics is the division of fundamentalist from feminist, for this boundary is in fact the shared site of common "exclusionary gestures"— insider/outsider, same/other, true/false, liberated woman/not-liberated woman. Such binary oppositions are the world- or meaning-making apparatuses intrinsic to the broader Western economy of sameness in which fundamentalist and feminist women participate. Neither group escapes the "general text," that "ether" as Armour calls it, "in which all western institutions—the family, the economy ... the political sphere, the church, the academy—are embedded and spoken."[123] Each camp's deceptively "full" presences and transcendent truths are really a sum of "in-betweens." That is to say, fundamentalist and feminist methods, and their respective notions of Woman similarly rely upon "the 'difference-between' ... various mirrors in order to function."[124] This dynamic of in-betweens "defers wholeness and plenitude of meaning indefinitely."[125] In derridean terms, fundamentalist/feminist meaning construction (e.g., definitions of Woman and "her" liberation) really occurs within a "trace" economy of "differences-between," also know as *différance*. This specular economy is the shared lifeblood, the most unlikely proximity, between both fundamentalist and feminist ideals and identities. This fundamental "ether" sustains both fundamentalist and feminist worldviews. Our variant drives for harmonic resolutions, criticized above, also point to this economy and its logics of mastery, clarity, and meaningful closure.

In the case of feminist and womanist meaning construction (Armour's thematic focus), deconstruction is definitive and productive insofar as it offers "new" resources for (de)constructing more emancipatory notions of divinity. For example, a God configured by the "play" of *différance* can challenge the hegemony of an eternal, omnipotent, omnipresent "guarantor of truth." This same hegemonic God dogs the topic at hand; as discussed above, Kintz limns the oppressive spin-off, that Judeo-Christian Book of the World that this Father God engenders.[126]

Given that deconstruction "render[s] legible the chains of intertextuality that constitute reading and writing,"[127] not to mention those that compose all of our conceptual notions of subjectivity, this recontextualisation of fundamentalist and feminist theologies within an economy of *différance* exposes our shared theoretical fragility. It thus thwarts any claims by either camp to higher methodological or teleological ground. (It is with a similar poststructuralist discourse analysis that Fulkerson challenges feminist theologians' standard readings of conservative Christian women as univocally oppressed or liberated.[128]) Displacing the hegemonic economy of sameness with this economy of *différance* shakes the most foundational tenets of both fundmentalist/feminist meaning systems. On the one hand, as I elaborate below, the ripple effects of this trace economy disqualify what I view as fundamentalist "prefaces" to the Bible. It is precisely this fivefold preface, and the "canonical reading regime" that it produces that are (of necessity) less central to Fulkerson's *positive* reassessments of certain Pentecostal women's emancipatory practices. The following critique of fundamentalism's mandatory scriptural prefaces thus serves a subordinate purpose in that it challenges Fulkerson's more benign portrait of Pentecostal women's resistant reading practices.[129] Such resistance in my view is very selectively applied; the interpretation of Leviticus 18, for example, is decidedly non-negotiable—its timeless, unilateral meaning enforced by the third fundamental of biblical inerrancy.

On the other hand, we shall then turn to the equally problematic *feminist* theological economy of sameness when we see how *différance* destabilises even the most sophisticated, radically inclusive feminist notions of Woman (as Armour herself scrupulously details). I shall thus briefly elucidate these two respective blindspots before refiguring Woman both across the divide, and in light of these chastening aporia.

Full-Fathomed Five: Fundamentalist Mirrors and Prefaces

Denying the archly contextual, ungrounded ground that Derrida and others reveal, fundamentalists devise their own set of mirrors, a specular trajectory, that will "block" undesirable, theological "chains of signification."[130] They do so by prefacing biblical texts with doctrinal fundamentals. In my view, these coordinates mime the dynamics that Derrida famously explores in his account of literary prefaces' unintended disruption of books' supposedly self-contained meanings. Derrida perceives similarly futile quests for identity, closure, and mastery driving medieval writers who composed encyclopedias. Armour has enlisted these same derridean exposés of encyclopedic and prefatorial logic to subvert the race/gender divide.[131] These precedents in turn exhibit the same self-defeating tactics of fundamentalist "prefaces" to the Bible. To explain:

Long before modern fundamentalists, medieval encyclopedists were key progenitors of "Russian-doll logic." As Derrida notes and Armour reprises, to medieval thinkers, God—the Ground of all Truth, and the perfect Unity of knower and known—is the Author of the Book of Nature. Nature, in turn, is "the central [cosmic] speculum in the divine economy," given that its "ordered unity mirrors the mind of the supremely intelligent being behind it." By writing "a universal Book," medieval encyclopedists could emulate their masterful author-God. They would create thereby "a second set of mirrors," that mirrored the cosmos that itself mirrored God. Driven by a longing for mastery and identity, these medieval authors brushed divinity's hem through their "complete cataloguing of all that was known about all that existed"[132] I perceive in this elegant medieval circuit(r)y the ancestor of fundamentalists' all-encompassing Judeo-Christian "Book of the World." For its "symbolic structure ris[ing] from the womb to the heavens" forges a more modern necklace of texts whose links—"God, family, mother, nation, and global duty"[133]—radiate, in Armour's words, "the [encyclopedia's] once and for all total disclosure of intelligible content through its sensible form."[134] However, as Derrida points out, and Armour reiterates, the earlier, medieval mirrors were always already cracked: "Encyclopedias are begun but never completed."[135] No book, however voluminous, can completely reflect a perfect, infinite, divine omniscience.

Similar self-sabotaging mechanics characterize the conundrum of literary prefaces. Prefaces, generally written *after* books are completed, are meant to mirror the books' contents by their own specular form and reiterations. They are, therefore, symptoms of "a desire for authorial mastery over the book-as-a-whole."[136] Yet, at the same time, the form and function of prefaces actually disrupt books' alleged plenitude of meaning and self-sufficient closure. Moreover, prefaces provide crucial completions as it were—guidelines and thematic "parameters" for the reader, thereby "protecting" the books' "insides" from any messy "excess in the form of misinterpretations."[137] Yet in this protective capacity, a preface contradicts a book's supposed completeness, and ironically undermines the author's assertions of mastery and control, even as the preface's very composition is meant to ensure the same. In my view, an analogous concurrence of mastery and subversion plagues fundamentalist "prefaces" to the Bible, namely, the prerequisite five fundamentals. These constitute the preface to their biblical Book of supposedly full disclosures. Much like the hegelian prefaces that Derrida discusses, fundamentalists' namesake "guard[s] against excess in the form of misinterpretation."[138] However, at the same time these prefatorial assertions acknowledge a lack, even as they mask and/ or fill it. As a result, this scriptural bodyguard belies the biblical Author's mastery, the latter—even more ironically—utterly crucial to fundamentalists' tenure of biblical inerrancy. While disrupting divine authorial intentions, the five fundamentals also flag human desires for unequivocal self-evident and self-sufficient absolutes, yet ultimately mar their existence. In the case of either divine or human intentionality, "prefaces double back on the aim of completion."[139] On either plane, the Bible's seemingly complete nature (*or* alternatively, its *revelatory* completion of Creation's *natural* mirroring of God) self-destructs, as did the encyclopedists' specular constructions.

In my view, another prefatorial dynamic is at work in fundamentalist discourse. The fundamentalists' "Judeo-Christian Book of the World" outlined by Kintz functions as a *cosmic* preface so to speak; it transposes (or "transcribes") the microcosmic preface-book dynamics to the macrocosm. For, like medievalists before them, this fundamentalist cosmic *imago* enforces *exact* reflections of a divine manuscript so as to preempt messier misinterpretations. Our proleptic world—God, family, mother, nation, global duty—must mirror and preface the Other-world.

But such logic, as Derrida's *différance* unveils, is erroneous. It also seems to me that, the notorious myriad of *divinely authored, contradictory* messages contained within this Bible further ruptures the economy of sameness that it conveys and upholds for fundamentalists. Dispersing its own polysemous "seeds of undecidability" on an ungrounded ground *of the Author's own design*, this sacred text is riddled with seminal slippages that sabotage mere mortals' traditionalist perceptions of its alleged perfection and plenitude of meaning.

Feminism's Solipsistic Economy and Irigaray's Partial "Remedy"

The five fundamentals, I have suggested, are a "graphic" subset of the shaky, because self-contradictory, structural necessities that circumscribe all meaning and interpretation. They flag the site of infinite, irreparable faultlines that Derrida exposes and interrogates for the sake of intellectual probity, and that Armour then enlists to subvert another misleading theoretical dichotomy, the race/gender divide. Turning now to *feminist* methods and ideals, Armour's derridean inquiries can help us to identify other specular masquerades that radically complicate fundamentalist/feminist distinctions. As mentioned earlier, Armour meticulously documents how, with few exceptions, race is usually *added* to feminist constructions of female subjectivity as a kind of subordinate clause, and is rarely treated as an equally formative "vector of power" (Judith Butler's term). Feminist constructions of Woman are thus inherently racist because of this twofold erasure, namely, those "of black women from whitefeminist analysis and of whiteness as a racial mark in need of analysis."[140] Even after swapping liberal notions of atomistic subjectivity for those decentered "in" multiplicity and difference (cf. Irigaray and Butler), these supposedly nonphallocentric, radically inclusive portraits of Woman do not overcome a chronic racial "(in)difference."[141] We learn from this intractable aporia that an "economy of racial sameness [i.e., "white solipsism"] ... continues to circumscribe whitefeminism."[142] To preempt such "additive analysis," and the theoretical erasure of feminsts' own whiteness, Woman must be reconfigured. The "vectors of power" that compose a raced, sexed, gendered Woman must be read together from the very beginning. No single "field of force" can take analytical or ontological precedence over another. Opacity must thus replace the clarity characteristic of feminist beginnings, means, and ends: "Whitefeminism can easily embrace putting man at risk, but has often balked at putting woman at risk as well. But if feminism is to follow its telos of becoming a platform for women in all their diversity, then woman must be put at risk."[143]

To take this (de)constructive risk, Armour consults and critically reworks precedents set by Derrida and Irigaray, both of whom have detected a "differing, deferring" Woman already circulating within the specular economy, more precisely, within the wider economy of *différance*.[144] According to Armour, where Derrida attends to "her" instrumentality in several philosophers' meaning-construction, Irigaray builds upon, criticizes, and extends Derrida's insights to portray this elusive Woman as the very (ungrounded) ground of *all* Western economies. Thus, Irigaray studies the wider "grammar of western culture" (philosophy, psychoanalysis, ethics, and economics)[145] to discover that, as Man's Other, Woman is never granted full subjectivity within this phallogocentric economy even though she is its most vital fuel. She is denied subjective (phallic) "plenitude," yet she is nevertheless continually used as a vital resource and currency for the same. For example, in both the specular economy's concrete transactions and their attendant accounts of physicality, as well as in its more abstract philosophical trajectories, Woman as Mother/*Mater* is conflated with Matter. As such, she becomes a raw, (re)productive material to be mastered by the male subjects whom *Mater* spawns. Later, in another "grammatical" empire, that of psychoanalysis, Woman embodies/reflects a castrated Lack or incompleteness that Man uses for validating his possession of the phallus. Turning then to *economic* discourse, in this field Woman enfleshes and fulfills commodified masculine desires via her inexhaustible exchange values as mother, virgin, whore.[146]

Occupying such confluent, object-positions, yet having no "real" essence (even within this non*postmodern* specular, phallocentric logic), Irigaray is actually heartened by the realization that Woman's non-fixity at least allows her to elude this economy's drives for mastery. Moreover, as Lack, Woman thwarts the economy's drives for consummation in fullness and satiety—plenitude. Irigaray thus reframes this "homelessness," this nonfixity and nonessence as comprising a powerful powerlessness. For, without Woman, Man would have no "othering" mirror for "self-location." And without her Lack, he has no confirmation of his own (phalli-cally defined) plenitude. Hence, in all of the above Western discourses, Woman's multipurpose polyvalence may seem an objectifying liability, but in fact, her unbounded nonpresence—her "resistance to circumscription"—can let loose "a disruptive excess" that prophetically reveals the flimsiness of specular borders and self-enclosed wholes.[147] As shape-shifting expedient, *woman can never be mastered*.[148] This is the rebellious, gynocentric double edge that Irigaray eventually harnesses in her own writing to "jam" the patriarchal sameness of the specular economy, including its hold over our imaginations. By extension, it is *this* "liber-ated" notion of Woman, variously enlisted by Derrida, Irigaray, and Armour to disrupt phallogocentric discourse and its attendant divides, that also lies beneath, and must replace, equally specular fundamentalist/feminist alternatives. Here too, Irigaray's strategic reconfigurations of Woman, and Armour's critical adaptations thereof, can teach us by example to reconfigure woman across the fundamentalist/feminist impasse.

Part Three
Diffuse and Tragic: Refiguring Woman across the Fundamentalist/Feminist Divide

Polyphonically reconfigured by Irigaray, this dispersed, differing Woman both creates and inhabits the fissures in specular discourses, a (non)position that Irigaray, for one, exploits to devise a makeshift female imaginary—the latter gal-vanized not somewhere "outside" the general text, but *in and through* the andro-centric economy of sameness. Thus, in her own writing, Irigaray playfully sketches this rebel Woman's contours in the aporia of Kant's, Nietzsche's, and Hegel's texts. More specifically, Irigaray scatters seeds of this new, interstitial imaginary by play-fully reiterating masculinist ideas about Woman yet with crucial new inflections produced by exposing their androcentric blindspots, and hence disrupting their Women's hegemony. Irigaray calls such exacerbations *mimétisme*.[149] As one ex-ample, she willfully toys with Nietzsche's masculinist misconceptions of Woman; Irigaray's woman becomes a coy "marine Lover" to a hydrophobic Nietzsche—he who makes arid quests for transcendence, "self-marriages … of light, drought, and hardness" far from the sea, atop transfiguring mountain peaks.[150] In these mis-guidedly specular self-marriages, Nietzsche in-flates Woman as an androcentrically wind-tossed vessel of Self-serving veils and sails:

> And all that she may say to you is: yes.
> From this "yes" of her flesh that is always given and proffered to suit your eternity, you draw your infinite reserves of veils and sails, of wings and flight…. Of sublimation and dissumulation….

…Spreading her out, folding her up, securing her, letting her flap freely, according to your fortune, or to the weather you're having.

Irigaray mocks such parched striving as airy dissimulation. She deflates Nietzsche's female foil, puncturing "her" (misdiagnosed) elementally airy frame:

But is that not your twilight—this nature that already mimics, for you, the dissimulation that attracts you? How will you imitate her if she is covered up by your workings…. If, having become skeptical, she merges into disguises that suit your taste and distaste for her—the deep one….[151]
…And this takes her away from her surfaces, her depths…. Becoming speech in your mouth, a stranger in her own body.[152]

Reviving the Circe whom Nietzsche smothers in distant veils and sails, Irigaray limns a slipperier, dispersed, intertextual Woman, even as she parrots Nietzsche's (in)famous metaphors for this Woman:

At the end, no sails, no skiff, no bridge remain in that breaking up and thawing of ice. And anyone who always relied on solid ground and stout moorings and lifejackets and who hung on to good and evil, to truth, illusion, pretense … and also to the meaning of the earth, is now drowning in a pleasure that he has not willed … is now sinking.
In me everything is already flowing, and you flow along too if you only stop minding such unaccustomed motion, and its song.

Thus Irigaray enters his texts as a decidedly nonacquiescent siren. For, in fact, as liquid diffusion she is the *eau de vie* that defines Nietzsche:

So remember the liquid ground. And taste the saliva in your mouth also—notice her familiar presence during your silence, how she is forgotten when you speak. Or again: how you stop speaking when you drink. And how necessary all of that is for you!
These fluids softly mark the time. And there is no need to knock, just listen to hear the music. With very small ears.[153]

Reading Irigaray's playful mimesis, we are shown the violent suppressions and distortions that phallogocentric discourse requires, and, by extension, those that perpetuate a theoretical divide between fundamentalist and feminist thought.

Conversely, whenever we detect, engage, or create "disruptive excesses" like those of Irigaray, we reclaim "the operation of the feminine in [an otherwise thoroughly phallogocentric] language."[154] Indeed, like Irigaray, Armour solicits this differed, deferring Woman to correct the methodological errors that perpetuate the *race/gender* divide in feminist discourse. In order for feminist theologians, for example, to redefine woman accurately, they must give simultaneous attention to race. To do so, we must reconceptualize female subjectivity as a polyvocal, historically processual, and *thoroughly concurrent* (vs. additive) intersection of multiple vectors of power. For Armour, Irigaray's Woman (once Irigaray's own racial myopia is corrected)[155] provides imaginative space in which to think other less exclusionary racio-sexual economies. I shall offer another specifically fundamentalist/feminist example of this mimetic play in my conclusion, but first, a much-needed summary, and a return, as promised, to Kathleen Sand's tragic heuristic.

Conclusion
Acquired Tastes: Four Unlikely Proximities

Fundamentalist women's contradiction of feminist hopes for radical inclusivity—the quandary that prompted this heuristic foray—has proven, paradoxically, symptomatic of deeper shared foundations between us. These are: (1) respective assertions of liberation and agency; (2) a common racist myopia/heritage; (3) divergent yet equally problematic ideologies of clarity and erotics of mastery; and (4) a shared immersion in both the Western economy of sameness and identity-thinking; all of which destabilize the divide between fundamentist and feminist women. This fourth commonality constitutes the "deepest" *fundamentum* we share, underneath which lies our more basic and common ungrounded ground. *Différance* lies at the heart of Woman, and chastens any fundamentalist/feminist clear-cutting obfuscations thereof: especially, for example, *fundamentalist* women's ideological *and* embodied reinforcement of both "man's desire-for-woman," as well as the phallus as "the standard of value" within the specular economy[156]; or conversely, *feminists'* perpetuation of white solipsistic constructions of Woman whose emancipatory strivings consist of specular, dehistoricized (albeit nondualistic) Goodness and Wholeness. With these "essences," both camps block the "abyssal chains" (Armour) that might liberate a very different because dispersed Woman that feminist dreams of radical inclusivity in fact mandate. Deconstructing this current divide unleashes the Pandora that both parties avoid, even though "her" polysemous traces and *suppléments* have always composed human logic, interpretation, and world-construction.

Perhaps the modest conclusion to draw from this meta-critical exercise then, is that *the fundamentalist/feminist divide serves a mnemonic purpose*: it chastens any lapidary reversions to oppositional logic, it chides us to figure Woman as "a perpetual site of contestation," and it reminds us to harness the latter's dispersibility in ways that will constantly "jam" phallogocentric discourse such that more genuinely inclusive economies might emerge.[157] *Freeing Her, how shall one extract loveable sinners from hateful sins?*

Tragic Reprise: Apples and Oranges

Offering more comfort perhaps than such rarefied deconstructionist remedies, we might also enlist Kathleen Sands's tragic heuristic and thereby reconfigure this divide as a tragic locus of reflection. This divide—paradoxical symptom of the ungrounded ground we share—stems, at least in part, from the rationalist and dualist (specular) logics that suppress the agonizing clashes of todays's terminally conflicting Truths and Goods. Either of these habits of thought spurns our tragic context. In the wake of the theoretical disruptions and gynomorphic dispersals above, Sands would nevertheless remind us (as would Derrida and Irigaray): "It is still not possible to live without boundaries, not possible to avoid saying no."[158] Meaning construction continues, and forces ethical choice. Consequently, like Sands we must ask: "How shall those boundaries be negotiated and defended? How shall new uprisings of difference within them be greeted? When enemies are frankly acknowledged as such, can the moral and intellectual costs of that be counted as honestly?"[159] However opaquely mediated rather than crystal clear, however discursively produced, Sands is willing to retain the category of the enemy.[160] Across the fundamentalist/feminist divide, more specifically, we witness these tragic costs in the blood ties that "family values" sever. Indeed, such estrangements "unmoored" both Sands herself, as well as another feminist religionist—Anne Gilson (mentioned above),[161] leading them to challenge the theological rationales that could sanction such divisive, heartbreaking violence, and to construct religious interpretive frameworks that, instead, might facilitate "a gentler touching of worlds."[162]

To that end, immersed as we are in tragedy, and finding fundamentalist/feminist boundaries now tougher to map, Sands advocates hard-won "practices of compassion." Compassion, redefined in a tragic world, is a "wound," because its formerly idealistic mold has been "broken" by the endless clash of proliferating truths and goods, and thus it is no longer "an item of metaphysical faith."[163] Compassion is impure—inevitably sullied because, as the work of human hands, it is entangled in and shaped by a variety of deleterious partisan forces: "political, economic, social, and legal."[164] All of us—however compassionate—are implicated to some degree in acts of "negation and destruction." Nevertheless, we can reconceive compassion as an arduous practice of intellectual and moral *askesis*. Cultivating compassion in a tragic world requires feminists and fundamentalists to attempt collectively, and quite simply, "to make the world go on."[165] To do so, *intellectually* we must accept the "hard, costly work of holding open boundaries of thought and care that are wider than the bounds of what we can choose and affirm."[166] *Morally*, we still exercise opposition, but "an opposition that is not benumbed to the enemy, [a] negation that dares to understand. [Compassion] cannot extract itself from the world of force, but within that world it counts the costs of violence to the seventh generation and beyond and chooses with open eyes."[167] Compassion is thus laced with an abiding guilt—there are no "clean hands"—and a haunting sense of loss. As such, however, intellectually and morally this compassion-as-wound remains simultaneously a "lure to healing." If we are willing to renounce the absolutes that forcibly produce illusions of clarity and sameness, of fullness and identity, compassion will enable us to cobble together "a *partial* wholeness."[168] In the context of the fundamentalist/feminist impasse, it seems to me that this salvage operation will be more viable through practices of compassion and mutual recognition than through resigned, despairing dismissals of our opponents.

For models of such compassion, and the means for "nonideal" meaning construction, Sands consults stories of all kinds—both sacred and secular, but especially women's stories. With these, we may "season our moral wisdom" by learning new, more emancipatory habits of thought, attention, and action. Indeed, I catch glimpses of a partial, patchwork wholeness, a style and practice of compassionate antagonism, even a rudimentary *mimétisme* in Jeanette Winterson's *Oranges Are Not the Only Fruit*—another welcome, narrative mnemonic for making all the faultlines discussed above more creatively tensile. In Winterson's semi-autobiographical novel, an adopted/spiritually-gifted/working-class/British/lesbian/fundamentalist laypreacher is orphaned a second time by family values (and lethal doses of Leviticus) when her "unnatural passions" "refuse" to be exorcised. Here (*pace* Fulkerson) we return to the heterosexist impasse that can violently divide Pentecostal mothers from daughters, feminists from fundamentalists, and that severely undermines more sanguine appreciations of fundamentalist women's homiletic, humanitarian, or missionary powers. Winterson's account of her mother's crusade against her lesbianism thus evokes the darker side of fundamentalist women's agency. And yet, concurrently, Winterson narrates a "negation that dares to understand," chronicling a ceaseless bleed-through between these women's boundaries, and thereby modeling for readers a dissonant, open-ended antagonistic compassion. To elaborate:

First of all, I see the jamming logic of Irigaray's nonphallogocentric mimeticism at play in the heroine's time-warped cohabitation of both mythical and "real" worlds. A turn of the page transports the reader from twentieth-century working class England into mythological thickets full of pagan/Christian heroes, quests, and symbols. Inhabiting the latter are syncretic heroes and villains who also reverse and/or conflate standard male-female roles. These mythical excursions spill into Jeanette's "real" life as her imagination exerts a "creativity within constraint" that keeps her alive. Readers also inhabit these dual, osmotic realms of subjectivity. And Jeanette herself, moreover, in her very flesh confuses fundamentalist and lesbian/feminist identities, thereby bamboozling her community's (and readers') binary logic and religiosity. In all these thwarted boundaries and spatio-temporal disruptions, trace elements of a female imaginary erupt. Like Irigaray, Winterson "undoes self-evidence,"[169] defying the conventional literary fixtures that readers—now narratively homeless—expect and desire.

This exploration of other sexualities/ textualities[170] continues as Jeanette's own volatile forcefield of fundamentalist/feminist energies are refracted by what I would deem the cracked set of mirrors provided by the story's veritable funhouse of other female personae. It is precisely their differences from and similarities to Jeanette that further her painful process of identity formation. Additionally, all of these women—friends, neighbors, and relatives—are mercurial in their tragically hybrid degrees of Christian orthodoxy and iconoclasm:

- Jeanette's Love/Hate, Wonder-Working, definitively "Old Testament" mother;
- "Testifying" (yet Closeted), Other-Worldly Elsie, who dies when Jeanette needs her most, leaving her nothing but a wool, tea-cozy helmet of salvation;
- Hilda, Nellie and Doreen—three poster-gals for connubial martyrdom;
- the three "Aunties"—Alice, May, and loose-legged Betty—near-kin turned foe;
- big-hearted, vermin-exterminating Mrs. Arkwright;
- the oboe-lipped realist Miss Jewsbury whose secret, unsolicited kisses salve and salt Jeanette's post-exorcism wounds;
- plain old "Miss"—schoolmarm absolutist who cannot abide contradictions, and thus must dam(n) both Jeanette's biblically inerrant roots, and the wildly creative artistic juices they spawn;
- the hyper-vigilant Mmes. White and Rothwell—sepulchral community pill(ar)s;
- Melanie and Katy—unrequited traitor-lovers;
- a revenant birth-mother—dubbed but a "carrying case" by Jeanette's "real" Pentecostal mother, the latter pre-empting their reunion with just one anointed fist that leaves Jeanette lying "on the lino."

Along with this dizzyingly profuse, differing Woman—the product of an interstitial female imaginary that continuously blurs moral and conceptual boundaries— *Oranges Are Not the Only Fruit* also offers a tragicomic "theater for shared inquiry about conflict."[171] From the oddly amusing yet brutal humiliations that Jeanette endures (an exorcism and public "inquisition" to name just two), there organically sprout visions of stranger, more compassionate economies that I shall discuss presently. As Sands has observed in other novels, here too in this story the protagonist's undeniably "spirit-scarring"[172] wounds become "lures to healing." In this case, the ever-widening wound between lesbian daughter and fundamentalist mother draws the two full circle in the book's final pages. Though the wound never closes, the daughter voices and practices a compassionate, because only partial, negation in the tale's final act. Her chosen visit home dares us to understand, and pays an ironic tribute "not benumbed to the enemy." Jeanette's Pentecostal household thus retains some familial value, entwined as mother and daughter inevitably are in a formative history, glued to each other by "the thickness of uneasy love."[173] For the reader, Jeanette incarnates/produces a nonideal form of (religious) hope, the kind that Sands sparely redefines as "our messy multiform continuance."[174]

Occupying multiple subject positions as author/narrator/heroine, Jeanette diffuses this bittersweet sustenance page by page, but especially in the book's closing ambiguities: a strangely endearing image of Jeanette's still militantly crusading mother barking her code name, *Kindly Light* into the CB radio. This tag is in fact part of the opening line from a well-worn Victorian hymn, one that Jeanette used to sing in her "glory" days. Its text was penned, ironically enough, by a decidedly non-Pentecostal dogmatist—the infamous Anglo-turned–Roman Catholic John Henry Newman: "*Lead kindly light*," the tormented cleric prays, anticipating the violent severance of treasured philial and ecclesial ties as he now "defects" to Rome; yet he also pleads for literal safe passage here, for he writes the hymn on board a ship, physically adrift off the coast of Italy, engulfed in suffocating darkness.[175]

Meanwhile, back on shore, mimetically disrupting phallocentric tales from beginning to end, the exiled, migrant Jeanette still manages to farm fertile ground, though it bears oranges, not apples—more polysemous fruit for Western imaginations—a genus that signals no promise of abundant, parousial harvests:

> On the banks of the Euphrates find a secret garden cunningly walled. There is an entrance, but the entrance is guarded. There is no way in for you. Inside you will find every plant that grows growing circular-wise like a target. Close to the heart is a sundial and at the heart an orange tree. This fruit had tripped up athletes while others have healed their wounds. All true quests end in this garden, where the split fruit pours forth blood and the halved fruit is a full bowl for travelers and pilgrims. To eat of the fruit means to leave the garden because the fruit speaks of other things, other longings. So at dusk you say goodbye to the place you love, not knowing if you can ever return by the same way as this. It may be, some other day, that you will open a gate by chance, and find yourself again on the other side of the wall.[176]

Enlisting tragedy and dispersal to reconfigure Woman across the fundamentalist/feminist divide has allowed us to uncover and make some sense of its paradoxical confluences, and, on the basis of these, sustain a metacritical practice of attention that tempers the divide's theoretical hegemony. It is my hope that a deconstructive re-reading of this impasse, and the recontextualisation of the latter in tragic terms, can encourage a double hermeneutic of both suspicion and generosity toward fundamentalist women—moral and intellectual practices of compassion that surpass what we might ever "choose and affirm."

These informed concessions may seem, at best, small advances. For, given our "tragic vulnerability," itself further redoubled by thought and meaning's terminal "dispersibility," whatever ideals we pursue—for example, the feminist project of becoming a "platform for women in all their diversity"—we chase our tails. More concretely, fundamentalist women's general refusal of dialogue renders all the above reflections an equally dizzying monologue. Yet, as acts of self-critique and hermeneutical refinement, this exploration is not entirely without value. Now, with each new abrasion, the fundamentalist/feminist divide can remind us to investigate its potentially disruptive excesses: when intelligibility "cracks" and "values collide,"[177] we can remember that each hermeneutic circle, however open or closed, always exudes a rich mixture of mastery and resistance, and, knowing this, we can redirect our energies toward harnessing these ambiguities more fruitfully, such that they allow "a gentler touching of worlds." In short, as we continue our irresistible, utopian quest for all women's flourishing, perhaps this tragically conceived, disseminal Woman can be a "ruddering interrogative"[178] that makes the tail-chasing more instructive, or at least less vertiginous.

Notes

* I would like to acknowledge my debt to the work of Ellen Armour whose subversion of the race/gender divide informed my own questioning of the fundamentalist/feminist theoretical dichotomy, and who very graciously read and commented on drafts of this essay. Profound thanks also to Drs. Jim Kanaris, Ron Griffin, Fiona Black, and Andrew Wilson for their helpful comments and criticism.

1. Rebecca E. Klatch is critical of this oversimplification: "Far from suffering from false consciousness, in fact, social conservative women are well aware of their interests and act to defend their status as women" (Rebecca E. Klatch, "Women and the New Right in the United Sates: Family, Feminism, and Politics," in *Identity Politics and Women: Cultural Reassertions and Feminisms in International Perspective* [Boulder, CO: Westeview Press, 1994], 380).

2. See especially the works of Nancy T. Ammerman, Brenda Brasher, Margaret Bendroth, and Betty DeBerg.

3. Here I am adapting Ellen Armour's terms. In a different context, seeking to destabilize another theoretical dichotomy, Armour "produces proximities" between the thought of Jacques Derrida and Luce Irigaray in order slowly to subvert the race/gender divide. Cf. *Deconstruction, Feminist Theology and the Problem of Difference: Subverting the Race/Gender Divide* (Chicago: University of Chicago Press, 1999), 105.

4. Linda Kintz, 137, discussing Jacqueline Rose's "Margaret Thatcher and Ruth Ellis, Why War?—*Psychoanalysis, Politics, and the Return to Melanie Klein* (Oxford: Blackwell's, 1993), 41–86. Kintz appropriates Rose's interpretive framework to analyze oversimplifications in the meaning systems of the Religious Right.

5. Ibid.

6. Ibid. Ambiguity and unknowing are healthy signs of "strangeness and difference," "evidence of mortal and vulnerable human bodies" and thus, ambivalent inescapable realities of the human condition (ibid.).

7. Mary McClintock Fulkerson, *Changing the Subject: Women's Discourses and Feminist Theology* (Minneapolis: Fortress Press, 1994). Defined *very* rudimentarily, discourse "is a set of statements that get their meaning via networks of differences, intersections with other discursive formations" (115). Given this complex generative matrix, the meaning of these sets of statements is hardly some isolated product of sign systems. It is composed out of "the signified as concept" and out of "signifying processes embedded in social relations, which are not only embedded in but indistinguishable from social practices" (75). Fulkerson summarizes: "The move to discourse, to signification, from the view of language as representation is best summarized as the claim that relations constitute meaning....

"The differences that construct signification are widened to include the discourses of a mode of production [e.g., postindustrial capitalism], the processes of the democratic state [e.g., legal codes and systems] and the 'ideological' discursive processes of the culture [e.g., patriarchy]" (93).

Discourse analysis thus forces a redefinition of women's experience. First of all, what we categorize as (meaningful) experience is not static but fluid, and impossible to essentialize; it is the confluence of social practices, meaning systems, power dynamics, and locations. In other words, experience is a constellation of "converging discourses, their constitution by differential networks, and their production of certain pleasures and subjugations" (115). Second, the "concept" of woman is reconceived as a "subject position" born of "discursive totalities," i.e., "discourses that make statements as well as pose binary oppositions, discourses that define whole regions of reality such as gendered bodies and heterosexually desiring complementary subjects" (85). Discursive totalities include, for example, medicine, science, religious traditions (90).

Power permeates discursivity. It operates both "hegemonically" and more "locally." In a Western context, "hegemony, or dominant discursive orderings ... refers to the role of processes of capitalist patriarchy in reproducing meanings and locations oppressive to women." And yet, the "poststructuralist move to discourse opens to view a form of power that is everyday, local, and omnipresent with discourse, power that is epitomized in the procedures of modern normalizing and disciplinary technologies" (93f.).

Given these redefinitions, discourse analysis forces another dramatic shift in feminist theology, namely its critiques of the bible; we can no longer "essentialize Christian texts" as, for example, inherently sexist or androcentric: "With a look at discourse ... communities' ways of reading the biblical text and the discourses of the social order and local place become part of the analysis. Once seen in these intertextual relations, the biblical text itself is no longer conceivable as a fixed container of meanings that are prior to the power relations in which subjects are embedded. The question of their oppressive or liberating character becomes more complex" (9).

8. Ibid., 237.

9. Ibid., 295. Fulkerson constructs a poststructuralist feminist theology of "difference" and "affinity" that requires the following crucial methodological revisions: "Feminist theology, then, cannot look only at the presence or absence of certain ideas about gender as a test of how women fare in a community. Judgement regarding what counts as women's

oppression and resistance to oppression requires more respectful attention to the *how* and *what* and *where*. It requires connecting every practice with the discursive possibilities available to women, the way in which being 'woman' is part of their oppression, and the distinctive scripture they hear as good news. Openings for emancipatory or liberating possibilities are found at the intersection of canonical codes and practices with the sufferings and desires of women's social location. These openings can look alien to the ideals of liberation feminism" (357).

10. Fulkerson's term for the "embedded social practice" (and knowledge production) of academic/professional discourse used throughout chapter 6 in her book.

11. Ibid., 357.

12. Ibid.

13. These are Fulkerson's rubrics for reassesing the "faith performances" of Presbyterian and Pentecostal women respectively in chapters 4 and 5. On page 11 of her introduction she describes "the practices of Presbyterian women as discourses of self-production and world transformation that resist certain oppressive patriarchal constraints on their subject position."

14. Ibid., 182. One specific discussion of the "transgression" of "rules" in a discursive "register" is that of Presbyterian women running powerful church organizations and resisting the "undermining process visited on the homemaker by patriarchal capitalism … its devaluing of the nurturing and other expressive functions of the mother and home" (233). "Register" is the term denoting the relationship between a "reading-performance regime" and a "canonical system." (178; see also 177–82)

15. Ibid, 357. Brenda Brasher's research (discussed below) in *Godly Women: Fundamentalism and Female Power* (New Brunswick, NJ: Rutgers University Press, 1998) offers very graphic evidence of fundamentalist hostility toward homosexuality. One woman whom she interviewed, and whose sister is lesbian, voiced the wider community's general attitude toward lesbians as follows: "If you accept homosexuality, you won't stop at anything. Even murder" (138).

16. On our discursive domestications of the Other, see Fulkerson, *Changing the Subject*, 382–83.

17. Ibid., 229.

18. Fulkerson would be amenable to this tragic heuristic, for she treats at length the inevitability that human "finitude" and "fallibility" will generate abuses of power within our discursive networks where power is "omnipresent." Still, her focus differs from mine in that she locates and focuses mostly upon this tragic dynamic as it plagues *feminist theological* discourses rather than feminist-fundamentalist estrangements (or more general, familial instances of the same like those that Kathleen Sands [*Escape from Paradise: Evil and Tragedy in Feminist Theology* (Minneapolis: Fortress Press, 1994)] discusses). Thus Fulkerson: "A feminist theology of finitude is a tragic account. Michel Foucault's more compelling accounts of the inseparable knowledge/power connection … displays the inescapable corruption that comes with finitude. Thinking about the finitude/power connection in this way makes it impossible to exclude ourselves, the privileged who produce knowledge, from this

realm of fallibility so as to mark as inevitable our complicity as subjected subjects—a complicity that accords with a feminist theo/acentric grammar of sin" (ibid., 366–68). Fulkerson does not enlist Sands, moreover, in her analyses (possibly because their works were published in the same year).

19. Ibid., 4.

20. Ibid.

21. See Brasher, *Godly Women,* 20–27.

22. Cf. as summarized in "Fundamentalism," *Harper Collins Dictionary of Religion,* ed. Jonathan Z. Smith (San Francisco: HarperSanFrancisco, 1995). These five fundamentals were established at "a Bible conference of conservative Protestants at Niagara, New York, 1895." More specifically, biblical inerrancy has led to the development of Creationism, and the expectation of Christ's return to the doctrine of premillenialism. In the case of the former, and in response to evolutionary theories, creationism tries to "harmonize Genesis 1 and certain scientific arguments." For example, "the geologic layers of the earth cannot be used to support the vast time sequences of standard earth science because the catastrophic flood of Noah's day were the source of much of the layering" (ibid.) Premillienialists believe that "Jesus will return to earth in visible form and establish a thousand-year kingdom" (ibid.).

The term "fundamentals" is also the title of "a series of volumes … by American, Canadian, and British writers (1910–15) [that] carried the discussion further by attacking Catholic doctrine, Christian Science, Mormon teachings, Darwin's theory of evolution, and liberal theology's critical study of the Bible and denial of miracles" (ibid.). See also Nancy T. Ammerman, "North American Fundamentalism," in *Media, Culture, and the Religious Right,* ed. Linda Kintz and Julia Lesage (Minneapolis: University of Minnesota Press, 1998); and Frank J. Lechner, "Fundamentalism," in *Encyclopedia of Religion and Society,* ed. William H. Swatos Jr. and Peter Kivisto, et al. (Walnut Creek, CA: AltaMira Press: 1998) for very good historical surveys of Fundamentalism. Ammerman prefers to outline four more general characteristics of the latter: evangelism, biblical inerrancy, premillenialism, and separatism (59–63).

23. Brasher, *Godly Women,* 11f.

24. Ibid., 10.

25. Ibid., 20–27. See also Ammerman, "North American Fundamentalism," 90–101. Traditionally Pentecostals (or charismatics) emphasize "'gifts of the spirit' (such as speaking in tongues and healing) as evidence of the believer's spiritual power.… [T]heir religious experiences go considerably beyond the 'rebirth' that noncharismatic evangelicals claim.… Pentecostals trust the revelatory power of experience more than do the more rationally oriented fundamentalists who seek to confine revelation to Scripture alone" (Ammerman, "North American Fundamentalism," 58f.).

Fulkerson posits upward socioeconomic mobility of many Pentecostal Christians as one partial explanation for the gradual erosion of differences between fundamentalist and Pentecostal theologies (Fulkerson, *Changing the Subject,* 242–52, and also 242n6). This economic advancement and correlated adoption of fundamentalist discourses has, however, hampered women's agency; they now have less "access to preaching ministry" (390). Her field work also indicates that within the poor rural Pentecostal communities, the earlier, more spontaneous biblical reading practices that distinguished Pentecostals from fundamentalists are still alive, and allow resistance of canonical regimes by Pentecostal women. See especially Fulkerson's section "How Pentecostalism differs from fundamentalism," 247–54. Controversy among scholars persists, however, as to whether Pentecostals were in fact significantly less doctrinally driven than their fundamentalist contemporaries.

26. Brasher, *Godly Women*, 19–24. See also Ammerman, "North American Fundamentalism," 56–59. This is also my own observation on the basis of the variety of multidenominational sources consulted below.

27. Here again, Fulkerson's data on Pentecostal women evidences notable exceptions. The rural, poor/working class congregations of Virginia that she analyzes seem decidedly not second-wave in that they remain otherworldly in their orientation and acutely aware of their status as almost abject outsiders to mainstream society. They therefore do not attempt to dialogue or assimilate with the latter.

28. Brasher, *Godly Women*, 22.

29. Ibid., 23. The second wave's more politically engaged religiosity developed during the '60s and '70s, particularly after the inauguration of "Southern Baptist" Jimmy Carter (1976), an event that prompted the oppositional formation of the Moral Majority and its spin-offs. This more widespread activism had formerly been pursued by only a minority of fundamentalist "political radicals" (Ammerman, "North American Fundamentalism," 96. See 88–101).

30. Brasher, *Godly Women*, 160.

31. Ibid., 12.

32. See Gastòn Espinosa's survey of these conflicting attitudes in "Your Daughters Shall Prophesy: A History of Women in Ministry in the Latino Pentecostal Movement in the United States," in *Women and 20th Century Protestantism*, ed. Margaret Lamberts Bendroth and Virginia Brereton (Urbana: University of Illinois Press, 2002), 25–48.

33. Here Espinosa cites as examples pioneers Juana Garcia Peraza, the Rev. Leoncia Rosad Rousseau who founded successful independent churches during the 1940s, and the continued, long-term successes (1940s 'til today) of Aimee Garcia Cortese ("Your Daughters Shall Prophesy," 36–38).

34. Ibid., 32.

35. Bendroth and Brereton, *Women and 20th Century Protestantism*, xii.

36. Espinosa, "Your Daughters Shall Prophesy," 33.

37. Fulkerson, *Changing the Subject*, 289.

38. Ibid.

39. Espinosa, "Your Daughers Shall Prophesy," 32f.

40. Paul Harvey, "Saints but not Subordinates: The Woman's Missionary Union of the Southern Baptist Convention," in Bendroth and Brereton, *Women and 20th Century Protestantism*, 5.

41. Ibid., 5. Fulkerson's study of (admittedly nonfundamentalist) affluent, conservative Presbyterian women evidences strikingly similar quasi-feminist humanitarian goals

mediated through self-critical/submissive rhetoric (*Changing the Subject*, 206–28; see more generally, ch. 4, "Decently and in Order").

42. Harvey, "Saints but not Subordinates," 5.

43. Espinosa, "Your Daughters Shall Prophesy," 40 and cf. also Harvey, "Saints but not Subordinates," 4. Fulkerson's study of both poor/working-class Pentecostal and affluent Presbyterian women corroborates this general antipathy across socioeconomic differences. See *Changing the Subject,* chs. 4 and 5.

44. Espinosa, "Your Daughters Shall Prophesy." 40.

45. Ibid., 42.

46. Sharon Welch, *A Feminist Ethic of Risk* (Minneapolis: Fortress Press, 1990), 21.

47. Harvey, "Saints but not Subordinates," 20f.

48. Ibid., 21.

49. See Welch, *Feminist Ethic of Risk,* chs. 2 and 4.

50. See Fulkerson, *Changing the Subject,* 234–38.

51. Sands, *Escape from Paradise,* 139.

52. Harvey, "Saints but not Subordinates," 20.

53. Cf. Welch, *Feminist Ethic of Risk,* chs. 1 and 2.

54. Colleen McDannell, "Beyond Dr. Dobson: Women, Girls, and Focus on the Family," in Bendroth and Brereton, *Women and 20th Century Protestantism,* 118–19.

55. McDannell, "Beyond Dr. Dobson," 128f. Here, McDannell is contesting Karen McCarthy Brown's conclusions ("Fundamentalism and the Control of Women," in *Fundamentalism and Gender,* ed. John Stratton Hawley [London: Oxford University Press, 1994], 175–201).

56. Anne Bathurst Gilson, *The Battle for America's Families: A Feminist Response to the Religious Right.* (Cleveland: Pilgrim Press, 1999), 102–6.

57. Bendroth and Brereton, *Women and 20th Century Protestantism,* xiii–iv. Fulkerson evidences similarly stellar (nonfundamentalist) humanitarian initiatives among conservative Presbyterian women; their global exercise of neighbor-love and care for the stranger has much to teach us, and is actually afforded by similar social "constraints"—women's "proper" places in both home and church (*Changing the Subject,* 237f; and ch. 4 more generally).

58. For a chronicle of this development, see "The Jesus Factor" documentary, Frontline documentaries, prod. by Aronowitz, PBS.org. For a discussion of the same, see "With Ben Franklin's Blessings: A Primer on Faith-Based Initiatives," Pew Forum on Religion and Public Life Event Transcript, May 23, 2005, pewforum.org.

59. See Brasher, *Godly Women,* ch. 4.

60. Ibid., 119.

61. See Ibid., 80–82.

62. Ibid., 122.

63. Ibid., 68 and 82.

64. Ibid., 137.

65. Ibid., 123f.

66. Ibid., 27.

67. Ibid., 89.

68. Ibid., 137. For a concrete example of this collective pressure in instituting wider congregational reforms, see ibid., 75–80 and more generally ch. 3, "The Hand that Rocks the Cradle."

69. Ibid., 20f.

70. Thus Fulkerson, *Changing the Subject*: "On the basis of the litmus test of my own feminist theological lexicon about empowerment of women, for example, the submissive-dependence and self-denigrating language of Pentecostal women looks to be a discourse of utter misogyny. Read intertextually and as socially graf(ph)ted on their situation, however, their practice appears different. For Pentecostal women the pleasures of their canon's reading of the Holy Spirit and the ecstasies afforded in their intimacy with God produce a place of well-being, in stark contrast with the marks of marginalization in their lives. It is not a place immediately compatible with liberationist practices, which are directed toward resisting socioeconomic marginalization, but it is a place of God-sustained integrity" (357).

As for Fulkerson's assessment of Presbyterian women: "In a fashion of gentility and nonconfrontation similar to that of the ladies of the 1910s and '20s, PW bypass the restrictions of the system and create their own community and public space. They transgress by taking up registers of authority by speaking, teaching, exhorting, and preaching in their own literature. They transgress the limits of their canonical system with the sheer productive work of running a woman's organization for almost a century. By creating a literature and a distinctive biblical practice, PW take up the subject position denied them by the church. They enter the public realm on their own terms of value" (233).

71. Bendroth and Brereton, *Women and 20th Century Protestantism*, xiii, and Espinosa, "Your Daughters Shall Prophesy," 31f.

72. Other scholars have focused on fundamentalism as a response to: theological liberalism, Darwinism, biblical criticism, postwar crises of meaning, intensified industrialization, and consumerism. DeBerg references Sandeen, Marsden, Loetscher, Szasz, Rudnick, Gatewood, Furniss, and most famously, H. Richard Niebuhr. Cf. Betty DeBerg, *Ungodly Women: Gender and the First Wave of American Fundamentalism* (Minneapolis: Fortress Press, 1990), 1–7.

73. Ibid., 8.

74. Ibid., 151ff.

75. Ibid.. 72.

76. Ibid., 62. On the "divinized home," see ch. 3.

77. Ibid., 152.

78. Ibid., 1.

79. The latter foregrounds a Johannine gospel, one that authorized women's witness to the empty tomb, the former enflesh Pauline and deutero-Pauline ecclesial trajectories. Elisabeth Schüssler Fiorenza asserts the authentic primacy of the former. Perhaps their contented membership among society's winners makes at least some fundamentalist women less inclined to excavate a forgotten past to discover prototypes for alternative visions of the

future. Cf. *But She Said: Feminist Practices of Biblical Interpretation* and *In Memory of Her: A Feminist Theological Reconstruction of Christian Origins.*

80. Rosemary Radford Ruether, "Is Feminism the End of Christianity? A Critique of Daphne Hampson's *Theology and Feminism*," *Scottish Journal of Theology* 43 (1990): 390–400.

81. Ibid., 397.

82. Ibid.

83. Ellen T. Armour discusses and/or references the following womanist scholars: bell hooks, Angela Davis, Hazel Carby, Patricia Hill Collins, Katie Cannon, Dolores Williams, Marcia Riggs, Cheryl Townsend Gilkes, Hortense Spillers, Barbara Christian, Evelyn Brooks Higginbotham. Cf. Armour, *Deconstruction, Feminist Theology and the Problem of Difference: Subverting the Race/Gender Divide* (Chicago: University of Chicago Press, 1999), chs. 1 and 6.

84. Ibid., 178.

85. Ibid., 179. Cf. also 166–79.

86. Linda Kintz and Julia Lesage, eds., *Media, Culture, and the Religious Right* (Minneapolis, University of Minnesota Press, 1998), 116; emphasis mine.

87. Cf. Phyllis Schlafly, *A Choice Not an Echo: The Inside Story of How American Presidents Are Chosen* (Alton, IL: Pere Marquette Press, 1964). This "circuitous" clear cutting demonizes ambiguity. As Kintz observes, Phyllis Schafly and Beverly LaHaye encode "ambiguity not only as subversive to a national security state but as a Satanic force that threatens Christian civilization itself," this by combining an "anticommunist Cold War framework" with "absolutist Christianity" (118).

88. Beverly LaHaye in Kintz, *Media, Culture, and the Religious Right,* 126.

89. Ibid., 132. LaHaye elaborates: "Those [pro-ERA] feminists had managed to convince Congress to spend five million dollars of our tax money to hold state conventions and then this grand finale at Houston, which seemed to be a Marxist/lesbian circus, manipulated and controlled from the beginning by a dissident group of feminists who were demanding federal intervention into our lives" (ibid.).

90. Here is the quote in full: "Someone once remarked that perhaps it is because God has implanted in a woman's heart and mind an aggressiveness that shows itself most obviously when her children or husband is threatened. Even in the animal kingdom, we see examples of lionesses fighting to the death to protect their offspring, and normally docile mother dogs will become vicious when they sense that their puppies are in danger" (ibid., 130).

91. For an exposition of Schlafly's reductionism, see Kintz, *Media, Culture, and Religious* Right, 120–27. For the actual political complexities in 1960s Brazil, see p. 129.

92. Ibid., 118.

93. Welch, *Feminist Ethic of Risk,* 111–12.

94. Ibid., 112.

95. Ibid. See 111–16.

96. Sands, *Escape from* Paradise, 115. Cf. also, chs. 4–6, especially 41–60.

97. Ibid., 64.

98. Ibid., 68f.

99. Quoted in ibid., 111f.

100. Quoted in ibid., 85.

101. Quoted in ibid., 109–12. In ch. 5, Sands critically analyses concepts from many of Ruether's works.

102. Ibid., 12.

103. Ibid., 109.

104. Ibid., 130. See Carol Christ, *The Laughter of Aphrodite: Reflections on a Journey to the Goddess* (San Francisco: HarperSanFrancisco, 1988); and "Toward a Paradigm Shift In the Academy and in Religious Studies," in *The Impact of Feminist Research in the Academy*, ed. Christie Farnham (Bloomington: Indiana University Press, 1987): 53–76. In ch. 6 of *Escape from Paradise*, Sands provides a careful, yet appreciative critique of several of Christ's works.

105. Sands, *Escape from Paradise*, 127.

106. Ibid., 130.

107. Ibid., 131.

108. Ibid.

109. Ibid., 63. So for example, Welch asserts the "option" for God, reconceived as radically immanent, contingent, manifested in a healing, relational power that we wield: "Choosing a side, [Welch] identifies the divine with goodness as a moral *quality*, not with ontic structures or processes. The goodness … possesses its own kind of power, but that power is only one among many" (ibid.). And yet, moral evils such as "racism, misogyny, or class privilege" are also relational powers. Sands thus is concerned by the "aura of absolute authority [that] still lingers around the ideals of 'justice'" (ibid.).

110. Cf. Kathleen Roberts Skerrett, "When No Means Yes: The Passion of Carter Heyward," *Journal of Feminist Studies in Religion* 12 (1996): 71–92.

111. Benjamin's level of analysis is psychoanalytical, addressing, more specifically, models of intersubjectivity. Between individuals, erotics of domination can be preempted when "true differentiation" becomes normative: "coming to terms with the existence of an Other—recognizing her without effacing ourselves, asserting ourselves without effacing her" (Benjamin, "Master and Slave: The Fantasy of Erotic Domination," *in Powers of Desire*, ed. Ann Snitow et al. [New York: Monthly Review Press, 1983], 280–99, 282). Here, however, fundamentalist and feminist subjects will perhaps be less likely to achieve a "praxis of mutual recognition," given that it requires acts of communication that ensue from the perception of at least some identificatory elements between self and other. (See also her more elaborate treatment of this topic in *The Bonds of Love: Psychoanalysis, Feminism, and the Problem of Domination* [New York: Pantheon Books, 1988].)

112. Kintz, *Media, Culture, and Religious* Right, 136 and 116 respectively.

113. Sands, *Escape from* Paradise, 10.

114. Armour, *Deconstruction, Feminist Theology and the Problem of Difference*, 69.

115. See Armour, ch. 2, relevant content of which I am summarizing here.

116. Ibid., 49. This is Rodolphe Gasché's coinage. (Here Armour enlists Gasché's *The Tain of the Mirror: Derrida and the Philosophy of Reflection* [Cambridge: Harvard University Press, 1986]; see Armour, *Deconstruction, Feminist Theology and the Problem of Difference*, 46–49).

117. Armour, *Deconstruction, Feminist Theology and the Problem of Difference*, 64.

118. Ibid., 64.

119. Ibid., 61.

120. Ibid., 71.

121. Armour emphasizes that it "is neither the otherness of absolute founding principles nor the otherness of negativity or opposition" (ibid., 51f.). Gasché carefully describes Derrida's "visions" of radical alterity as follows: It "has nothing of an essence or truth.… [It] is irretrievably plural and cannot be … *thought as such*, and hence put to work by the system of metaphysics. [It is] more and less than negativity … *less* because it has no meaning, no signification … *more* because it is the 'medium' (the nonmediating medium) in which philosophy comes to carve out its … contradictions" (Gasché quoted in ibid., 52).

122. My thanks to Dr. Jim Kanaris for his very helpful and deft elucidation of these critical nuances. Regarding Derrida's "solicitations," Armour notes that the French *solliciter* "means to question, to disturb, to exacerbate, to shake up, to cause to tremble … in order to reveal what constitutes [e.g., the book] and what exceeds it." So, for example, in his treatment of medieval encyclopedists, Derrida seeks to "coax out the 'deep structures' of a cultural imagination that would allow the *idea* of the pursuit of a universal book of truth to occur." Note, however, that this strategy is not tantamount to "making judgements as to the feasibility (or lack thereof) of such a project" (ibid., 55).

123. Ibid., 184.

124. Ibid., 61.

125. Ibid.

126. Armour: "The effects of the Father God reach to the level of basic presuppositions of western thinking … 'nothing outside the text' of metaphysics also means that institutions, economies, … families, and such, also bear marks of inscription by the text of metaphysics, its economy of truth, and its Father God" (ibid., 72).

127. Ibid., 50.

128. See especially Fulkerson, *Changing the Subject*, 357.

129. Fulkerson discusses their resistant biblical practices on pp. 280–82, but afterward readily acknowledges that belief in the divine inspiration of the "entire scripture" and its "use as literal prescriptions" will never allow "a radical Spirit-authorized women's regime of reading" or "an 'anything-goes' experiential religion of excess." Also a constraining factor is the community's "doctrinal rigidity" (ibid., 286). Nevertheless, in her conclusion she still emphasizes (where I would not) that "Scripture will continue to be a living Word in these (temporary) stabilizations of gospel practice." I am less inclined to stress such impermanence, but again, her case studies of Presbyterian and Pentecostal women do give counterexamples by way of her chosen reading strategy: "Instead of locating the stabilizing

authority of scripture in its canonical form as a written discourse, I point to practices that create spaces for well-being" (ibid., 370).

130. Armour, *Deconstruction, Feminist Theology and the Problem of* Difference, 66f.

131. See ibid, 61–63 and 77–78. Very briefly, Armour demonstrates the absolute necessity of thinking race and sexual difference together, as "equiprimordial" "fields of force" that compose human subjectivity. With the economy of *différance* as the new context for reconceptualizing the concept of Woman, "she" must be consciously "held open as a figure of undecidability" and a "site of contestation" despite the negative ideological trajectories that this may invite. This "differed and deferring Woman" will allow constructions of more accurate racio-sexual economies. (Terms synthesised here are from the passages referenced above.)

To this theoretical end, Armour enlists "an ontological site where both [race and sex] converge," namely a derridean-inflected *Dasein*. See chs. 5 and 6.

132. Armour discusses medieval encyclopedists, and Derrida's reading thereof on 54ff.

133. Ibid.

134. Ibid., 49.

135. Ibid., 55.

136. Ibid., 56.

137. Ibid., 60.

138. Ibid.

139. Ibid., 39.

140. Ibid., 56.

141. Ibid., 180.

142. Ibid., 134.

143. Ibid., 163.

144. Ibid., 128.

145. This is Irigaray's term. Ibid., 110.

146. Ibid., 119f.

147. Ibid., 117.

148. Ibid., 116f.

149. Elizabeth Grosz lucidly distills this philosophico-poetic technique: "[Irigaray's] texts not only demand but also enact the overflow of meaning, structure, argument, putting phallocentric oneness into question." (*Sexual Subversions: Three French Feminists* [Sydney: Allen and Unwin, 1989], 127). Irigaray's poetic interventions in other philosophers' prose blur "the borders between poetry, fiction and knowledge" and create the necessary conditions for "the positive inscription [and exploration] of the female body" in language and discourse more generally (ibid., 130).

150. Luce Irigaray, *Marine Lover of Friedrich Nietzsche*, trans. Gillian C. Gill (New York: Columbia University Press, 1991), 33.

151. Ibid.

152. Ibid., 36.

153. Ibid., 36ff.

154. Irigaray quoted in Armour, *Deconstruction, Feminist Theology and the Problem of Difference,* 126.

155. Ibid., 125.

156. Armour's terms, pp. 77 and 62 respectively.

157. Ibid., 162. Here Armour recuperates a derridean reading of *DaSein*—there-being —that connotes this originary dispersibility.

Fulkerson deploys differences among her three discursive networks—feminist theologians, Presbyterian women, and Pentecostal women—as similar touchstones or "cautionary ciphers," *but limits their scope to feminist aporia rather than using at least some variation thereof to chasten fundamentalist reductionisms as well:* "The stories of the Pentecostal woman, the Presbyterian woman, and the academic feminist are cautionary ciphers— warning spaces about the dangers of academic discourse" (*Changing the* Subject, 385). Nonfeminist conservative Christian women "stand as iconic reminders of the blunderings and harm that we do as objectifiers who veil our projects with good will and intentions" (ibid., 386). "Lest it reproduce Christianity in its own image, feminist theology beyond liberalism requires an iconoclasm that refuses to way what a 'real' woman is, even as it testifies to possibilities of liberation" (ibid.). See her final chapter in full: "Beyond Inclusion: A Feminist Theology of Difference."

158. Sands, *Escape from Paradise,* 166.

159. Ibid.

160. The dominant perception with which Fulkerson's more benign portraits of conservative Christian women left me (and perhaps other readers) is that no strongly oppositional critique of Christian others can be wagered or defended. Sands by contrast foregrounds antagonisms rather than "affinities" (the latter a specifically theological term which Fulkerson deploys in her conclusion). Again, it is possible that my perceived difference between Sands and Fulkerson results more from our respective thematic preferences rather than any intended categorical exclusions on her part. (My thanks to Jim Kanaris for pointing out Sands's willingness to retain this more negative version of the Other (i.e., "the enemy"), and for our discussion of its abiding poststructuralist utility/value.

161. Gilson's project is partially a response to the painful rift she currently experiences between her quasi-fundamentalist blood sister (*Battle for America's Families,* 3–5) while Sands's reformulation of our world as tragic stems at least partly from her participation in protests of "injustices … suffered by lesbians and gay men," and her attendant realization that, in battling the Religious Right's homophobia, "there is no higher ground from which to adjudicate the differences between me and my opponents over what is 'natural' or 'just'"(Sands, *Escape from Paradise,* ix.).

162. Sands, *Escape from* Paradise, 136.

163. Ibid.

164. Ibid., 61.

165. Ibid.

166. Ibid., 168.

167. Ibid.

168. Ibid., 165.

169. Elizabeth Grosz's phrase describing Irigaray's writing strategies (*Sexual Subversions*, 127).

170. Grosz appreciates Irigaray's enactment of other "sexualities/textualities" thus: "In demonstrating that there are other possibilities (of sexuality/textuality or pleasure/production), Irigaray makes clear the violent appropriation by masculine representational and libidinal economies of a richly heterogenous field of possibilities" (ibid., 130).

171. Sands, *Escape from* Paradise, 174.

172. Ibid., 12.

173. Ibid., 143.

174. Ibid., 169.

175. See G. C. Faber, *Oxford Apostles: A Character Study of the Oxford Movement* (New York: AMS Press, 1976) on Newman's "defection," ch. 10, and the annotations for "Lead Kindly Light" in Maurice Frost, ed., *Historical Companion to Hymns Ancient and Modern* (London: Wm. Clowes, 1962).

176. Jeanette Winterson, *Oranges are Not the Only Fruit* (New York: Grove Press, 1985), 123, italics added.

177. Here I paraphrase Sands: "To stand over the cracks of intelligibility and there to think, to position oneself where values collide and there to discern—these I believe could be among the distinct contributions of theology to the moral and intellectual quality of life" (*Escape from* Paradise, 10).

178. Ibid., 166.

CHAPTER 6

Miniskirts and Fundamentalist Fashions: Clothing the Muslim Canadian Woman

Reem A. Meshal

Introduction

For as long as the "Orientalist" has peered into the harem and imagined the veil a symbol of the Muslim woman's eroticism and oppression, Muslims have grappled with the utility of veiling. In 1898 the Egyptian Qasim Amin's *Tahrir al-Mar'a* (*The Liberation of Women*) triggered wide debate in the Arab world by invoking women to remove the (*hijab*) veil and "advance" into the "modern" age. Thirty years prior, in 1869, Nazir Ahmed's Mir'at al-'Uroos, published in British India took a similar position to Amin's, adopting "the bourgeois virtues of thrift, sacrifice, forbearance and meticulous attention to child-rearing."[1] In the ensuing maelstrom of endorsement and protest aroused by such works, Muslim women have weathered a barrage of voices from '*ulama* (Islamic scholars), government agencies, intellectuals, and of course feminists (Muslim and non-Muslim), entreating them to accept or reject the veil. In spite of the initial controversy, Amin's message appears to have found a wide mark in much of the Muslim world for the first half of the twentieth century. Turkey and Iran went so far as to pass laws prohibiting women from wearing the *hijab* while in many more Muslim countries the veil had become the attire of a small minority of urbanites. The pendulum had already begun to swing even before Iran's 1979 Islamic revolution, considered the dramatic culminating point of what scholars of Modern Islam refer to as "Muslim revival."

The following study will not revisit, challenge, or confirm the arguments made for or against the veil as a requirement in Islam. Rather, it approaches the issue solely from the perspective of the Muslim women in the West, concerning itself with their personal reasons for wearing or declining the *hijab*. Furthermore, the scope of the inquiry is restricted to women in the Canadian Muslim Diaspora, a strategy that changes the focus of inquiry from the subject of "gender equity in Islam" to "the consolidation of identity in the West." What is revealed is that the veil in Canada is conspicuously worn as a religious symbol, but more than that, consciously articulated as an "alternative feminism."

Also revealed is the tension it evokes within the Muslim community between its advocates and detractors, reflecting the doctrinal debates that preoccupy Muslims over what constitutes "modernity" and how that is to be harmonized with Islam? Before we broach this debate, a word on Muslim scripture and the doctrinal origins of veiling and seclusion in Islamic history is in order.

Section 1: The *Hijab* in Sacred Texts and in History

O ye who believe! Enter not the Prophet's houses—Until leave is given you—for a meal, (and then) not (so early as) to wait for its preparation: but when ye are invited enter; and when ye have taken your meal disperse, without seeking familiar talk. Such (behaviour) annoys the Prophet: he is ashamed to dismiss you, but God is not ashamed (to tell you) the truth. And when ye ask (his ladies) for anything ye want, ask them from before a screen (*hijab*): that makes for greater purity for your hearts and for theirs.[2]

Reference to the term "*hijab*" in the Qur'an has led contemporary scholars to one resolute conclusion. Given that the word occurs in relation to a screen, which divides space as in the Indo-Persian concept of *purdah*, rather than a reference to a woman's attire, they argue that the doctrine of *hijab* has evolved since Prophetic times, the main catalyst being the cultural and social exigencies of later times and non-Arabian spaces. Nevertheless, a history of the doctrine of the *hijab* remains elusive. For example, although veiling and seclusion were part of the elite cultures of the ancient Near East (e.g., Hellenic, Sassanian, Byzantine) and their influence has been taken into account, the specific contributions of individual cultures and their role over time has not been identified in detail. What is clear, however, is that prior to the nineteenth century, Muslim legists did not debate the question of female dress as a particular category of analysis. Instead they discussed dress as part of a broader discourse on the place of women in public life, focusing on the question of whether women had a role to play in public or whether it was best to practice seclusion. This would only change on the heels of colonial interventions, when Victorian norms, for example, would challenge the concept of seclusion, and the introduction of "European" dress would spark the debate over correct outward attire for "Muslim" women.[3]

To demonstrate the evolution of the doctrine of *hijab*, a brief review of the secondary literature will illustrate the variety of arguments involved. Regarding Muslim textual sources, the secondary literature roundly suggests that the Qur'an and the Hadith are either "vague" or, in the latter case, "suspect." As evidence, such scholars as F. Mernissi and M. Shuhrur and others point to the ambiguity and imprecision of the two Qur'anic chapters surrounding "modesty."[4] The first, chapter 24, *Surat al-Nur*, verse 31, reads:

> And say to the believing women that they should lower their gaze and guard their modesty; that they should not display their beauty and ornaments (*zinah*) except what (must ordinarily) appear thereof; that they should draw their veils (*khimar*) over their bosoms (*juyub*), and not display their beauty (*zinah*) except to their husbands, their fathers, their husbands' fathers, their sons, their husbands' sons, their brothers, or their brothers' sons, or their sisters' sons.

Evidently, the most crucial terms in determining the standard of modesty implied by the above verse are *khimar, juyub,* and *zinah*. According to Mernissi and Shuhrur, therefore, the "founding discourse" on *hijab* can be located in the earliest Qur'anic commentaries (*tafsir*), such as the work of al-Tabari (d. 923). M. Shuhrur has examined al-Tabari's commentary, representing the earliest complete, extant example of this genre, showing how the work expends time pondering the meaning of "apparent adornments," which are ultimately defined as anything but a woman's hands, face, and neck. Shuhrur, however, points out that adornments are generally considered "external to the original" when used in the Qur'an. Moreover, the latter identify *juyub* as the cleavage between the bosom.[5] As such, all the contemporary scholars make the point that the time and place in which the commentators wrote played a large role in his definition of modesty, reflecting a different ethos from that of the Prophet's time. However, while S. Hajjaji-Jarrah argues that a scholar like al-Tabari was limiting what is acceptable for women, L. Clark takes the opposite perspective, arguing that he was in fact choosing from the among the most liberal interpretations available to him.[6] Either way, al-Tabari's work illustrates a departure from the ethos of the Prophet's time and place in favor of latter-day, non-Arabian norms.

Another manner in which the "founding discourse" is argued to differ from the ethos of the Qur'anic text is by virtue of its ahistoricity. For example, Mernissi points to chapter 33, *Surat al-Ahzab*, verse 59:

> O Prophet tell thy wives and daughters and the believing women that they should cast their outer garments (*jalabib*) over their persons (when abroad), that is most convenient, that they should be known (as such) and not molested.[7]

Mernissi makes the point that these measures were adopted at a specific historical juncture when the "hypocrites" (opponents of Muhammad in Medina) were waging hostilities toward the Muslims. To avoid harassment, Muslim women were instructed to identify themselves, but this "draconian" measure, adopted in a state of emergency, has come to serve as the basis for justification of veiling and seclusion. Mernissi also points out that slave Muslim women were excluded from adopting this measure, indicating in her view, the abandonment of the slave Muslim woman and her exemption from the community's protection. K Abu al-Fadl has also highlighted the fact that slave women were not only exempted from veiling, they were forbidden to wear it.[8] That is to say, the veil was a measure rooted in particular circumstances, temporal and class-bound, rather than the general injunction upheld by the founding discourse that arose later.

In the case of Hadith—narrative, literary reports about the life and sayings of the prophet—L. Clarke has made virtually the same case. She argues that the number of Hadith that actually address the issue of women's clothing are meager when compared to the number discussing the need for men to cover their *'awarh*, or the thigh. Furthermore, "the outstanding theme of the Hadith related to the concealing of women's physical being, is not … clothing as such, but restriction of women's movements, that is of their 'space.'"[9] That is to say, *hijab* in the Hadith, as in the Qur'an, is a reference to an abstract concept, or institution, not an article of clothing. Thus, based on the fact that only the reports admonishing women on dress are quoted and recycled in the works of later Muslim scholars (such as Ibn Taymiyya) she begins to make the case for the cultural forces shaping this "selective" reading.[10] The case is nowhere more resoundingly made than in the body of Hadith used in the debate on women attending mosques. One reads, "Do not prevent your women from attending the mosque," while a variant adds, "but their houses are better for them."[11] Clarke and others read such variances as examples of interpretations due to actual social debate, but her final point is that latter-day Muslim scholars drew from the second, while ignoring the first variant.

Clarke is also important to this discussion for drawing one's attention to ties between the "founding discourse" and that of "modern" Muslims. Echoing other studies on the subject, Clarke shows that the attitudes of such scholars as al-Tabari and Ibn Taymiyya, rather than the ethos of the Prophet's time and place, underpin current attitudes. However, as previously noted, it is apparent that the founding discourse has been transformed by more contemporary influences. In particular, the doctrine of *hijab* has been transmuted from an "institution" or "space" into a mode of "apparel." Clearly, this suggests that the earlier debate over the "public" or "private" role of women has been somewhat set aside in favor of allowing for a public role. Thus, the issue of the day largely revolves around the correct attire for a publicly active "Muslim" woman. In this light, the *hijab* of today represents a compromise between the seclusionism of the founding discourse and the public role promoted by contemporary "Western" feminism.

Section 2: The Social Significance of the *Hijab*

Great differences mark the analytical approach of modern scholars when it comes to the question of the *hijab*'s social significance. Is the *hijab* a regressive patriarchal garment or, conversely, progressive attire toward indigenization in the quest for an authentic Muslim feminism? Both positions have their proponents. To begin with the latter, Abu Odeh describes the act of donning the *hijab* as a show of defiance against the social corruption and consumerism of Western-oriented economies.[12] Y. Haddad argues that the "return to Islam" symbolized by the *hijab* allows a Muslim woman to access, or at least agitate for, the economic and marital rights guaranteed her under Islamic law.[13] For many, the Muslim woman in *hijab* represents the "non-Westoxicated" model for Muslim feminists, a protagonist in the shaping of her own distinct identity.[14] In the same vein, H. Hoodfar and K. Bullock see the *hijab* as a legitimate alternative for Muslim women negotiating a place between private sexuality and public space.[15] Others still have argued that for lower-class women, the *hijab* represents an affordable alternative to Western consumer fashions, an equalizer between classes. Of course, not everyone shares these perspectives.

Counterarguments to the above abound as well. El-Saadawi, for instance, writes, "veiling and nakedness are flip sides of the same coin. Both mean that women are bodies without a mind and should be covered or uncovered in order to suit national or international capitalist interest."[16] H. Moghissi concurs with this view of the *hijab*, sharply criticizing scholars who would defend it as "shaped by a postmodern relativism which dominates European and, particularly, the North American academy." Moreover, she continues, their analyses are marked by, "an uncritical pursuit of the culturally exotic and the untouched."[17]

The disparate views outlined above encapsulate the academic, albeit normative, debate on the politics of the veil. What remains to be seen is how this discourse is altered in the context of a Muslim immigrant minority.

Section 3: The Diaspora

In the West, the act of donning the veil (*hijab*) renders a Muslim woman more physically conspicuous even as it shrouds her body. Veiled, she is marked and identifiable, not just to her Muslim community, but also to the wider Canadian society. *Hijab* "is a flag," said one woman, and when, in the current climate, controversies over immigration and Islam in the West bring intolerances to the fore, women in *hijab* are the first identifiable targets.[18] This was amply demonstrated following the attacks of September 11, when assaults on Muslim women were reported in most major North American cities. Little wonder then that the increasing number of Muslim-Canadian women choosing to don the *hijab* has generated wide debate both in mainstream Canadian society and in Muslim communities. In these debates, the voice of the group at the center of the controversy, Muslim women, is often drowned out. Little is known of their motivations in wearing or declining it, their sense of identity, or their level of comfort both within their community and within mainstream Canadian culture in making that decision freely.

In pursuit of information on the above questions, an eleven-page questionnaire was designed and distributed across ten Canadian cities to 129 respondents between the ages of 18 and 30–60 of whom who wear *hijab* and 67 who do not.[19] While I strove to garner a representative sample of young Canadian Muslim women, the target group for the survey consisted of university students. Each section of the questionnaire included a set of multiple choice questions as well as space for the respondent to elaborate on her answers. The multiple-choice responses were later quantified by percentage.

In answer to the questions, who are the Muslim women wearing or declining the *hijab* in Canada and why, matters of identity and assimilation, conditioned by socioeconomic indicators, including income, education, family, and access to religious information, come to the fore. In this paper, however, we pay special attention to the formation of identity as measured against levels of discrimination and integration, including, the number of non-Muslim friends a woman has, the labels she uses to identify herself, her views on questions of feminism, gender relations, and her place in Canadian society.

For Muslims in Canada, the issue cannot be separated from questions of cultural assertion and assimilation, nor shorn from the global inter-Muslim dialogue on the *interpretation* of public symbols of Islam and "Muslimness." However, it must be remembered that as an immigrant community in the North American setting, Muslim grapples with the added difficulties of cultural exclusivity, assimilation, discrimination, and identity. As such the cultural debate on the future of the Muslim Diaspora in the West must be broached.

In the "Institutionalization of Islam in the Netherlands, 1961–86," Jacque Waardenburg forecasts an "Islam without ethnicity," where the twin processes of communication and migration foster an increasingly homogenous Muslim community.[20] However, the views of J. Waardenburg and others, which insist on the emergence of a monolithic Islam, and an increasingly homogenous Muslim community in the West, are proven only half true. That more than one Islam, or more than one interpretive understanding of Islam exists is amply demonstrated by the rival views of the women who participated in this research. Nonetheless, Waardenburg's thesis is born out in this study by the Muslim population that subscribes to the "orthodoxy" advocating *hijab*. Among this group, one is far more likely to encounter an Islam which de-emphasizes normative cultural, racial, and national traits (the *hijab* itself is not worn in any national style but is most often culturally neutral), while subscribing to a singular interpretation of scripture on this and many other issues of controversy within Islam.

Yvonne Haddad sees Waardenburg's scenario as improbable, pointing to a set of crosscutting affiliations (racial, linguistic, cultural, and sectarian) that divide Muslims in the present.[21] Many secular Muslims, it has been argued, show an attachment to their national culture that transcends the attachment to religious identity. Nonetheless, the applicability and relevance of Waardenburg's claims for a large cross section of Muslims cannot be disregarded.

Moreover, the employment of certain identifications, like "secular" when speaking of Muslims is problematic when branded discursively to the subject of identity. What does "secular" mean in this context? Does it define those who believe in the separation of church from state, but are themselves conventional practicing Muslims? Can it be said from the perspective of culture that a Muslim who fails to perform his liturgical duties or who even fails to possess "faith" is no longer a Muslim? Moreover, is the answer to this question the same when posed in a majority or a minority Muslim setting? The following study makes no such presuppositions as no woman in the following survey identified herself as "secular and non-Muslim."

Nonetheless, the results of the survey indicate that while objective measures of levels of assimilation—the language spoken at home, for example—are similar for both groups of Muslim women, those who do not wear *hijab* feel more integrated into Canadian society, are somewhat more inclined to call themselves simply Canadian, and claim to have more non-Muslim friends. This is further corroborated by the views of the women on issues of work and home, gender roles and gender equality. As will be shown, the majority of women who wear the *hijab* described themselves as career-minded, while more of their counterparts emphasized the importance of marital home life. When explaining their positions on gender equality, the women fell into the same neat categories. Those wearing the *hijab* often repeated the phrase "equal but different," while those who did not made no such qualification and described men and women as "equal in all respects." It would be a mistake to assume from these statements that women who do not wear the *hijab* are "modern" feminists or to dismiss their counterparts as "traditional" women. Those who wear the *hijab* insist that they are not rejecting the fundamentals of feminism, or passively accepting of a tradition that would assign them an inferior role. In fact, many of them sharply criticized the inherent male biases of Muslim culture, which thrive they argue, in spite of, and not because of, Islam. In other words, they are articulating the view that the "ideal/ethical" voice of Islam acknowledges gender equality, and that it is only in the "interpretation" of these doctrines that man's corrupting hand distorts the ideal.

Rejected by the women who wear *hijab* is the notion of a "universal" feminism that can be exported by the West to the rest of the world. Where the issue of the *hijab* arises, the debate spills over into the discourse on women and sexuality. The question Muslim women are asking is, which is more feminist, emphasizing feminine sexuality or de-emphasizing it in public space? Which affords a woman greater freedom when moving in public? These are some of the questions posed by women who wear *hijab* and who claim to feel greater sexual autonomy when covering all but their hands feet and face, arguing that it forces people to deal with them as intellectual rather than physical beings.

When one considers that there is no historical precedent for the present form of dress known as *hijab*, it is clear that this is a form of dress no less "modern" than jeans.[22] The lack of "historical precedent" refers to the fact that the *hijab* is not rooted in any regional or national costume. As understood by most Muslims, the requirements of the *hijab* entail long, loose garments and a scarf to be worn over the hair and to cover the throat. Whether that garment is an Arab *jilbab* or a South Asian *shalwar-kumiz* or for that matter loose Western pants or skirt is generally left to the individual's discretion. In Canada, the vast majority of women between the ages of 18 and 30 adapt Western clothing (i.e., skirts, blouses, and pants) to their Islamic wardrobe. The essential element for all concerned is the scarf, or the garment with which the hair and neck are covered. Here again, there is no standardized "veil." One can observe a variety of lengths, colors, and styles of scarves. As such, it is often difficult to attach national or regional identities to women in *hijab*. In whichever style it is worn then, the *hijab* becomes a universal Muslim symbol. Its relationship with "modernity" is that of a "Muslim" alternative to the "fashions" normative in Canada and the West. Nearly half the women in this survey have appropriated that symbol and have also articulated its significance for an alternative "Muslim" feminism.

Section 4: Manufacturing Orthodoxy

Despite the fact that, across time and space, different Muslim societies and classes have responded to Qur'anic injunctions for modesty in very different ways—from face veils, to seclusion, to far more liberal interpretations—a new consensus has emerged. In the last century, a new "orthodoxy" has taken shape on the question of the *hijab* and may be seen as part of a larger push for "authenticity" against what Mohammad Arkoun terms the consolidation of European imperial power and the hegemony of European culture.[23] As part of that orthodoxy the doctrine of veiling (*tahajub*) is upheld—enjoining a woman to cover her entire body except for her face and her hands—in the presence of males, save immediate and some extended male family members.[24]

In Canada the *hijab* seems to be increasing, and while one would expect to find disparities in the incidence of *hijab* depending on ethnic or national origins, that is not the case. The use of *hijab* among all ethnic groups suggests that cultural origins play a diminishing role in shaping attitudes toward this practice. In this study, 52 percent of the Arab women surveyed wear the *hijab*, compared with

40 percent of Pakistani/Indian women; most of the other groups were evenly split, except for European Muslim women, where five out of six wear *hijab*.[25]

As described, many scholars theorize that this Muslim mosaic will assume more and more the contours of a Muslim melting pot. This argument may help explain why women of vastly different cultural and ethnic backgrounds are opting for a standardized "Islamic" mode of dress as opposed to traditional costumes, which are often as modest. Certainly, the question of female dress in Islam reveals a growing parity in religious interpretation between Canadian Muslims of various backgrounds, as is evidenced by the ranks of women from diverse national backgrounds wearing the *hijab*. This is further supported by the fact that every convert in the survey wore the *hijab*.[26] Metcalf notes that this idea of a standardized Islam "has been the goal, indeed the expectation, of some Muslim leaders, who have hoped that in a new setting, particularly when Muslims from different areas were joined together, individuals would examine their practices in light of scriptural norms and focus on what was sanctioned and could be common to all."[27]

Canadian mosques, our respondents confirmed, appear to accept and promote the *hijab* as the ideal for a Muslim woman. A third of those surveyed reported that sermons on the *hijab* are delivered on a regular basis at mosques. Overwhelmingly, both groups of women (74 percent of those who do not wear *hijab* and 79 percent of those who do) concurred that the mosques are "in favor" of *hijab*. One woman noted that the subject [of *hijab*] will often be alluded to as part of an overall sermon on topics such as "Conduct in Islam" or "What is a Muslim." Another described how, "One of the patriarchs at my local mosque has, on several occasions, suggested that I wear the hijab or duputta (south Asian head scarf/shawl)." According to Metcalf, "mosques increasingly represent Islam in the West to Muslims and non-Muslims alike."[28] The message the respondents claim is propagated by mosques has found its mark in national and campus organizations, which are also largely pro-*hijab*. Sixty-eight percent of women reported that campus organizations are "in favor" or "strongly in favor" of the *hijab*.[29]

To whom does this orthodoxy appeal and more importantly, how do such individuals internalize and harmonize between its tenets and the demands and norms of life as a Canadian, a Muslim, and a woman? One of the preliminary findings of the study was that women *born in Canada* are **less** likely to wear *hijab* (37 percent) than immigrant Muslims (54 percent).[30] Without assuming that there is a definitive way of "being Muslim" in Canada, one may still separate those who adhere to Islam as culture from those who adhere to it as spiritual ethos and, yet again, from those who adhere to Islam as an orthodox, ritual-based faith. In this context, "practice" signifies those aspects of *ibadat*, or worship, common to both Sunnism and Shi'ism, the two prominent sects of Islam. As seen from table 2, a majority of the women wearing *hijab* claim to fulfill their daily prayer and fasting requirements. At first glance, the claim that women who wear the *hijab* do so "for purely spiritual and religious motives," as some of our respondents stated, seems to be substantiated.

Of the women surveyed who do not currently observe *hijab*, almost half said that it was possible they would adopt it at a future date, suggesting that second-generation women are also increasingly accepting of the prevailing twentieth-century Islamic orthodoxy. That acceptance is either greeted with reinforcement or censure from the woman's coreligionists and from mainstream society. Her formulated responses to the inevitable challenges she confronts make clear the ideological and cultural symbols relevant to that particular woman's notion of self.

Section 5: Returning the Mainstream Gaze

When it came to individual encounters in the mainstream, the women described a range of reactions, from tolerant, respectful, and highly supportive to rude, disdainful, and even insulting. Sixty-five percent of women in *hijab* reported experiencing from mild to overt discrimination at work, 73 percent from their non-Muslim peers, and 61 percent from their professors. While it is possible that the instances of discriminatory behavior, cited in table 4, may be related to other factors such as race, ethnicity, accents in speech, etc., as opposed to the *hijab* per se, nearly half the women (47 percent) reporting harassment said discrimination rose significantly upon their adoption of the *hijab*. This seems to be substantiated by the converts to Islam in our sample, all of whom reported experiencing prejudice after putting it on.[31] Among other women, almost 30 percent said that non-Muslim men had negative reactions and 32 percent said that non-Muslim women responded negatively. Consider the words of the these three women:

> Some of them have this stereotype that all of us are ignorant, submissive fools and this is apparent in their treatment of us.

> Aside from [people] trying to prove my insanity for converting to Islam and wearing the hijab, either they felt it wasn't necessary or they thought I was trying to imitate "someone from one of those countries." But to me it was a step forward.

> They don't understand why I wear it. They think that I'm oppressed.

It is difficult to make a clear link between discrimination and the *hijab* when almost half (49 percent) of the women who do not wear the *hijab* also report encountering racist attitudes. In summary, women who adopt the *hijab* encounter little in the way of positive feedback from the wider, mainstream society. Whatever support or encouragement they are given for wearing the *hijab* is found at home, or in the Muslim community. Non-Muslims react at best with tolerant indifference, and at worst with hostility. Non-Muslims were fixated on the *hijab* as a mark of

"Islam's oppression of women," complained many of the women. As well, some of them (27 percent) told us they had experienced overt coercion from non-Muslims to remove the *hijab*. As one woman said, "A lot of people try to 'save' me. They don't understand that this is my decision and that they are the ones [who are] interfering with my freedom."

Due to the largely negative portrayal of Islam and Muslim societies in the media, Muslim women are hesitant to openly critique the veil. This may also explain why so many women who do not wear the *hijab* defend its presence as a symbol of their community. It has not escaped the attention of Muslim women that the controversy that plagues their community because of the *hijab* has not, for instance, affected the Orthodox Jewish community, which also requires women (once married) to cover their hair and to wear long loose garments. One unveiled woman wrote, "What is the debate here? I fear it is not the superficiality of the veil, it is rather the fear of Islam itself. We do not, for example, fear nuns in their habits nor do we want to rescue hem from the male oppression of the church." Another wrote, "I live in a Hasidic neighborhood and I see them [Jewish women] covering their hair with wigs and wearing long modest dresses. Where is the concern for their human rights?"

Resentment for what is seen as blatant vilification of Islam and Muslims by the West spurs members of the community, even those who do not wear the veil or practice the faith, to close ranks in defense of their coreligionists' inalienable right to do so. But the *hijab* evokes as much controversy within Muslim circles as it does in mainstream society in Canada, with the women themselves acting as principal protagonists. How do Muslim women from either side of the veil view each other? How do they interpret and internalize the mainstream attitudes they encounter in Canada?

Section 6: Woman to Woman

Under half (38 percent) the women who wear *hijab* made negative judgments about Muslim women who do not, pronouncing them "wrong." Those who wear the *hijab* used the words "*impious*," "*weak*," and phrases like "*badly brought up*," to refer to bare-headed Muslim women. Reflecting this tension, one woman said, "The debate in our Muslim community is around [this question] … is a Muslim woman a good Muslim if she doesn't wear hijab? Some of the Muslim hijabee [*sic*] women sometimes look down upon other non-hijabee women in the mosque and outside too. It sometimes feels that the issue will never be resolved because of people always judging others."

As one woman put it, "Women who wear it like it, and women who don't wear it, don't like it." Almost a third of the women who decline the *hijab* reacted with a mixture of neutrality and negativity to the woman in *hijab*. Many of them described their *hijab*-wearing coreligionists as "*backward*." One woman in *hijab* remarked, "The women who themselves do not wear the hijab, but know that it is obligatory, respect and admire me. As for those who dismiss the hijab altogether, well they hate me and consider me a fundamentalist." A woman who is not veiled writes, "I didn't ask God to create me female. I cannot imagine that God would be so unfair as to put restrictions on me that don't exist for men. Also, the interpretations of the Quran given for the hijab is a chauvinist one given by men. Any woman who accepts this is blocking the way to a better interpretation of the Quran. Most of the women who veil cannot even explain why these Quranic passages are read this way. Sometimes they do not even know it [the correct verse or chapter]." And another says, "This is the twentieth century. The veil is old fashioned and stands for ideas I do not consider progressive."

Implicit here are notions of modernity, progress, and feminism to which, in the mind of this woman, the *hijab* does not conform. More importantly, as the woman before her indicated, not everyone accepts the prevailing consensus of the '*ulama* (religious scholars) on the veil. A minority of modernist, Muslim academics (both male and female) have challenged this interpretation, fashioning a new historiography that appropriates text and symbol to provide a new reading of the sacred scripture. For others, however, the bareheaded Muslim woman merely parrots her Western counterpart, bringing little that is original or critical to the "modern" discourse on gendered space and sexual politics. One veiled woman wrote, "The Muslim woman who is in a mini-skirt is just a slave to western fashions. I don't believe she has given any independent thought to her actions." These exchanges notwithstanding, it must be said that just over a quarter (28 percent) of the women not wearing *hijab* were positive in their appraisal of those who choose to wear it. This high number is logical when we reflect on the number of women who say they are open to the possibility of donning it in the future.

However, whether or not they disapproved of it, the unveiled women in our sample consistently supported their coreligionists right to wear it without fear of harassment or discrimination in university classrooms, work places, etc. Not one woman in this survey thought that either Quebec, France, or Turkey had the right to bar women in *hijab* from schools or universities. Does this suggest that the women are advocating a pluralistic modernism, where every woman has the right to choose what is or is not appropriate for her? Yes, but only to a point. First we must recall the barbs Muslim women exchanged above. Moreover, one must consider that when asked whether Saudi Arabia or Iran, two Muslim states that enforce the *hijab* even upon non-Muslims, should be held to the same standards as France or Quebec, the result was split. Unveiled women almost unanimously agreed that they should be held to the same standards and respect the right to choice of Muslim and non-Muslim alike, while more than half (54 percent) of their veiled counterparts felt that the comparison was unjustified. The rational one woman gave, "By asking someone to cover the hair you are not forcing them to violate any of their religious beliefs. It is no different from asking them not to go topless." Apparently, to some respondents there seems no contradiction between denying one state's right to impose set norms derived from secular values while upholding another state's right to impose norms derived from religious values. It should be stressed, however, that the majority of respondents intuitively recognized that the underlying principle in both cases was the right to choice.

Section 7: Faith, Alternative Feminisms, and Nation

When asked to choose a national label for themselves, the women lent credence to the argument that religion serves as a component of one's ethnic identity when the group in question is a religious minority. For the overwhelming majority (75 percent) of all women in this survey, the answer seems to be **Muslim-Canadian**. Only a quarter of the women who do not wear the *hijab* identified themselves by national origin—e.g., Iranian-Canadian—while an even smaller number of the women who wear *hijab* did so. No woman in *hijab* identified herself as merely "Canadian," although a small number of unveiled women did.

Hence, for the linguistically, racially, and culturally diverse women who filled out the survey being "Muslim" signified an ethnicity. Only a quarter of the women who do not wear the *hijab* identified themselves by country of origin as an appendage to Canada, while 52 percent of them identified themselves as Muslim-Canadian. The process of assimilation underway within the Muslim mosaic has already occurred on one fundamental level. Diverse groups are identifying as one. Second-generation Iranians, Pakistanis, Palestinians, etc., are no longer identifying with their country of origin, but are indistinguishable from their coreligionists under the common label "Muslim." To what extent is this process a reaction against an alien, and often alienating, dominant culture?[32] Mustapha Diop and Laurence Michalak argue "almost all Latin American migrants to the U.S. in recent years have been 'Christian,' but religion plays no part … in the American discourse on [their] migration.… If migrants speak as 'Muslims,' finding such an identity natural and effective in the new context where they live, we must see that in part as a label thrust upon them."[33]

Metcalf asserts that Muslims are pronouncing the differences between Islam and the West as a way of expressing dissatisfaction with the "totalizing culture of the nation-state."[34] What we are concerned with here are the ways in which the answers to the questions posed above touch on a woman's motive in wearing the *hijab*. Is a woman's sense of integration, or lack thereof, in Canadian society, already reflected in her attire? We are better positioned to answer this after a perusal of the patterns of integration into which the women surveyed fall.

Not surprisingly, women who did not wear the *hijab* reported feeling more integrated into Canadian society. More than a quarter (29 percent) of this group called themselves "very integrated," while the remainder consider themselves "integrated to some degree." Only 4 percent described themselves as "not integrated at all." Conversely, a substantially lower percentage (10 percent) of women who wear the *hijab* felt "very integrated," while a substantially higher percentage claimed they were not integrated at all (21 percent). The number of non-Muslim friends the women counted was also taken as an indicator of levels of integration. The same patterns reveal themselves here. Women who do not wear the *hijab* are twice as likely to have over ten non-Muslim friends. Over a third (35 percent) of those wearing the *hijab* said they had only one to three non-Muslim friends.

That women who wear the *hijab* feel less integrated into Canadian society is perhaps self-evident. To extrapolate further from this information we must consider another indicator: the gender roles to which the women subscribe and the cultural references that these entail.

When questioned about their professional or domestic aspirations, almost half (40 percent) of those who wear the *hijab* cited their primary ambitions was to be a housewife and mother, compared to just 7 percent of the women who were unveiled. This staggering discrepancy gives reason for pause. It speaks to us of the cultural gulf that separates the woman in *hijab* from her coreligionist. A substantial number of the former perceive of their role and place in society as wives and mothers, while the latter express an almost unanimous interest in careers outside of the home. Note, however, that over half (60 percent) of the women wearing the *hijab* also depicted themselves as career oriented. Having said this, we must still ask why so many more of these women prioritize their lives differently. The word "prioritize" is used here in view of the fact that three quarters (75 percent) of women wearing *hijab* reported having been employed, while 60 percent claimed to be interested in working outside the home. The remaining 40 percent have, in their own words, worked because they have been obliged by economic imperative. What is the cause of this discrepancy?

Clearly, any answer to the above question must touch on the issue of gender identity. In view of the fact that more recent immigrant women are wearing the *hijab*, it may be a reflection of conventional gender roles in the country of origin. This is born out by the fact that the respondents born in Canada, who wore the *hijab* in fewer numbers and exhibited a career-minded outlook, appear to have imbibed the feminist ideals of the local culture to a greater degree. On the other hand, of those born outside Canada, a full 50 percent do not subscribe to so-called "traditional" gender roles either or wear the *hijab*. It is telling to note that of the Egyptian, Iranian, and North African (Algerian, Moroccan) immigrants—all from countries weathering strong Islamic revivalist movements—only a fraction wear the *hijab*. Second-generation Canadian respondents from these backgrounds were far more likely to wear the *hijab* than those born in the country of origin. Thus, we must assume that the forces of these gendered identities are found in Canada itself.

From the foregoing, we may deduce that Muslim women, like all women, are defining their sense of self in reaction to, or against, societal currents. What are these currents? In the Muslim East, women are contending with two trends: one, a process of Islamic revivalism that often entails certain gender roles; the other, a process of Westernization, often packaged as modernization, that espouses Western feminist values. In Canada, the latter is ensconced as a feature of the dominant culture. The relatively fewer number of women in *hijab* who saw their futures in terms of career and work are signalling that: "Its [Western feminism] objectives and values do not represent me!" This should hardly come as a surprise given the criticism to which feminist theory is subject even within the West, namely its neglect of low-income brackets and members of visible minorities.[35] Thus, it may be concluded that on a profound level, the answers of the women in *hijab* are as significant for what they reveal of the values that are adopted in the Canadian context as they are for highlighting those that are rejected.

The answers given to the final question in our survey, "Do you believe that men and women are equal?" support the proposition that women who did not wear the *hijab* were far more likely to employ feminist terms familiar to the Western ear. The answers, however, do little to elucidate the women's views on the equality of the sexes nor do they provide evidence of the strength of their feminist convictions. A number of women—from both sides of the veil—qualified answer (a), for instance, by adding, "Men and women are equal but they have different duties and responsibilities." In other words, equal but different. Others marked "in some respects," but made sure we understood that "equal in some respects" alluded only to anatomical differences. The following women had this to say:

Men and women are not equals. There are areas (where) women are superior and areas where men are superior. There should be a balance.

We are equal but we are not the same.

The rights and duties of men and women are similar and under certain circumstances one will take precedence over the other. Under no circumstances are the rights and duties of one more important than those of the other.

Equality –> complementarity

The answers are significant, however, not for what they inform us of a woman's feminist convictions, but rather, for what they convey of her cultural and, by extension, political terms of reference. That women seem more likely to say "men and women are equal in all respects" suggests that they are comfortable with a key tenet of Western feminist thought; i.e., the deconstructionist argument that reduces all gender roles and traits to social, environmental conditioning; biological differences signify little and men and women are essentially the same. This argument boasts its fair share of critics and by no means represents the only line of feminist thought in the West. For many Muslim women unfamiliar with the substantive content of feminist theory, the feminist slogans and the sexual objectification of women in the West suggest that "liberation" equals nudity. For Muslim women who are aware of the history and underpinnings of feminist movements in the West, and the critiques they make of modern Western culture, Western feminist theory still harbors biases that betray Euro-centric, as opposed to universal, paradigms. We noted with great interest, for example, the number of women who defended the *hijab* as a garb designed to desexualize a woman's presence in society and, thus, to promote her as an intellectual being rather than a sexual object.

> *Hijab* gives me freedom to spend more time on development of my spiritual and intellectual self. That is more important to me than wasting time and money on my physical attraction. It protects me from being taken for my beauty rather than brains, making me a … liberated feminist in the true sense of the word.

> I question the legitimacy of this so-called debate on the issue of *hijab*. Why not debate instead the sexualized clothing of Western consumer culture? We should closely examine the fashions foisted upon women to entice men.

> Living in a western world [I find] far too much emphasis on looks and size. I guess we all have to look like Cindy Crawford [a popular fashion model] to be accepted. How absurd these [Western] women are. And they claim to be feminists? I'd rather be judged for what and who I am.

From these and other direct statements made by the women, we may infer that two mutually antagonistic remedies to the "problem" of sexuality, feminism, and public space have come to a head. Western society, for all testaments to the "sameness" of the sexes, revels, as Western feminists themselves charge, in the promotion and commercialization of feminine sexuality. The Muslim women who wear the *hijab* are identifying what they consider to be dissonance between the doctrine of absolute equality in Canada and the vagaries of practice. Moreover, they are boldly questioning the alleged egalitarianism of mainstream sexual norms, particularly the politics of attire, norms that they conclude exploit and exaggerate feminine sexuality while obscuring the feminine intellect.

Equally critical of attitudes within Muslim society, many of the women who wear the *hijab* censured their male coreligionists for overriding the tenets of Islam on equality in favor of misogynistic local practices. As one woman wrote, "Islamically, I agree we are equal according to the Qur'an, Hadith, and sunna, but this is not always practiced or acknowledged due to ignorance and (popular) culture." Others attacked what they considered to be the double standards entertained by a community over indulgent of its males: "I believe more Muslim women would wear the *hijab* if they thought there was a balance with (respect to) Muslim men's dress. How ridiculous it is to me to see a Muslim man in jeans, a leather jacket, loafers, T-shirt, and cologne, walking with his wife who is covered from head to toe in black clothing." Or in the words of another, "Men use their culturally and socially derived privileges to deprive women of the rights given by Allah. I don't think Islam is practiced in its true form. I think … male dominance in society has caused Islam to be practiced by communities (not by individuals) in quite a male-biased, male-glorifying fashion." The tone adopted above is analogous to that taken by a number of Western feminists in their critiques of contemporary patriarchy. However, the distinctions in rhetoric illustrate the logic by which Muslim women who wear the veil negotiate the terms of their assimilation with the mainstream and within their own communities. It is not the women who must be liberated through the shedding of these distinctive garments, but Muslim men who must be made to strive for that "ideal" Islam that affords all "equality based on difference."

Thus, the Muslim women who wear and who do not wear the hijab in this survey employ a decidedly feminist rhetoric in defending their respective positions. Whether the rhetoric she uses is "Western" or "Muslim" is important as it shapes and defines the parameters of the dialogue between the woman and her society on the final question, her identity.

Conclusion

We have seen that newer immigrant women wear the *hijab* in greater numbers. We have also seen that 49 percent of second-generation Canadian women said they might don the *hijab* at some future date. Attempting to explain this phenomenon, we made reference to Waardenburg and Metcalf's views on the consolidation of a Muslim Diasporic "orthodoxy" and identity, for which the *hijab* becomes a potent symbol. We cautioned, however, that this analysis fails to account for a sizable number of Muslims who neither attend mosques nor partake of tradition or orthodoxy and yet who have not ceased to identify as Muslim. Moreover, as argued by Diop, even those who would not identify as such find the label "Muslim" thrust upon them by the dominant culture. Thus "Muslim" becomes an ethnicity in itself, as demonstrated by the majority of women who engaged in this study, much as "Jewish" has functioned for centuries in the West. How that dimension of the women's identities manifests in their ideological and cultural choices was explored through their wardrobes.

The side of the veil a woman chooses does, it was argued, reveal the cultural and ideological references to which she subscribes. It follows that women who are less integrated into Canadian society, either because they are recent immigrants, or because they are second-generation Muslims who question mainstream values, are more likely to wear *hijab*. Recall that among the latter group, women who defended the *hijab* did so in feminist terms, arguing that it "desexualized" public space, making it a safer and more intellectually hospitable environment for women. Declining to accept the paradigms of Western feminism, veiled Muslim women have not abandoned feminist rhetoric, but have appropriated its arguments to construct an alternative feminism, born of an alternative Muslim modernity.

Appendix of Tables

Table 1: Ethnicity

South Asian	Arab	European	Irani	African	Turkish	Other
57%	34%	5%	2%	2%	1%	4%

Table 2: Sources of Islamic Knowledge

	Veiled	Unveiled
Qur'an and Had'ith	82%	44%
Family	35%	18%

Table 3: Is *Hijab* Prescribed by Islam?

	Veiled	Unveiled
% claiming knowledge from Qur'an and Hadith	94%	73%
% who believe *hijab* is prescribed in Qur'an	79%	32%
% who could identify relevant verses of Qur'an or Hadith	37%	3%

Table 4: Incidents of Discrimination Reported by Women Wearing the *Hijab*

	Yes	No
Work	34%	35%
Peers	63%	27%
Professor s	39%	39%

Table 5: Forms of Self Identification

Label	With *hijab*	Without *hijab*
Muslim-Canadian	76%	52%
Canadian	0%	10%
Ethnic-Canadian (e.g., Arab-Can.)	19%	25%
Other	15%	13%

Table 6: Are Men and Women Equal?

	With *hijab*	Without *hijab*
a) In all respects	52%	79%
b) In some respects	37%	21%
c) In no respect	8%	0%

Notes

1. Cited in S. Tharu and K. Lalita eds., *Women Writing in India 600 B.C. to the Early Twentieth Century* (New York: Feminist Press, 1991), 165.

2. Yusuf Ali, trans., The Holy Qur'an, vol. 2, chapter 33, *Surat al-Ahzab*, verse 53.

3. For example, see Leila Ahmed, *Women and Gender in Islam* (New Haven, CT: Yale University Press, 1992), chapters 3–6.

4. See M. Shuhrur, *al-Kitab wa-al-Qur'an: qira'ah mu'a·sirah* (Damascus: Ahali lil-·Tiba'ah wal-Nashr wal-Tawzi', 1990); and F. Mernissi, *The Veil and the Male Elite: A Feminist Interpretation of Women's Rights in Islam* (New York: Addison-Welsey, 1991).

5. Ibid.

6. L. Clarke, "Hijb According to the Hadith," in *The Muslim Veil in North America* (Toronto: Women's Press, 2003), 221; and S. Hajjaji-Jarrah, "Women's Modesty in Quranic Commentaries" in the same volume, 181–211.

7. Yusuf Ali, Holy Qur'an, vol. 2.

8. K. Abu al-Fadl, *Speaking in God's Name: Islamic Law, Authority and Women* (Oxford: Oxford University Press, 2001), 241.

9. Clarke, "Hijb According to the Hadith," 229.

10. Ibid., 218.

11. Ibid., 235. Quoted from Abu Dawud, *Sunana, Kitab al-Salah,* hadith no. 79; Ibn Hanbal, *Musnad,* hadiths 5211, 5214

12. Abu-Odeh L., "Crimes of Honour and the Construction of Gender in Arab Societies," in *Feminism and Islam: Legal and Literary Perspectives,* ed. M. Yamani (New York: New York University Press, 1996).

13. Yvonne Haddard and J. I. Smith, "Women in Islam; 'the Mother of All Battles,'" in *Arab Women Between Defiance and Restraint,* ed. S. Sabbagh (New York: Olive Branch Press, 1996).

14. The term "Westoxicated" was coined by Iranian intellectuals responding to the changes overtaking Muslim culture under the influence of European modernism. See Negin Nabavi, *Intellectual Trends in Twentieth Century Iran: A Critical Survey* (Gainesville: University Press of Florida, 2003).

15. Homa Hoodfar, "More than Clothing; Veiling as an Adaptive State," in *The Muslim Veil in North America,* ed. S. Alvi, S. McDonough, and H. Hoodfar (Toronto: Canadian Scholars Press, 2003); Katherine Bullock, *Rethinking Muslim Women and the Veil: Challenging Historical and Modern Stereotype* (Herndon, VA: International Institute of Islamic Thought, 2002).

16. Nawal El-Saadawi, *Women at Point Zero* (New York: Zed Books, 1997), 139.

17. Haideh Moghissi, *Feminism and Islamic Fundamentalism; The Limits of Post-Modern Anaysis* (New York: Zed Books, 1999), 47.

18. See Zuhair Kashmeri, *The Gulf Within: Canadian Arabs, Racism and the Gulf War* (Toronto: James Lorimer and Company Publishers, 1991).

19. The cities included Vancouver, Edmonton, Saskatoon, Toronto, Oakville, Mississauga, Kingston, London, Halifax, and Montreal.

20. Jacque Waardenburg, "The Insitutionalization of Islam in the Netherlands, 1961–86," in *The New Islamic Presence in Europe,* ed. T. Gerholm and Y. G. Lithman (Stockholm: Centre for Research in International Migration and Ethnicity, 1988)

21. Haddad and Smith, "Women in Islam."

22. Historical terms are usually culturally specific: *burqah, chador, niqab,* etc., and refer to items of clothing that vary, from complete body covering to partial facial covers. Moreover the style of each is specific to the local culture.

23. Mohammad Arkoun, *Rethinking Islam,* trans. R. D. Lee (Boulder, CO: Westview Press, 1994).

24. See F. Mernissi, *Veil and the Male Elite.*

25. Waardenburg, "Insitutionalization of Islam in the Netherlands, 1961–86." In this article, Waardenburg describes what he foresees as an "Islam without ethnicity," wherein the processes of communications and migration foster an increasingly homogenous Muslim identity in the West.

26. Converts, by virtue of their newcomer status, generally subscribe to mainstream interpretations of a faith, and thus provide good indication of its normative patterns of belief and conduct.

27. Barbara Metcalf, "Sacred Words, Sanctioned Practice, New Communities," in *Making Muslim Space in North America and Europe* (Los Angeles: University of California Press, 1996).

28. Ibid., 18.

29. Muslims in Canada include the following nationalities: Bengali, Indian, Pakistani, Egyptian, Syrian, Jordanian, Palestinian, Turkish, Irani, Indonesian, east European, East African, Carribean, and Canadian-born. As well, this pluralistic "group" adheres to a number of sects within Islam: Sunni, Shi'ite, Druze, and Isma`ili. Followers of the latter two sects do not acknowledge the *hijab* or veil as an Islamic proscription. Most Muslims in Canada are of Asian descent, with Indo-Pakistanis comprising the largest group at 42.1 percent. Arabs follow at 22.8 percent.

30. Women who do not wear the hijab generally come from more educated families in higher income brackets. Fifty-nine percent of those who **do not** wear the hijab had mothers who had completed university or post-graduate work, while their veiled counterparts had almost half the number of educated mothers (31 percent). Seventy-seven percent of those who do not wear the hijab had fathers who had completed university or post-graduate work, as compared to 58 percent of those wearing hijab. For more on the socioeconomic place of Muslims in Canada, see Husaini, Zohra, *Muslims in the Canadian Mosaic* (Edmonton: Muslim Research Foundation, 1990); and A. Rashid, *The Muslim Canadians: A Profile* (Ottawa: Statistics Canada, 1985).

31. Ten percent reported neutral reactions from non-Muslim women, 14 percent from non-Muslim men; 19 percent reported mixed reaction from non-Muslim women and 6 percent reported mixed reaction from non-Muslim men.

32. Remy Leveau draws parallels between the experiences of Jews and North African Muslims in France. See Remy Leveau and Gilles Kepel, *Culture Islamique et Attitudes Politiques Dans la Population Musulman en France: Enquete Effectuee Pendant le Mois du Ramadan* (Paris: Fondation National des Sciences Politique, 1985).

33. Mustapha Diop and Laurence Michalak, "Refuge and Prison: Islam, Ethnicity and the Adaptation of Space in Worker's Housing in France," in Metcalf, *Making Muslim Space*, 74.

34. Metcalf, *Making Muslim Space*, 16.

35. Razia Aziz, "Feminism and the Challenge of Racism: Deviance or Difference?" in *Knowing Women: Feminism and Knowledge*, ed. Helen Crowley and Susan Himmelweit (Cambridge: Polity Press, 1992); Sandra Harding, "The Instability of the Analytical Categories of Feminist Theory, " in Crowley and Himmelweit, *Knowing Women: Feminism and Knowledge*.

Postscript: Reading from Both Right and Left to Center

Katherine K. Young

In this postscript I will relate the general discussion of my introduction on fundamentalism to the insights now available from evolutionary psychology. This is in the nature of a thought experiment—speculative by nature—and interdisciplinary.

Is there any approach that would provoke deeper insights into the two poles represented by feminism and fundamentalism—or even to reconcile them? One way, I suggest, is to understand more about the dynamics of stress. There are three basic reactions to stress: adaptation, fight, or flight; faced with threats to their identity, groups either adapt (which, if successful can eliminate the source of stress altogether, though it might leave them with no identity), withdraw to a marginal realm, or, failing that, fight back. Closely related to threats to religious identity are threats to masculine identity, moreover, which can also trigger fight or flight. My interest here is mainly with "fighting back."

One important example of "fighting back," men's reaction to stress, happened during the rise of early states. Urban men were in danger of losing their masculine identity. This occurred because male size and strength, on which their identity had been based, were no longer necessary in daily life. The major markers of masculinity, therefore, were the ways in which it was culturally distinct from femininity. This led to sexual segregation, distinctive forms of dress for each sex, denial of education to women, and so on. These became deeply embedded in elite culture. In later centuries, these restrictions have increased in times of stress and decreased in time of less stress but have usually had serious implications for women, especially elite women, by reducing their identities to motherhood.

Nyitray points out that "the history of political control over women/females in China is well documented: on the level of the family, mechanisms to properly 'educate' women accelerated during periods of social stress and cultural upheaval." This education included exhortations to obedience, chastity, and so forth.

Colonialism certainly caused enormous stress for colonized people, because all identities—including the gender identities of men and women—were attacked. In this case, fighting back by men required creativity and positive overtures to their own women—especially because colonial rulers blamed these societies for their historical mistreatment of women. According to Bartholomeusz, "We find that the anxiety over the condition of the female among Sinhala Buddhists toward the end

179

of the nineteenth century hinged on the rhetoric of shame and promise." Something similar happened to Hindu women during British rule. (The British shamed Hindu men for their mistreatment of women, which inspired the men to institute reforms.) And, according to Nyitray, the renewal of Confucianism in China as a reaction against Marxism can be attributed partly to "government fears of declining morals in the face of rising capitalist tendencies" and to the desire for a regional identity (including that of other Confucian-influenced cultures such as those of Japan and South Korea) to counter Western influence.

Attacks on identity have proven stressful in the past, and those on the identity of men in particular (which led to a consolidation of their power) have had serious implications for women over the centuries. When it comes to identity, men have projected their stress onto women, who come to embody the problem. As Simone de Beauvoir has noted, women "tend to carry the projections of 'all that is undesirable or threatening in human existence—sexuality, emotion, pollution, sin, and mortality'—necessitating their control and containment."[1] Commenting on this, Nyitray in this volume observes that "It is not surprising, therefore, that … [men's] response to perceived external threats encompassed a heightened sensitivity to internal threats as well." (It could be argued, of course, that sometimes women project their stress onto men as well, as contemporary expressions of misandry in popular culture reveal.)

Stress, therefore, can cause men to "fight back." They might want to help the women in their communities and therefore be reform-oriented (a kind of adaptation), or they might want to project their own stress onto women and therefore reassert the original solution to stress: segregating women and denying them rights in order to ensure that women remain under their control as a way to maintain identity (women would have less opportunity, for instance, to marry outside the group). Because the underlying problems are not addressed, however, this is a temporary solution. Although control of women established some general trends that prevailed until modern times, these were often relaxed in times of security but rigidified in times of stress. The higher the stress, I suggest, the greater the urge to distinguish between men and women as antidote, which would lead to real male dominance. The lower the stress, the greater the equality. But there is a corollary: the higher the stress created by alien critiques of the treatment of women, the greater the urge to include women in "fighting back" as equal partners to prove their equality (which makes it likely that women will come along rather than defect), although this equality is sometimes short-lived if the original identity problems remain unsolved.

Now it could be argued that modernity is causing historically unprecedented stress through urbanization, industrialization, capitalism, the shrinking intergenerational family, and the weakening of masculine identity. As for masculine identity, that was problematic in the second half of the nineteenth century. Even then, men complained about the feminization of culture in general and of Christianity in particular. Colleen McDannell[2] shows that the artifacts of homes and churches were overtly sentimentalized during this period and covertly feminized. Not surprisingly, men were alienated. They were alienated even more by the fact that women not only firmly controlled the home but also set the tone of theology, and publicly crusaded against the shortcomings of men (often arguing that women were innately morally superior to men).

According to Anthony Rotundo (and others),[3] moreover, sexual segregation was partly caused by the fact that men went off to work in factories and offices, leaving women at home to care for the children. With largely absent fathers, the major influence on boys now came from mothers. Boys were dressed like girls (producing the Little Lord Fauntleroy look), which restricted mobility of any kind, let alone rough-and-tumble play. By the age of five, however, boys were not easy to control. Many rebelled to such an extent that they were described as "wild" and even "savage." As "Red Men," they associated themselves with ferocity, which became a source of identity. These boys were so violent and sadistic that adults became afraid of them and took steps to control their subculture. Although these new controls helped to some extent, not all boys made the transition. They faced new kinds of anxiety, moreover, in early adulthood: how to cope with rejection in courtship, how to find the middle-class jobs on which masculine identity and status were based, and confusion over what masculinity really was. Many of those who could not achieve marriage, suitable employment, and a healthy masculine identity withdrew into the home for rest and recovery. (The term "male neurasthenia," which appeared in 1869, referred to the debilitating effects of this stress: fear of failure, insomnia, tension, depression, fatigue, effeminacy, and so forth.) This is an example of the flight response to stress.

And once again, machismo was the antidote. At this stage of life, however, it was practiced secretly in fraternal lodges such as the Odd Fellows, the Freemasons, the Knights of Labor, the Grand Army of the Republic, the Lions, the Elks, the Shriners, the Order of Red men, and so forth. According to Mark Carnes,[4] entrance into these lodges was a ritual of initiation into manhood. (It is striking that they fostered the machismo of their earlier games as boys. These men once again pretended to be "Red Men," for instance, or warriors from ancient Babylonia, Greece, or even the American Civil War.) This identity crisis and the heroic romanticism that it spawned were overcome partly during the Spanish-American War of 1898 and again during World War I and World War II, when men's bodies were once again valued by society (even though the ultimate value was given to dead ones). Other ways of overcoming these identity problems included secret male cults of machismo, competitive sports, organizations such as the Boy Scouts, and sexually segregated schools. These things provided support for the identity of boys and men but often, once again, by withholding it from that of girls and women. This means that it would surely make sense for women, both feminists and fundamentalists, to take seriously the problem of stress and masculine identity.[5]

———————•◦•———————

Underlying the expressions of stress that I have just mentioned is an even deeper reality of interest here. This consists of several interrelated problems that are caused by the human condition itself: maleness, femaleness, and reproduction, which necessitates male-female bonding. I suggest that the deep structure of fundamentalism is linked with these stresses, especially as they have been challenged by modernity. As a result, they cannot be explained simply as the most extreme form of "patriarchal evil."

Earlier sources of masculine identity are now obsolete. Elsewhere, Paul Nathanson and I have discussed the underlying problem of masculine identity.[6] Cross-cultural evidence suggests that a healthy identity for any individual or group must be based on at least one distinctive, valued, and publicly celebrated contribution to society as a whole. For women as a class, the basic source of identity has been motherhood; because only women can gestate and lactate, survival (of the family, community, and species) depends more immediately on them. The functional equivalents for men have usually been based on being protectors, providers, and progenitors.[7] Although most societies have appreciated the first two, these functions do not rely exclusively on maleness; societies have used culture, therefore, to bolster masculine identity either by exaggerating their importance or by banning women from certain cultural activities. Otherwise, how could *men* form masculine identity as providers and protectors of women? The state now does these very things. The identity of men as progenitors, moreover, is now threatened by sperm banks, new reproductive technologies, and women's push for reproductive freedom—that is, autonomy—through either single motherhood by choice or the legalization of marriage for female couples (although the legislation would include male couples). It is important to acknowledge that there are problems for both men and women if the identity of women is reduced to biology and that of men relies mainly on culture. In the former case, women are virtually denied culture by excluding them from education and jobs and in the latter cultural props for identity can be easily deconstructed given modern knowledge and the intellectual fashion of deconstruction.

Nathanson and I predict that the loss of not one or two but all functions traditionally defined in terms of masculinity will create unprecedented stress for men. The signs are already evident: soaring dropout rates of boys from schools, for instance, and high suicide rates among men. But we can also predict a growth in fundamentalism. In that case, we can also predict that one major response—at least in those religious communities that remain intact—might be the attempt by men to re-create some form of exclusivity that will provide them with at least one course of healthy identity. In other words, they will fight back, perhaps under the more broad religio-political banner of fundamentalism. Some might combine all this with machismo to hide their vulnerability or correct their identity problem by reasserting separate spheres and privileges for men.

Another approach, however, is flight. Both dropping out from school and suicide are examples, after all, of flight. Remember Rotundo's account of the nineteenth-century lodges as safe havens for secret ritualized machismo? That is the response of men today in some religious circles. In liberalized wings of Judaism, reports Fishman, congregations have become startlingly feminized. With women occupying many of the religious and organizational leadership positions, men in many cases no longer seek out these positions. More seriously, she observes, worshipping congregations are composed largely of women. This phenomenon is found not only in liberal forms of Judaism but also in liberal forms of Christianity—especially those of Protestantism (something that had already happened in the nineteenth century). For religions that want men to participate, this is surely a major problem, not only a sociological one but a theological one as well. It is not a problem, of course, for those feminists who believe that women are better off with each other than with men—and that if men refuse to meet radical feminist demands, then so be it.

But there is an even deeper problem underlying that of masculine identity. Today, we are witnessing a historically unprecedented breakdown of the cultural support for bonding not only between men and women but also between men and children. According to Don Browning,

> These ideals may be collapsing wherever modernization and globalization spread. In some places, modernity's threat to males does more than disconnect procreation from care and male sexuality from long-term commitment to wife and child. Modernity threatens other male prerogatives because it also beckons women into the market and loosens traditional restrictions on their thoughts and actions. Modernity is a threat to men; it makes women a threat as well. Such dynamics are in the background of the great confrontation between religious fundamentalism of various kinds and the emerging dynamics of modernization and globalization. This conflict, often viewed as one between the United States and Islamic fundamentalists, is more a conflict between modernity and those using religion to form a dogmatic reaction to it. Nonetheless, one of the consequences of modernity has been to aggravate the problem of male responsibility—what I have called the "male problematic." This is the threat of modernity to loosen further the already archaic and fragile tie of males to offspring and their offspring's mothers. This also accounts for the reaction of traditional males to modernity's threats to their customary patterns of responsibility and privileges.[8]

Insight can be gained into the problem (including men's reaction of wanting dominance when extremely stressed) by looking at a key development in evolution.

The fidelity of women to men—often a fundamentalist platform, I suggest, was not originally based on a demand made by men (and therefore an expression of male dominance) but rather on a primeval contract made with men but *by women* and *for women*. Support for this idea comes from evidence of our primate ancestors and the prehistory of our species.[9]

According to David Geary and Mark Flinn, females across species invest more in parenting than do males whereas as males invest more in mating effort because they gain from obtaining additional mates (due to the difference between large amounts of sperm and fewer eggs). Among mammals, females have even less opportunity than males for multiple mates because of internal gestation and obligatory postpartum care (such as lactation) and this makes them more interested in male parental investment. Geary and Flinn surmise—based on an examination of the changing sex differences in the fossil record of various primates (including those in hominid evolution) as well as contemporary primate behaviors—that some aspects of the social behavior of [the proto-human] Australopithiecines might have been more like that of gorillas than in chimpanzees or bonobos, especially patterns of male parental investment (which is strong in both gorillas and humans). The social organization with male gorillas is single-male harems. Males control the females in their harem by preventing the access of other males and thereby ensuring that the offspring are their own. Not surprisingly, male gorillas provide far more parental investment than other primates do. In addition, coalitional behavior, which is found in both chimps and humans, might have developed independently in the latter. These two developments help to explain why human families have been characterized generally by male-female bonding, marriage, and parental involvement.

The need for male dominance (fighting other males to create their harems) gradually declined among proto-human males. Among the factors that differentiated them from other primates were less obvious signs of estrus among females, which no longer attracted many males (and therefore led to less fighting for male dominance and access to females), less difference in size between males and females, and so forth. This made emotional bonding between males and females more important than sheer male power and dominance. With a longer gestation period came a greater need, moreover, for provision and protection of females through pregnancy. In addition, the much longer period of childhood development required even more attention to provision and protection.

With the development of human intelligence, women must have realized that it was to their advantage to form enduring bonds with men and gain the resources (provisions and protection) that men could provide. To ensure the advantages of men's parental investment without their physical dominance, women came to the conclusion that their own fidelity could be exchanged for the parental investments of men. This was probably the first social contract. Eventually, it became deeply embedded in culture and given the highest authority possible (ancestral, religious, or legal). This continued throughout human prehistory and early history. The gorilla social structure of harems did not completely disappear. Now kings, much like gorillas, had harems, which expressed their total dominance over both other males in the society and the females of their harem.

With the development of male dominance, especially after state formation, however, voluntary female fidelity was changed to female obedience. The contract's original reasons became obscured. This made it seem, once modern feminists revealed the "patriarchal" aspect of history, that men's desire for power over women was the raison d'être for all their actions (and that all of human history could be understood in the stark but simplistic terms of a conspiracy of men against women).

Keeping this evolutionary history in mind, let us return to Browning's link of modernity, masculinity, and fundamentalism.

> The fundamentalist reaction to modernity's threat to male prerogatives and responsibilities contains a grain of insight. It at least raises a very important question: How can male family involvement be maintained in the face of the challenges of modernity without absolutizing male patriarchy on the one hand or dismantling, in the spirit of an anomic new freedom and equality, male responsibility on the other? The dogmatism of traditional paternalisms may be no worse than the new message being shouted from the rooftops that says both men and women are equally entitled to be self-regarding yet tentative about marital, family, and parental commitment. The fundamentalist reaction intuitively understands the importance of this question even though its solution is unjust to women and children and wrong in its interpretation of both tradition and modernity.[10]

Because religions have regulated reproduction through the institution of marriage and fostered male-female bonding, their fundamental critique by feminists is obviously deeply threatening to the men of these communities (and by extension to the men of all communities). So is the feminist demand for reproductive autonomy by which some feminists mean that women should have total control over reproduction. This discussion of the historically unprecedented threat to an underlying social contract between men and women helps us to understand why gender is the fault line in every modern society.

The stakes around identity are indeed high, which is what the rhetoric of demonization reveals. For this reason, I think, we need more deep thinking about the important insights provided by both feminism and fundamentalism. To avoid the extremes, we must acknowledge that the fundamentalists rightly intuit reciprocity (which they call complementarity) and want to safeguard it, without referring to evolution. In any case, we should give them credit for their insight and courage in this regard, as we think about the true significance of any social contract between men and women.

But we must also remember the Achilles heel of the fundamentalist position: that there is an inherent danger of *real* male dominance arising from the relegation of women's identity and activity to biology and the private sphere, which could again create all the problems of androcentrism in the past. Now that the mask of male dominance is off, fundamentalists should recognize that only when women have real choice will they enter willingly into a new social contract with men.

Men should take all this seriously, of course, because women can already virtually cut them out of the reproductive process. As a result, men should learn to live with, or appreciate, the important contributions of feminism: its critique of misogyny and feminine stereotypes; its insistence on education for women along with the possibility of well-paying jobs and careers for them; its warning of the need to stop violence against women and children; its demand that we eliminate double standards, and so forth. If this argument is not convincing, remember that male gorillas paid a heavy price for access to reproduction. They had to fight other males to become the alpha reproducer. The losers, of which there were many, well, died; others just had to do without sex and offspring.

But the social contract's breakdown can be threatening to heterosexual women for additional reasons. It would eliminate marriage, which not only brings men and women together but also encourages paternal investment in family life and children. Given what we know about evolution and the role of world religions in protecting the reproductive cycle, which lies at the heart of human existence, the new scenario would create a very different future. Better reform than revolution, I suggest, so that both women and men can renew their social contract but without the hierarchical accretions.

Notes

1. Karen McCarthy Brown, "Fundamentalism and the Control of Women," in *Fundamentalism and Gender*, ed. John Stratton Hawley (New York: Oxford University Press, 1994), 188, citing Simone de Beauvoir's *The Second Sex*.

2. Colleen McDannell, *Material Christianity: Religion and Popular Culture in America* (New Haven, CT: Yale University Press, 1996).

3. E. Anthony Rotundo, *American Manhood: Transformations in Masculinity from the Revolution to the Modern Era* (New York: Basic Books, 1993).

4. Mark C. Carnes, *Secret Ritual and Manhood in Victorian America* (New Haven, CT: Yale University Press, 1989).

5. Some feminists do recognize that bolstering traditional notions of gender as a way of dealing with the (male) stress of rapid social change is related to fundamentalism. Epstein, for instance, refers to the historian Betty DeBerg who argues that fundamentalism's preservation of traditional gender roles in the wake of their collapse during the "turbulent, fast-paced change" of the nineteenth century "preeminently fuelled fundamentalism's widespread appeal." Epstein has no sympathy for this response, however, because "clergy

strove to 'masculinise' Christianity over against its deleterious 'feminisation.'… To do so, they not only used misogynist rhetoric, but also curtailed women's range of public and ecclesial activities." Epstein is right; swinging to the opposite extreme is no real correction. If gynocentrism is wrong, so is androcentrism (and vice versa).

6. Paul Nathanson and Katherine Young, *Spreading Misandry: The Teaching of Contempt for Men in Popular Culture* (Montreal: McGill-Queen's University Press, 2001), 87–88; 231.

7. David D. Gilmore, *Manhood in the Making: Cultural Concepts of Masculinity* (New Haven, CT: Yale University Press, 1991), 75–76.

8. Don S. Browning, *Marriage and Modernization: How Globalization Threatens Marriage and What to Do about It* (Grand Rapids, MI: William B. Eerdmans Publishing Company, 2003), 75–76.

9. The following discussion is based on David C. Geary and Mark V. Flinn, "Evolution of Human Parental Behavior and the Human Family," *Parenting: Science and Practice*, nos. 1 and 2 (2001).

10. Browning, *Marriage and Modernization*, 75–77.

Index